Routledge Revivals

The History of the Anglo-Catholic Revival from 1845

First published in 1932, *The History of the Anglo-Catholic Revival from 1845* is a sober and judicious history of the Catholic Revival in the Church of England by a very well-known Anglo-Catholic scholar with an established reputation. The scope of the book is clearly shown by the chapter headings— The Movement after Newman's Secession; The Apostolic Succession; The Decisions of the Courts on Doctrine; The Rise of Ritualism; Eucharistic Vestments; Confessions to a Priest; The Treatment of Ritualism; Three Representative Documents of the Revival; The Spiritual Independence of the Church; The Movement in the Twentieth Century; and Conclusion.

The History of the Anglo-Catholic Revival from 1845

W. J. Sparrow Simpson

First published in 1932
by George Allen & Unwin Ltd

This edition first published in 2024 by Routledge
4 Park Square, Milton Park, Abingdon, Oxon, OX14 4RN

and by Routledge
605 Third Avenue, New York, NY 10017

Routledge is an imprint of the Taylor & Francis Group, an informa business

© 1932 W. J. Sparrow Simpson

All rights reserved. No part of this book may be reprinted or reproduced or utilised in any form or by any electronic, mechanical, or other means, now known or hereafter invented, including photocopying and recording, or in any information storage or retrieval system, without permission in writing from the publishers.

Publisher's Note
The publisher has gone to great lengths to ensure the quality of this reprint but points out that some imperfections in the original copies may be apparent.

Disclaimer
The publisher has made every effort to trace copyright holders and welcomes correspondence from those they have been unable to contact.

A Library of Congress record exists under LCCN: 33004612

ISBN: 978-1-032-90721-5 (hbk)
ISBN: 978-1-003-55943-6 (ebk)
ISBN: 978-1-032-90723-9 (pbk)

Book DOI 10.4324/9781003559436

THE HISTORY OF
THE ANGLO-CATHOLIC REVIVAL
FROM 1845

by

W. J. SPARROW SIMPSON, D.D.

LONDON
GEORGE ALLEN & UNWIN LTD
MUSEUM STREET

FIRST PUBLISHED IN 1932

All rights reserved
PRINTED IN GREAT BRITAIN BY
UNWIN BROTHERS LTD., WOKING

CONTENTS

CHAPTER		PAGE
I.	THE MOVEMENT AFTER NEWMAN'S SECESSION	9
II.	THE APOSTOLIC SUCCESSION	25
III.	THE DECISIONS OF THE COURTS ON DOCTRINE	46
IV.	THE RISE OF RITUALISM	67
V.	EUCHARISTIC VESTMENTS	83
VI.	CONFESSION AND ABSOLUTION	105
VII.	THE TREATMENT OF RITUALISM	124
VIII.	THREE REPRESENTATIVE DOCUMENTS OF THE REVIVAL	161
IX.	THE REVIVAL OF CONVOCATION	175
X.	THE SPIRITUAL INDEPENDENCE OF THE CHURCH	186
XI.	THE REVIVAL OF RELIGIOUS ORDERS IN THE ENGLISH CHURCH	230
XII.	THE MOVEMENT IN THE TWENTIETH CENTURY	246
XIII.	THE PAST AND THE FUTURE	281
	INDEX	297

THE HISTORY OF THE ANGLO-CATHOLIC REVIVAL FROM 1845

CHAPTER I

THE MOVEMENT AFTER NEWMAN'S SECESSION

THE Catholic Revival in the Church of England during the nineteenth century was fundamentally an endeavour to restore certain elements in the Church's faith and practice which had for the time become obscured. It was by no means the first revival of its kind, but one of a series of Movements in which the Institutional and Sacramental and Ministerial aspects of Religion were set in the forefront of religious thinking.

The history of the English Church since the Reformation displays a succession of reactions. A remarkable Catholic Revival occurred in the time of Bishop Andrewes and Archbishop Laud. It was followed by a violent Protestant Reaction in Cromwell's time. That was followed by a Catholic Revival at the Restoration, when such leaders as Bishop Cosin, Bishop Jeremy Taylor, Archbishop Bramhall, Bishop Wilson brought forward out of the Church's inheritance many neglected principles. The secession of the Nonjurors, for reasons connected with the State, deprived the English Church of a large proportion of its Catholic elements, and left its future in the power of the men of latitude. Then came in due course the Evangelical Revival under the Wesleys. But whereas

The History of the Anglo-Catholic Revival

the Puritanism of the sixteenth and seventeenth centuries had been strongly institutional, the Evangelical Movement of the eighteenth century lost this institutional idea. It was conspicuously individualist. It was concerned with the separate soul, but not with his incorporation into a Divine Community. In spite of Wesley's High Church beliefs the Wesleyan Movement tended to make men Methodists, not members of the English Church. So long as an individual was converted, the Evangelical appeared indifferent about the particular Communion in which he might enlist. Thus the Evangelical did not inherit the corporate sense of his Puritan forefathers. Evangelicalism within the English Church created powerful centres of religious life, as at Cambridge, at Islington, and at Clapham. But it cannot be said that the Movement controlled the Nation. The old-fashioned High Churchmen continued. The rationalising tendencies of the age extended. It has been said that "the time had come for a reassertion of Church Authority, and of the meaning of the Church as a Divine Institution. The Evangelicals were powerless to meet this growth of a liberal theology. They had never been thinkers. . . . They were lacking, moreover, in any adequate theory of the Church. The key-note of their system was individualism."[1]

Protestantism in the nineteenth century had largely lost belief in the Church as a supernatural institution transmitted from one century to another. It fixed attention on the first century as described in Scripture, and regarded the following centuries down to the sixteenth more or less as deviations from the Gospel. The History of the Church was constantly represented as departure from

[1] Storr, *Development of English Theology*, p. 251.

The Movement after Newman's Secession

the mind of Christ. Thus attention was fixed first on the Apostolic Age, and next on the Reformation, the long interval of the centuries being overlooked as debased, and the subsequent period commended as pure and reformed.

This was a popular outlook when the Oxford Movement began. What Evangelicals had left out Anglo-Catholicism endeavoured to restore.

Keble, in his sermon on National Apostasy, declared: "I do not see how any person can devote himself too entirely to the cause of the Apostolic Church in these realms."[1]

Pusey said that the object of the Movement of 1833 was "the Catholicising of England: that is, to bring all to that one faith of the Primitive Church, which the Homilies say is specially to be followed, as most incorrupt and pure or, in scientific language, the rule of Vincentius, . . . the one faith which had been held by all everywhere always."

The Tractarian was no innovator. Originality was the last thing to which he aspired. He had not the smallest desire to construct a New Theology. On the contrary, his object was to restore the old. Newman, dedicating a volume of his sermons to Hugh James Rose, Principal of King's College, London, expressed his admiration for him as one "who, when our hearts were failing, bade us stir up the gift that was in us, and betake ourselves to our true Mother."

The Church was a Divinely created corporate Institution, with distinctive characteristics essential to its integrity. Its Dogmas were supernaturally determined,

[1] Keble, *Sermon on National Apostasy*, 1833.

The History of the Anglo-Catholic Revival

its sacraments divinely appointed, its ministry apostolic and transmitted from Christ with His Authority. The identity of the Church in all these three respects with its primitive original was fundamental to the Anglican position.

It follows, of course, that stress was laid on the Apostolic Succession, but only as one element in the Church's constitutional identity. To the Tractarian the identity of the ministry was part of the Christian inheritance, like the identity of the Creed. The Christian centuries which retained the Sacraments retained also the ministry to which they were entrusted. This was the aspect of Religion which the Tractarian Revival endeavoured to restore. The Church was the accredited organ for the perpetuation of Truth, and for the communication of life to the individual soul.

Tractarianism, therefore, was an appeal to History. It was, as has been said, an appeal not limited to any age. Yet it was specially an appeal to the Doctrine and Practice of the Primitive Church, to those generations which drew their inspiration most directly from the Apostles, and which produced the greatest succession of interpreters of the Christian Faith. The originators of the Revival held in profound veneration the great saints and bishops and theologians of the early centuries. They acknowledged the dogmatic decisions of the great Councils of Christendom. The Witness of the Undivided Church possessed immense authority. As Cuthbert Turner said,[1] we could not conceive of the Oxford or Tractarian Movement as continuing to exist without this appeal to history.

This conception of the Church, as a Spiritual Institu-

[1] Cuthbert Turner, *Catholic and Apostolic*, pp. 77–98.

The Movement after Newman's Secession

tion divinely created with its own distinctive principles and purposes, involved the problems of the true relation between the Church and the State: problems which underlay the whole course of the following century. Bishop Hamilton of Salisbury did not publish his celebrated charge to the clergy until 1864, but he expressed the true Tractarian spirit.

"When I speak of the Church," he said, "I am speaking of the visible Kingdom of the Mediator; and when I speak of its authority I mean that it has the power and responsibility of defending the truth of God, and that this real since delegated and inalienable power is wholly spiritual, and owes nothing to any temporal source.

"But this Kingdom, which is not of this world, was to find its place in the midst of the Kingdoms of the world, and, when placed in them, had to exercise its independent authority in juxtaposition to the august and equally independent authority of the State."

Thus Nationalism was subordinate to Catholicism. The essential thing was not what appealed to the English disposition, but what represented the universal qualities of the supernatural Institution. To those who held the prevalent view of the subordination of the Church to the State, such a conception was strange and repellent to the last degree. But it dominated the Tractarian theology.

Fr. Benson exactly represented the Tractarian outlook when he wrote: "I know of no English Church to which I owe any loyalty distinct from the loyalty which I owe to Truth and the Church Catholic of which I believe the English Church to be a part."[1]

"As for being *loyal* to Church of England principles,

[1] *Fr. Benson's Letters*, i. 28.

The History of the Anglo-Catholic Revival

I hope we always have been; but it is a phrase which admits of some misconception. It cannot mean being loyal to the exact phraseology for praise or blame of any particular age, as Edward VI, Charles II. There is no reason why we should be loyal to any particular age. Our loyalty is due to Truth, and to the great principle of Truth which the Church of England enunciates i.e. the tradition of the Undivided Church, especially the first five centuries."[1]

The rise of the Catholic Revival within the limits of University circles has been immortalised by Newman in his *Apologia*, and by Dean Church in his *History of the Oxford Movement*. It is a story which they, and they alone, could adequately tell. But what concerned them was the Academic period, ending with Newman's secession. The development of the Catholic Revival in the Nation at large was, according to Dean Church, almost more important than the history of the Movement at its beginnings, for, besides vindicating it, the generation that followed "carried on its work to achievements and successes which, even in the most sanguine days of Tractarianism, had not presented themselves to men's minds, much less to their hopes." But that story, added Dean Church, must be told by others.

It is well known that the Catholic Revival in the English Church did not begin among the Bishops. Like the Wesleyan Movement it began among the priests. And in neither case did the Bishops of the period appreciate it. In the course of the Oxford Movement we encounter, in the Charges addressed by the Bishops to their clergy, judgments of great severity and inability to

[1] 1871.

The Movement after Newman's Secession

appreciate. A formidable collection of extracts from Episcopal Charges during the years 1833-42, extending to some seven hundred pages, was published by Bricknell in 1845. But there is another side to this. Even in the early stages of the Revival there were memorable recognitions of the benefits which the Movement conferred upon the Church.

Connop Thirlwall, Bishop of S. David's, addressing his assembled clergy in his primary Charge in 1842, defended the right of a Churchman to criticise the defects of the English Church.

"It cannot, indeed, be denied that expressions have been deliberately used which clearly imply a certain degree of dissatisfaction with the present state of the Church, a certain desire of change, a certain regret mingled with disapprobation at the course pursued by some of our Reformers and especially at the extent to which they were swayed by foreign influence. But I have yet to learn that such views and feelings are inconsistent with the obligations of a Minister of our Church, or with a sincere attachment to her."[1]

Thirlwall went on to quote Arnold of Rugby on the imperfection of the Reformation.

Arnold of Rugby, severe critic though he was of Newman's methods, was, none the less, the author of some remarkable reflections on the losses incurred at the Reformation. "No wise man doubts," he said, "that the Reformation was imperfect, or that in the Romish system there were many good institutions, and practices, and feelings, which it would be most desirable to restore among ourselves. Daily Church services, frequent com-

[1] *Primary Charge*, p. 70.

The History of the Anglo-Catholic Revival

munions, memorials of our Christian calling continually presented to our notice, in crosses and wayside oratories; commemorations of holy men of all times and countries; the doctrine of the Communion of Saints practically taught; religious orders, especially of women, of different kinds, and under different rules, delivered only from the snare and sin of perpetual vows; all these, most of which are of some efficacy for good even in a corrupt Church, belong no less to the true Church, and would there be purely beneficial."[1] This was written between 1835 and 1840.

Edward Denison, Bishop of Salisbury in 1842, told his Clergy that, much as he dissented from some of the Tractarian opinions, and disapproved the manners in which they had been expressed, yet he could not refuse to acknowledge that in several and weighty respects Churchmen were deeply indebted to them.

"They have been the chief instruments in reviving the study of sound theology in an unlearned age. They have raised the standard of the ministerial character, by teaching men to trace the commission of the Clergy, through His Apostles, up to our Blessed Lord Himself, and to see in this the sure warrant for their work. They have impressed upon the Clergy the obligation of walking orderly, according to the laws and regulations of the Church in which they are commissioned to minister. They have successfully vindicated the important truth of the nature and constitution of the Church from the vague and lax notions which used too generally to prevail respecting it. They have given the Sacraments their due place in the scheme of our holy religion, as contrasted

[1] Thomas Arnold, *The Christian Life*, 1878, Introduction, p. xlv.

The Movement after Newman's Secession

with those who would make them little else than bare signs and symbols, instead of channels of regenerating and sanctifying grace."

If we contemplate the Oxford Movement at the date of John Henry Newman's secession in 1845 we find that many contemporaries believed that it could never survive. Newman drew others after him. Stanley, afterwards Dean of Westminster, was convinced that the Movement was at an end. On the Nation at large the secession produced reaction not merely from Rome but from Catholicism in any form whatever. The Romeward tendency of certain individual Tractarians gave plausibility to the assertion that the entire Movement would end that way, if indeed it was not being deliberately promoted to secure that result. Consequently, the secessions to Rome made the progress of the Movement in the Nation at large more difficult.

But on the Movement itself its effect was to consolidate and unite its members as a whole into closer and firmer loyalty to the English Church. It is singular to recall that this result was exactly what Newman himself had predicted as sure to happen in such a case. Long before he made up his mind to depart he wrote in a letter to De Lisle the following warning words: "If there is any one thing calculated more than another to extinguish all hope of a better understanding between Rome and England, by discrediting us with our own people and rendering us suspicious of yourselves, it would be the conversion by you of some of our members. If your friends wish to put a gulf between themselves and us, let them make converts; but not else."[1]

[1] *Life of A. P. de Lisle*, i. 229.

The History of the Anglo-Catholic Revival

A writer in the *Christian Remembrancer* at the time of Newman's secession insisted that the Catholic Movement "sprung up out of the genuine English soil; it had its origin there; and no foreign material, either in the English Church or out of her, produced it. It was of the genuine substance of our Church; it grew upon genuine, though enlarged, Church of England feelings and sympathies; and it extended far and wide in the Church, because it had that solid connexion with, and that native origin in her. But this Movement was taken up by a school of mind which was not thus congenial with, and had not this mental basis in our Church. First of all, at the very outset, Mr. Newman took it up: he took it up, as distinct from originating, and joined, as distinct from creating it. . . . He was their convert originally, and not their teacher; and a convert of a particular kind: that is to say, never to the absolute acceptance of their ground, but only to the trial of it. In this way Mr. Newman adopted a movement, threw himself into it, and lent the whole force, fertility and richness of his mind to it."[1]

But "if we are asked how the Church Movement stands affected by the loss of Mr. Newman, the answer is that it has lost a most powerful and telling organ; one who could bring out, explain, illustrate, spread it, and carry it into people's hearts. But it is its organ that has gone, and not itself. It does not cease to be because it has been left."[2] "The organ gone, the unexpressed, indefinite feeling in the body falls back upon itself; and is thrown upon its own vague strength; but it is there: because it is unexpressed for a time, it is not, therefore, unsubstantiated; its substance remains, abides, endures,

[1] *Christian Remembrancer*, 1846, p. 214.   [2] Ibid., p. 216.

The Movement after Newman's Secession

to find out its own expression somehow or other, and use those that are left, instead of those who are gone. Such is the state of things with our Church."

The opposition of the Bishops to the Catholic Revival is to a large extent accounted for by the policy of the State, which was to select for the Episcopate men who were of the Broad or Evangelical School.

There is an instructive passage in the Greville *Memoirs* showing the impression which the exclusion of High Churchmen from higher offices in the Church made in 1856 upon a distinguished man of the world who certainly had no leanings towards Anglo-Catholicism.

"Great astonishment has been excited by the appointment of a Mr. Bickersteth as Bishop of Ripon, against whom nothing can be said, nor anything for him, except that he is a very Low Churchman. All the vacant sees have now been filled with clergymen of this colour, which is not very fair or prudent, as it will exasperate the moderate High Churchmen and set them strongly against a Government which appears determined to shut the door of ecclesiastical preferment against all but the Lowest Churchmen."[1]

At a later period, from 1856 to 1862, Lord Shaftesbury[2] exerted an immense control over the Church of England by his influence with Lord Palmerston in the appointment of the Bishops. Palmerston appointed no less than twenty Bishops and Archbishops in the English Church. And in all their appointments Shaftesbury was his adviser. The Shaftesbury Bishops were notoriously of Evangelical tendencies. In Palmerston's opinion an

[1] Greville, *Memoirs*, vol. viii. Ed. 1888, p. 69.
[2] Hodder's *Life of Shaftesbury*, iii. 194.

essential qualification for the episcopate was a man who would get on well with the Nonconformists. Almost every appointment made by him excited deep resentment among the Tractarians, and indeed among High Churchmen. Bishop Wilberforce, writing to Gladstone, complained of "Lord Palmerston's wicked appointments."[1] Every sound Churchman felt that the Government insulted the Church almost every time it had to recommend to the Crown for a Bishopric. The political utility of this exclusive selection is carefully noted by Shaftesbury. "The first appointments were so successful that they influenced elections, turned votes in the House of Commons, and raised around him (Palmerston) a strong party in the country."[2] The first Bishops appointed by Palmerston, says Shaftesbury, "were decidedly of the Evangelical School; and my recommendations were made with that intention." But he confesses that the range was limited. Tractarians perpetually called for learned men. That limited the range still more. This demand was sustained by almost every newspaper. "I suggested to him Tait for London," says Shaftesbury. "I did so as believing that the Broad Church ought to be represented ... and selected Tait as the mildest among them. It is an appointment," he reflects, "in some respects to be regretted, in others to be commended."

Professor Goldwin Smith[3] noted that the High Church party had been desperately put out by Palmerston's wholesale appointments of Evangelicals to bishoprics. Shaftesbury was the recognised leader of the Low Church

---

[1] *Life of Wilberforce*, iii. 85.
[2] *Life of Shaftesbury*, iii. 196.
[3] *Goldwin Smith* by Haultain, p. 34.

The Movement after Newman's Secession

party, and Palmerston saw that there were votes to be got there, so he made Evangelical Bishops by shoals.

The occupant of the English throne during this period, revered and beloved as she deservedly was, felt deeply-rooted repugnance to the revival of Anglo-Catholic beliefs and practices. The sympathies of Queen Victoria were with the moderate or the liberal school. Her correspondence with Disraeli is illuminating as to the treatment which the Oxford Movement received during many years from the Crown and from the politicians. The Queen desired that that distinguished author, the Rev. Charles Kingsley, should be appointed to a canonry; "his religious views are liberal and enlightened."[1] The Premier for the moment objects. "His preferment just now (1868) would be seriously prejudicial to Mr. Disraeli." He recommends appointments which would "gratify the Conservative party generally." Disraeli recommends one who "has been for many years a shining light of the Protestant party," and of late has gained golden opinions by his commanding advocacy of the Royal Supremacy. But the Queen had misgivings, and objected because he was too strong a partisan. Disraeli returned to the encounter and prevailed. Nevertheless, the royal diary expresses general satisfaction since Disraeli sees the force of the Queen's arguments in favour of moderate and distinguished men. Yet the Queen declined the nomination to the Episcopate of one characterised by herself as "an insignificant Low Churchman." Disraeli writes to say that he has fine opportunities of feeling the pulse of public opinion on the subject of Church appointments. Dr. Bright is appointed Professor of Ecclesiastical

[1] *Letters*, i. 519 ff.

The History of the Anglo-Catholic Revival

History at Oxford since, though a High Churchman, he is perfectly constitutional in his Church views and is a warm and influential supporter of the Conservative party. On the death of Archbishop Longley the Queen wrote at once to Mr. Disraeli to say that there is no one so fit to succeed him as Dr. Tait, Bishop of London. Disraeli is decidedly averse to this proposal. But the Queen refused to alter her opinion. Disraeli still resists. He finds Dr. Tait "as an ecclesiastical statesman, obscure in purpose, fitful and inconstant in action, and evidently, though earnest and conscientious, a prey to constantly conflicting convictions." He asks the Queen, "Is this the Prelate who can lead the Church?" The Queen persisted, and her Prime Minister gave way. So Dr. Tait became Archbishop and Dr. Jackson succeeded him in London. Liddon's comment on both was: "They are miserable appointments. I feel sure," he added, "that all sorts of troubles are ahead. Both the Puritans and the Rationalists are more bitter and menacing than ever, and, what is worse, our own people are very far from wise."[1] "It really seems as if everything were going against the Catholic Party in the Church of England." Disraeli felt the public pulse, and wrote to inform the Queen that "the High Church Party are much enraged with the Episcopal appointments, and are endeavouring, in consequence, injuriously to influence the Country elections."[2] He thinks, therefore, that the preferment of one whom he represents as "a High Churchman but staunchly Conservative," would be "well timed and advantageous to your Majesty's Government." This was too much for the Dean of Windsor, who remarked to the Queen his

[1] *Life of Liddon*, p. 116. [2] *Letters of Queen Victoria*, i. 554.

The Movement after Newman's Secession

great regret that Disraeli had not some more fixed principle about his Church appointments than the mere political bias they may have one way or other.

This instructive correspondence has only recently appeared. But as long ago as 1880 complaints were made in print[1] as to "frequent attacks upon a widowed Sovereign whose beloved Consort was a Lutheran and a Presbyterian, for sharing that Consort's belief that Presbyterian Churches are as valid as Episcopalian." Her Majesty, added the writer, occasionally worships and even communicates in Presbyterian Churches. "It should be remembered that many of her nearest and dearest relatives are Presbyterians—Lutheran Presbyterians, indeed—but still members of a Presbyterian Church. But that is not all: the husband of her youth, the guide and stay of her maturer years, was reared a Presbyterian, and probably ever remained one in heart."[2]

As a natural result, this crowding the high places of the Church with Bishops whose tendencies were everything except Catholic disabled the Episcopate from capacity to appreciate the true character of the Catholic Revival. Conflict between an Episcopate selected on these principles and the leaders of the Catholic Revival was inevitable. But it is only right to remember that the overwhelming majority of the Nation were with the Bishops and against the Tractarians.

Fr. Benson of Cowley, reflecting on the History of the Movement, said: "I think the Church Party would have been much more advanced in the present day if there

[1] Pamphlets, 1880.
[2] Archer Gurney, *First Principles in Church and State*, 1880, pp. 16, 27.

had been more respect shown to the parental authority of the Bishops. At the same time we must remember that the bishops have often forfeited all claim to have their judgment respected by trying to enforce their *personal* judgment instead of the judgment of the *Church*, their *ministerial* judgment. The *personal* judgment of a bishop is really of no more weight than that of any other priest, although one ought always to give it, even when wrong, respectful consideration."[1]

It did not need much penetration to see, in 1845, that troublous times lay before the Catholic Revival.

[1] Fr. Benson's *Letters*, i. pp. 29, 30, 1871.

CHAPTER II

THE APOSTOLIC SUCCESSION

THE Tractarians have been subjected to much criticism for the great stress which they laid on the principle of Apostolic Succession. And yet, in appealing to this principle, they were by no means innovators, but inheritors of the Anglican Traditional belief. They were well aware that the Apostolic Succession had been taught and reiterated in the Church of England by a series of its theologians from the seventeenth century. Pusey collected an impressive catena of passages from more than forty authoritative English Churchmen, including such names as Bishop Andrewes, Archbishop Laud, Archbishop Bramhall, Bishop Sanderson, Bishop Jeremy Taylor, Bishop Pearson, Bishop Beveridge, Archbishop Wake, a whole series of the Nonjurors, Bishop Wilson, Bishop Horsley, Bishop Jebb, down to Bishop Van Mildert, the last prince-Bishop of Durham. These teachers of the Church of England had impressed upon their contemporaries in a variety of ways the principle of ministerial commission derived from the Apostles, and transmitted through its recipients right down the Christian centuries. They agreed that the Apostolic function is not decayed, and cannot be wanting in the Church of God (Bishop Wilson). That the power to ordain entrusted to the Apostles was not personal, but committed to ecclesiastical persons (Bishop Andrewes). They called on members of the Church of England to hold to Episcopacy as a holy institution of their blessed Saviour and His unerring

The History of the Anglo-Catholic Revival

Apostles (Bishop Hall). They called on those who did not possess the Apostolic Succession not to put it to more question whether they have ordination or not, nor to desert the general practice of the Universal Church when they may clear it if they please (Archbishop Bramhall). They declared that Episcopal Government is not to be derived merely from Apostolical practice or institution, but that it is originally founded in the Person and Office of our Lord (Bishop Sanderson). They wrote about the Divine right of Episcopacy. They said that the Government of the Church was delegated to the Apostles by Christ, and that this power so delegated was not to expire in their persons. That the Apostolate might be successive and perpetual, Christ gave the Apostles a power of Ordination, that they might impart that power which they had received (Bishop Jeremy Taylor). If you ask the Fathers who they were that were accounted in their times and ages the successors of the Apostles, they will with one accord make answer that the Bishops were (Heylin). Where the same order and ministry is, there is the same Church (Bishop Pearson). They said we live in a Church wherein the Apostolical line has through all ages been preserved entire, there having been a constant succession of such Bishops in it as were truly and properly successors to the Apostles (Bishop Beveridge). They declared that it is the Bishop's part only to ordain (Archbishop Wake). This was an Archbishop's exposition of the doctrine of the English Church. They said that Christ's commission of the Apostles plainly contained the authority of ordaining others, and a power to transfer that commission upon others, and those upon others to the end of the world (Nelson, author of *Festivals*

The Apostolic Succession

and Fasts). Jurisdiction was conveyed to Bishops and Priests; and this succession has continued without interruption for above sixteen hundred years (Collier, the historian). The Apostles ordained successors to themselves and took measures for perpetuating in the Church a standing ministry of divers orders and gradations (Bishop Van Mildert, Bampton Lectures).

It is, therefore, plain from all this evidence, which might easily be vastly increased, that when the Tractarians laid impressive stress on the Apostolic Succession they were only reminding their contemporaries of the belief widely held in the post-Reformation period of the English Church.[1] It is certainly true that the Tractarians brought out into unusual prominence this principle of uninterrupted succession. But their conviction was that in this matter, as in certain others, they were only restoring to its rightful place what a previous generation had undervalued or neglected. Professor Cuthbert Turner, indeed, did not hesitate to claim that the Apostolic Succession "is as prominent a theme in the argument of Hegisippus or Irenaeus as it is in the argument of the English Tractarians."[2]

The Catholic Revival by no means rested content merely with the consensus of Anglican post-Reformation theologians to the principle of Apostolic Succession. The Tractarians appealed to the witness of the Primitive Church. In the writings of the Fathers the doctrine of Succession from the Apostles holds a most impressive place. Much study has been concentrated on the subject

[1] See Canon Mason, *Episcopacy in the Church of England*.
[2] In Swete, *Essays on the Early History of the Church and the Ministry*, p. 95.

The History of the Anglo-Catholic Revival

since the days when Arthur Haddan published his important work on *Apostolic Succession in the Church of England* (1869). He dealt quite slightly with the doctrine in the primitive centuries. Every fragment of early evidence has since then been subjected to a critical scrutiny of the most rigorous kind.

I

The History of the Ministry must not be isolated from the Institution in which it exists. It will not be rightly appreciated apart from the Church. There is a natural order in approach to truth. In the present case it should always be first the Church, then the Sacraments, and then the Ministry. The Church appeared at the beginning of the Christian era in the form of an Institution containing within itself a Creed, Sacraments, and Ministry. As Heiler says, "The primitive Jerusalem Community contained in germ three elements fundamental to Catholic institutionalism: Dogma, Hierarchy, and Sacrament" (*Der Katholizismus*, p. 47). The Dogma was the product of the impression of Christ's personality. The Sacramental principle was attributed to His direction. The ministry to His personal immediate commission. Ministerial authority was at first retained by its original Apostolic recipients, and afterwards gradually imparted by the principle of transmission from its possessors. If there is anything mechanical in the Apostolic Succession it is a method to which the Apostles themselves were committed. S. Clement was only formulating the actual development when he maintained that God sent Christ, Christ sent the Apostles, and the Apostles sent those who should minister

The Apostolic Succession

after them. The relation of the ministry to the Sacrament was taught by S. Ignatius as early as A.D. 110 in the direction: let that be counted a valid Eucharist which is ministered by the Bishop or by one to whom the Bishop has entrusted it. Tertullian, in A.D. 200, profoundly impressed by the universal development of all the local Churches into identity of Creed, reflected: "Is it likely that so many Churches, and they so great, should have gone astray into one and the same faith?" Error of doctrine in the Churches must necessarily have produced various results. Giving his well-known illustration of the same flower growing in widely separated lands, Tertullian argued that identity of product implies identity of seed.[1] This argument, which Tertullian applied to Creed, is applicable also to the ministry. There are few more wonderful facts in the history of the Church than the universal development of the ministry into identity of form and principles. Christendom matured into the same Creed, the same Sacraments, and the same ministry, name, and thing. There was over a considerable period difference of opinion with regard to the Canon of Scripture. There was no corresponding diversity about the principles of the ministry.

It has often been said of late that Apostolic Succession as understood in the second century meant succession to a predecessor, and not to an ordainer. And there is in this no doubt a considerable element of truth. The point on which the early apologists of the Faith laid very great stress was that the Bishops held and taught precisely the same faith as the Chief Pastor who held that position before him. Tertullian, in often-quoted words, challenged

[1] *De Prescriptione*, xxviii.

The History of the Anglo-Catholic Revival

men who held doctrines differing from those of the Church to prove the Apostolic character of their teaching by their Apostolic ministerial succession. "Let them unfold the roll of their Bishops, running down in due succession from the beginning in such a manner that their first distinguished bishop shall be able to show for his ordainer and predecessor (*auctorem et antecessorem*) some one of the Apostles or of Apostolic men."[1]

It is impressive that Tertullian, in the words ordainer and predecessor, unites the two ideas involved in Apostolic Succession. He does not only think of a Bishop as occupying the position previously held by an Apostle, but also as having received his ministerial commission from an Apostle. Indeed, it is quite inconceivable that Tertullian would have regarded a minister as a legitimate successor of the Apostles merely because he occupied the Apostles' place, unless also he had received from an Apostle the ministerial commission. The two meanings attached to Apostolic Succession were separable in theory, but in fact they were united. Tertullian contemplates Bishops who, as he says, had been "appointed to their episcopal places by Apostles."

It was, and continued to be, the universal consent of Christendom that no man might consecrate the Eucharist unless he were a priest, and that no man could be a priest unless he were ordained by a Bishop, and that no man could be a Bishop unless he were consecrated by the Episcopate. An intimate, indeed inseparable, relation between the Sacrament and the Apostolic Ministry was everywhere an accepted principle.

This conception of the ministry and its functions

[1] *De Prescriptione*, xxxii.

The Apostolic Succession

persisted without a rival down to the sixteenth century. When the East and the West parted company from one another, both alike retained the same principle of Apostolic Succession. The impression that the Apostolic Succession has been disproved is entirely contrary to the fact. It has never been disproved. Bishop Gore, after a life-long study, could write: "I totally disagree with those who say that modern historical criticism has tended to weaken the distinctive Catholic position about the Apostolic Succession of the ministry, or the place of the episcopate. Really I think the effect has been the opposite."[1]

In support of this decision Bishop Gore referred to four writers—Batiffol, Duchesne, Turner, and Hamilton.

The passages to which reference is made are presumably such as the following:

Duchesne[2] concludes that "the view that the Episcopate represents the Apostolic Succession is in accordance with the sum-total of the facts as we know them."

Batiffol[3] maintains that "the deposit of revealed faith ... was, by divine right, entrusted to the guardianship of the Bishops, the successors of the Apostles." Contending at the same time that his investigation "is conducted, as no one has ventured to deny, in full accordance with the historical method."[4]

It has to be remembered, as Professor Cuthbert Turner pointed out, that the precise conditions required to make a Bishop a successor of the Apostles were not definitely raised until instances had occurred in which uncertainty

[1] Bishop Gore, *Basis of Anglican Fellowship*, 1914, p. 30.
[2] *Early History of the Church of England*, 1909, p. 66.
[3] *Primitive Catholicism*, English translation, 1911, p. vii.
[4] Ibid., p. viii.

31

was actually felt in regard to the genuineness of some particular claim. But there is no reason to doubt that, from the earliest period, wherever succession was recognised at all, two conditions, and only two, were implicitly assumed as necessary elements in the case. To be a Bishop in succession from the Apostles it was necessary to possess a right relation to the local Church, of which he claimed to have been constituted the head, and a right relation to the Universal Church, of the Episcopate of which he claimed to have been constituted a member. If he had not received ordination to the Episcopal office he had no right to exercise Episcopal functions, because, without this *charisma* of his ordination, he and his community had nothing to stand upon but their own basis: with it they possessed the whole fellowship and life and virtue of the Church Catholic and Apostolic.[1] "Conversely if, although genuinely ordained to the office of a Bishop, he was not the lawful occupant of any particular See in the communion of the Church and represented no body of Christian people, then he was not really in any line of the Apostolic Succession."

To these may be added the light thrown upon the principle of Apostolic Succession by experience in the Mission Field, as described by Bishop Palmer of Bombay before the Conference on Reunion at Lausanne:

"The whole Christian world at the end of the second century believed the bishops of certain sees to be the successors of Apostles in those places. It is true that these, and other items which might be cited, are only fragmentary pieces in favour of what tradition says.

[1] In Swete, *Essays on the Early History of the Church and the Ministry*, p. 107 1918.

The Apostolic Succession

But no one can live on a mission-field, so long as I have, without seeing that tradition is right. The order of proceedings is universal. First the missionary itinerates, secondly he or his successor settles in suitable headquarters, and from there superintends the Church in the surrounding district, thirdly, that duty of supervision passes into the hands of a local minister. That is the normal, natural, almost necessary development. That is exactly how the authority of the Apostles passed into that of the bishops. . . . I feel no reason to doubt, but every reason to accept, the tradition that the Bishops succeeded the Apostles in everything that they could succeed to."[1]

II

The changes which took place at the Reformation with regard to the Ministry of the Church did not originate in any desire to reject the doctrine of Apostolic Succession. It was not Episcopacy as such that the Reformers desired to abolish, but the medieval encroachments upon it, and the secularities with which the Episcopate had become identified. The Augsburg Confession of 1540 makes this distinction perfectly plain. In the section on the power of the Bishops, the German Reformers say that the Bishops could easily secure lawful obedience if they did not insist on maintaining traditions which could not be maintained with a good conscience. The Reformers expressly declared that they did not seek that Bishops should lay aside their Episcopal dignity, but only that they should cease to impose unjust burdens,

[1] Bishop Palmer of Bombay at Lausanne Conference. Bate, *Faith and Order*, p. 238.

The History of the Anglo-Catholic Revival

which are novelties and outside the custom of the Catholic Church. The principal grievance of the German Reformers was that the Bishops would not allow them to preach the pure doctrine of the Gospel. Accordingly, the Reformers complained that the Bishops imposed upon them the alternative to choose between obedience to the Episcopate and obedience to Christian Truth.

In this dilemma they argued that their duty was to obey God rather than man. Hence they dissociated themselves from the Historic ministry. It is important to lay stress on this fact that the Reformation nowhere began with a desire to introduce new principles about the ministry.

When the Reformers found themselves severed from the Historic ministry they were compelled to construct a ministry of their own. They did what in their circumstances was the obvious and natural thing. They appealed to the Scriptures. They endeavoured to reproduce, as far as they could, the ministry as they conceived it to have existed in the Apostolic Age. Out of these efforts to construct a ministry on the evidence of the New Testament two distinctive theories were created. One theory clung to the principle of succession, but denied that the succession depended upon the Bishops. Or rather it maintained that the power to ordain resided in every minister alike, and although it had not been exercised by ordinary pastors for many centuries, yet still the power was there, and could be put in practice in occasions of emergency. Hence arose the ministry of the Presbyterian.

The other theory abandoned altogether the principle of Apostolic Succession, and decided that ministerial authority belonged to the whole body of the Church, which

The Apostolic Succession

could confer it in such ways and on such persons as the community might choose. Hence arose the ministry of Congregationalism.

Neither the Presbyterian nor the Congregationalist conception of the ministry was the original reason for separation. They were the consequences of the same. In the reaction, the non-episcopal Communions—as modern phrase describes them—came in controversy to repudiate the Historic ministry and its principles in terms which were not deficient in force. There was much regrettable denunciation on either side.

Professor Briggs[1] observed that the separation of the Bishops from most of the Continental Churches of the Reformation left those National Churches in such an abnormal condition that the only ordained ministry left to them was obliged to exercise all the functions of the ministry. On the basis of this necessity he claims that their acts, even if irregular and disorderly, were not the usurped authority of individuals, but the Authority of organised National Churches, in accordance with natural law and order. But, as Bishop Gore contended, it cannot be maintained that the acts of ordination by which presbyters of the sixteenth or subsequent centuries originated ministers were covered by their commissions. And, of course, it may be added that the power of a local Church to authorise such actions is the question at issue. Necessity may compel a temporary expedient, but it cannot create equivalents, nor permanently justify continuance of that which was admittedly introduced under abnormal conditions.

The theory of the Ministry which Calvin thought he

[1] *On Unity*, p. 89.

The History of the Anglo-Catholic Revival

found in Scripture was that the Apostles were the Architects who laid the foundation; the Prophets were exceptional exponents of Revelation; Evangelists were inferior to the Apostles, but next to them in rank, and occasionally their substitutes.[1] But none of these three functions were instituted to be perpetual. The ministers who were designed to be perpetual were Pastors and Teachers. The Church could never dispense with these. The difference of function between these two kinds of minister was that the Teacher was not concerned with the administration of the Sacraments, but only with the interpretation of Scripture.[2]

On Calvin's theory the inevitable Anglo-Catholic comment was concisely and forcibly uttered by Bishop Palmer of Bombay at the Lausanne Conference that "Calvin made the most amazing mistake for an able man when he tried to reform the Church by reconstructing it after the pattern of the Apostolic age *minus* the Apostles."[3]

It may, indeed, be argued that the implicit logic of their position led those who were parted from the Apostolic Succession to formulate new theories of the ministry, and then, quite naturally, to claim for these new theories an authority independent of the ancient ministry of the Historic Church. But this theoretical defence was rather the sequel to their separation than its original and primary cause. A partial parallel may be seen in Wesley's change of principles from the High Churchman with his episcopal ordination to the Presbyterian ordainer of others when the English Church had unhappily lost him.

[1] Eph. i and ii.
[2] *Institute*, Bk. IV, ch. iii, par. 4.
[3] Bate, *Faith and Order*. Lausanne, 1927, p. 238.

The Apostolic Succession
III

As to the maintenance of the Apostolic Succession in the English Church, a few examples will suffice to illustrate what has been held since the Catholic Revival.

Bishop Stubbs's words are weighty as a historian of Episcopacy. In his first Visitation Charge to the Diocese of Oxford in 1890, he reminded the clergy that up to the period of the Reformation "there was no other idea of episcopacy except that of transmission of Apostolic commission," and that "the historic episcopate, not merely as a method of Church government—in which sense it could scarcely be called historic—but as a distinct, substantive, and historical transmission of the commission of the Apostles, in and by which our Lord formed His disciples through all generations into a distinctly organised body or Church—the historic episcopate is of the very essence of the Church of England."[1]

In the answer of the Archbishops of England to the Apostolic letter of Pope Leo XIII on English Ordinations, an answer addressed to the whole body of Bishops of the Catholic Church, it was explained with regard to our Ordinal that "the succession and continuance of these offices from the Lord through the Apostles and the other ministers of the primitive Church is also clearly implied in the Eucharistical prayers which precede the words 'Receive the Holy Ghost.' Thus the intention of our Fathers was to keep and continue these offices which come down from the earliest times, and reverently to use and esteem them, in the sense, of course, in which they were received from the Apostles and had been up to that time in use."[2]

[1] *Visitation Charges*, p. 130.   [2] P. 32.

The History of the Anglo-Catholic Revival

It is, of course, a fact that this Answer of the English Archbishops was a document for which the two Primates were responsible, and that it had not behind it the Synodical support of Convocation. Yet it cannot be denied that it was one of the most official Anglican utterances since the Reformation, issued at the crisis when its Orders were repudiated at Rome, when therefore a declaration about ministerial succession, and the intention to retain the ministerial inheritance, in the sense in which it had been received from the Apostles, and had been up to the time of the Reformation in use, could only mean a deliberate claim to identity of principles with the centuries previous to the sixteenth, and would have been no answer whatever to Rome if it had meant that the Church of England did not retain the Catholic conception.

Bishop Hall of Vermont taught his clergy that "If ordination by Bishops is only a matter of spiritual convenience or ecclesiastical order, like the consecration of Churches, then we have no right to stand by our own preferences, if they prove an obstacle to more harmonious working with others. If, on the other hand, the handing on of the ministerial commission by those who have duly received it, is a principle of the Kingdom of Christ, and a necessary guarantee for the validity of ministrations (i.e. for God's pledged sanction and ratification of them) it is an altogether different matter, and we ought to be ready to bear misunderstanding and misrepresentation while we bear witness to what, if a part of God's design for His Church, must be a necessary element in any sound and lasting reunion."[1]

[1] Bishop Hall of Vermont, *Charge on the Apostolic Ministry*, 1910, p. 36.

The Apostolic Succession

At the Church Congress at Cambridge in 1910 Bishop Gore felt bound to say that "the Anglican communion would certainly be rent in twain on the day on which any non-episcopally ordained minister was formally allowed within our communion to celebrate the Eucharist, and any Colonial Church of our communion which recognised in this way the validity of non-episcopal orders, would either be disowned by others parts of the Anglican communion or, if that were not the case would cause ... a division within our communion at home." The impression which that opinion made on those who held other theories justified Bishop Gore's later reflection that "those who most resent that so it should be have not been able to deny that so it is."[1]

Quite consistently with this, Bishop Gore, expounding the Basis of Anglican Fellowship, regards the ministerial succession as fundamental to the constitution of the English Church. "In the preface to the Ordinal it claims that the Orders of Bishops, Priests, and Deacons have been in the Church from the Apostles' time, and it asserts its intention that they should be continued in the Church of England; and it admits to its ministry all persons who 'have had formerly episcopal consecration or ordination' without any further ordination, but ordains *de novo* all others; and within the threefold ministry it restricts to Bishops Ordinations and Confirmations, with other minor functions, and it restricts to priests the ministry of the Eucharist and of Absolution."[2]

"It is quite true that the Church of England imposes upon the clergy no obligation to hold the dogma that only episcopal ordinations are valid, and only priestly con-

[1] *Basis of Anglican Fellowship*, 1914, p. 35. [2] Ibid., p. 34.

secrations of the Eucharist, and that Bishops are of the *esse* of the Church, but it has acted, so far as concerns its corporate action, always in such a way as to satisfy those who hold these doctrines, and to impose a severe restriction on the action which those who do not hold them would naturally wish to take.... If you hold the Lutheran or the Calvinist theory of the ministry, you naturally desire to recognise practically the essential indifference of all forms of ministry; but the Church of England, by its requirements for ministry, most severely restricts such inclination. Also, the whole coherence of the Church of England depends on the maintenance of those severe but Catholic principles."[1]

Another Anglo-Catholic representative, the late Canon Lacey, taught as follows: "I conclude that the Episcopate is indispensable for one reason alone; it is the Apostolate, the one fundamental ministry of the Church, the only one of Divine institution, given to the Church by the ascended Lord, set in the Church by God Himself."[2]

IV

But if we are to appreciate the Anglo-Catholic insistence on Apostolic Succession, it must be remembered that this principle concerning the Christian Ministry is regarded as essential both in the Roman Church and also in the Orthodox Churches of the East.

The German theologian Möhler was, in the latter half of the nineteenth century, a very celebrated advocate of Catholicism as against Protestantism. Möhler's *Symbolism*

[1] *Basis of Anglican Fellowship*, 1914, p. 94.
[2] Lacey, *Essays in Positive Theology*, p. 228.

The Apostolic Succession

was highly valued among the later Tractarians, and warmly commended to their followers. He may be taken as one of the ablest modern German exponents of the principle of Apostolic Succession.

Möhler declared the faith of the Church on this subject to be that the Apostles were sent forth by the Saviour, they in their turn instituted Bishops, and these appointed their successors, and so on down to our own days. "By this episcopal succession, beginning from our Saviour, and continued on without interruption, we can especially recognise, as by an outward mark, which is the true Church founded by Him. The Episcopate, the continuation of the Apostleship, is accordingly revered as a Divine institution."[1] Möhler's work was first published in 1832, and ran through many editions in the German, besides being translated into English.

But it is not difficult to show that the Greek Church is no less tenacious of the principle of secession than the Latin.

Androutsos is certainly one of the ablest of the modern Greek theologians. His exposition of the doctrine is that the Apostles, conscious of their direct commission by our Lord, not only had power to celebrate the ministry entrusted to them in the name of the Lord, but imparted the priestly authority to others, appointing in the Holy Spirit deacons and presbyters, and establishing successors of their apostolic functions.[2]

Stephen Zankow, professor in the University of Sophia, in his lectures delivered in the University of Berlin, sums up the doctrine of the Ministry as held in the Greek Church in two principles. First that in its

[1] Par. xliii. [2] Androutsos, *Dogmatiké*, Athens, 1907.

The History of the Anglo-Catholic Revival

origin, doctrine, and essential constitution the Greek Church has continued true to the Apostolic doctrine and constitution, and will continue to do so. Secondly, that this continuity with the Apostles and their spirit is maintained through the Apostolic succession.[1]

The Archpriest Sergius Bulgakoff, professor in Paris, writing in 1931, explained that according to the Orthodox faith no approval of men, and no election by man, can confer on any person authority to celebrate the Eucharist.[2] Approval is, indeed, a preliminary condition to Ordination. But only the Divine omnipotence of Christ, which was bestowed upon the Apostles, and which is extended in the succession of Apostolic Ordination, can bestow this sacred power.

The representatives of the Eastern Church at Lausanne formulated the Orthodox doctrine of the ministry in the following terms:

"The Orthodox Church, regarding the ministry as instituted in the Church by Christ Himself, and as the body which by a special *charisma* is the organ through which the Church spreads its means of grace, such as the Sacraments, and believing that the ministry in its threefold form of Bishops, Presbyters, and Deacons can only be based on the unbroken Apostolic Succession, regrets that it is unable to come, in regard to the ministry, into some measure of agreement with many of the Churches represented at this Conference; but prays God that He, through His Holy Spirit, will guide to union even in regard to this difficult point of disagreement."[3]

[1] Zankow, *Das Orthodoxe Christentum des Ostens*, 1928, p. 79.
[2] Bulgakoff in *Die Hochkriohe*, August 1931, p. 259.
[3] Bate, *Faith and Order*, p. 427.

The Apostolic Succession

The recognition of Anglican Orders by Authorities in the Eastern Church is one of the most remarkable advances of the twentieth century. Meletios, Ecumenical Patriarch of Constantinople, in his letter to the Archbishop of Canterbury, July 1922, informed him that the Holy Synod had concluded that the ordinations of the Anglican Episcopal Communion possess the same validity as those of the Roman, Old Catholic, and Armenian Churches, "inasmuch as all essentials are found in them which are held indispensable from the orthodox point of view for the recognition of the *charisma* of the Priesthood derived from Apostolic Succession."[1]

This letter was followed, in 1923, by another to the same effect from the Patriarch of Jerusalem.[2] The Archbishop of Cyprus, with his Holy Synod, concurred in the same conclusion. In all these three letters stress is laid on the Apostolic Succession.

V

Looking back on this outline of the belief in Apostolic Succession it is obvious that this Anglo-Catholic belief has been and still is the belief prevalent all over the Episcopal Communions of East and West. Whatever criticism has been urged against the Catholic Revival on the ground that it made this principle unduly prominent, the fact remains that East and West are deliberately committed to the doctrine that the Episcopate is part of the organic constitution divinely imposed on the Church, and that this constitution is perpetuated from Christ

---

[1] Bell, *Documents on Christian Unity*, 1924, p. 94.
[2] Ibid., p. 97.

The History of the Anglo-Catholic Revival

through the Apostles by means of the Apostolic Succession. If this is so it follows that the prospect of Reunion in the Historic Episcopate without any interpretation of its meaning is hopeless. Neither the Roman nor the Orthodox Church could value the Episcopate as they do without its basis in the fact of the Apostolic Succession. And this is what Anglo-Catholicism has been maintaining.

When the time arrives that complete Reunion has been accomplished with the Orthodox East, the Roman Catholic rejection of Anglican Orders will be neutralised in face of facts. If Rome recognises the Orders of the Eastern Church, and the Eastern Church not only recognises but identifies itself with the Anglican, the attitude of the Roman controversialist in this matter will be bound to change.

Rightly understood the Apostolic Succession is neither mechanical nor merely legal, but deeply spiritual. It must never be dissociated from the Apostolic Faith and the Apostolic Sacrament. It is no mere question of external forms and the laying on of hands, but of the Divine Commission transmitted through its possessors, the continuity of the Divine Organism of the Church in its ministerial Constitution.

Among German Evangelical writers no one has entered more sympathetically into the conception of Apostolic Succession than Friedrich Heiler. He sees that the principle of evolution has been at work on what existed originally in an undeveloped state. Just as the Christological doctrine, and the Trinitarian doctrine, and the sacramental principle, have all gradually matured into clear and definite expression, so also the Apostolic Ministry. All these different spheres—Credal, Sacra-

The Apostolic Succession

mental, Ministerial—have undergone a similar development, with the result that in all three alike the Church of the twentieth century is united to the Church of the first century.[1]

Heiler recognises in the Apostolic Succession a wonderful Symbol of the uninterrupted unity of life between the Church of to-day and the Church of the Apostolic Age.[2] If the principle is liable to over-valuation, it is also liable to be insufficiently esteemed. Incorporation in the Apostolic Succession is an essential in all Catholicising aims.

[1] Heiler, *Im Ringen um die Kirche*, 1931, p. 491.
[2] Ibid., pp. 504, 505–6.

CHAPTER III

THE DECISIONS OF THE COURTS ON DOCTRINE

ON three conspicuous occasions the Privy Council pronounced decisions concerning the doctrines of the Church. It is well that these should be grouped together and considered apart from decisions on ceremonial, since in the doctrinal sentences the respective authority of the secular and the spiritual is apparent in its acutest form.

Before approaching these doctrinal decisions of the Privy Council it is advisable by way of introduction to recall the attitude of the State towards the Church's defence of its Faith displayed in the Hampden Controversy. Dr. Hampden, Bampton lecturer in 1832, was described by a contemporary Oxford writer[1] as avowing the boldest latitudinarianism and placing Socinians on a level with all other Christians. In 1836, says the same writer, the University of Oxford was "electrified by the intelligence that Dr. Hampden had been appointed to the vacant chair" of the Regius Professor of Divinity. "This measure seemed a designed insult to the University for its resistance to the Ministry in the preceding years. It was like an attempt to force latitudinarian principles on the Church. It was to place in the chair of Divinity, with the power of instructing and guiding half the rising clergy of England, one who would undermine the authority of our Creeds and Articles." What

[1] William Palmer of Worcester, *Narrative of Events*, 1843, p. 28.

The Decisions of the Courts on Doctrine

Oxford thought of Hampden was proved when he was pronounced by the Vice-Chancellor to have treated theological subjects in such a manner in his published works that the University in this respect had no confidence in him. This censure was passed by an overwhelming majority. However, the fact that Hampden was under censure by his own University for unorthodox opinions did not prevent the Premier, Lord John Russell, from recommending him in 1847 for the Bishopric of Hereford. Lord John was satisfied that this appointment was "calculated to strengthen the Protestant character of our Church." The Archbishop of Canterbury (Dr. Howley) sent a remonstrance to the Premier against the nomination. Thirteen Bishops of the Church of England sent a united Protest to the same effect; 1,650 priests of the English Church appealed to Dr. Sumner, who in the interval had become Archbishop in Dr. Howley's place, imploring him to refuse to consecrate. The appointment was resented by Evangelicals as well as Tractarians. When the *Congé d'Élire* was received at Hereford, Dr. Merewether, the Dean, protested against the election. The thirteen Bishops represented to the Head of the Government their earnest conviction that if the appointment of Dr. Hampden to the Episcopate were completed, the peace of the Church would be in danger, and the confidence both of clergy and laity in the exercise of the Royal Supremacy would be weakened.

Lord John Russell replied that if he withdrew his recommendation, which the Queen approved, he would virtually assent to the doctrine that the Supremacy which is now by law vested in the Crown was to be transferred to a majority of the members of one of our Universities.

The History of the Anglo-Catholic Revival

Many of the objectors had joined the Church of Rome. At which he did not seem concerned. And he could not sacrifice the rights of the Crown, and what he believed to be the true interests of the Church, to a feeling founded on misapprehension and fomented by prejudice. His letter showed no deference whatever to the remonstrances of the Primate of the English Church and the collective Protest of thirteen of its Bishops.

After that treatment of the Episcopate it was not to be expected that the protest of a Dean would have much influence. The Dean of Hereford appealed to the Queen, begging to be relieved from the necessity of proceeding to the election of Dr. Hampden until the published writings of the same had been submitted to the judgment of Convocation. The only reply to that appeal was a brief note informing the Dean that his letter had been laid before her Majesty, and that the Queen had not been pleased to issue any commands thereupon.

So the State prevailed, rode roughshod over the Church, and inflicted upon the Spiritual Institution a person considered by the responsible authorities of that Institution quite unqualified to teach its Faith and principles.

Nothing can illustrate more conclusively the complete submission of the Authorities of the Church to those of the State. It is inevitable to ask why the Primate of the English Church and thirteen Bishops who protested against the nomination to the Episcopate of one whom they regarded as utterly unfit for the Apostolic office consented, nevertheless, to consecrate him. We may speculate what the History of the Church would have been if the whole Episcopate had resolved that Hampden's

The Decisions of the Courts on Doctrine

consecration must be refused. Their inability to resist the arbitrary action of the State illustrates both the blindness of the Secular Authorities to the Church and its principles, and the powerlessness of the Spiritual Authorities to hold their own against the State when a crisis came.

It was on a background of this nature and with traditional despotic dealing of this kind, that the Judicial Court of the Privy Council entered on its pronouncements on the Sacramental doctrine of the Church.

I

The first of the three Doctrinal Judgments was in the Gorham case in 1850.

In 1850 the Catholic-minded within the English Church were deeply disturbed and distressed by the Gorham judgment on the Sacrament of Baptism.[1] According to the Court which tried the case, Gorham was said to hold that the grace of Regeneration does not so necessarily accompany the act of Baptism that Regeneration invariably takes place. The grace of Regeneration might be granted before or after Baptism. It was held by the Court that the Church of England at the Reformation was harassed by a great variety of opinions concerning Baptism,[2] which rendered it difficult even if it had been desirable not to allow some latitude of interpretation;[3] that the queston at issue was among the points left undecided; that the thanksgiving "that hath pleased Thee to regenerate this infant"[4] did not determine the

[1] Broderick and Freemantle, *Eccles. Judgments of the P.C.*
[2] Ibid., p. 91.   [3] Ibid., p. 95.   [4] Ibid., p. 100.

case of adult persons,[1] that upright and conscientious men cannot in all respects agree upon subjects so difficult; and therefore it was not the duty of the Court to be minute and rigid in cases of this sort. It was decreed accordingly that the doctrine held by Mr. Gorham was not contrary or repugnant to the declared doctrine of the Church of England as by law established.[2]

On the Gorham case a singularly outspoken letter was sent by the Bishop of Exeter (Phillpotts) to the Archbishop of Canterbury.

"My Lord, I shall not be thought to impute wrong motives to your Grace, beyond the common infirmity of our nature, if I aver my belief that other motives besides mere justice and truth, swayed this sentence of your Grace in your advice upon it. I cannot imagine that English judges could have been betrayed into so grievous a perversion of justice, or your Grace into sanctioning it, had there not been some very powerful motive which, through the kindly feelings of our nature, blinded their and your eyes to the evil of tampering with justice. Common report said that such principles were even avowed. It was feared lest, if a true judgment should be given, a large number of clergymen would be driven to resign their office—perhaps to leave the Church. And so a temporising measure was adopted which, it was thought, would satisfy both parties, and leave the position of both untouched."[3]

It is instructive to recall the reflections of an eminent lawyer who was one of the Privy Council Judges in this

[1] Broderick and Freemantle, *Eccles. Judgments of the P.C.*, p. 101. [2] Ibid., p. 105.
[3] Quoted in *Christian Remembrancer*, 1868, p. 228.

The Decisions of the Courts on Doctrine

Gorham case. "I found myself called upon," said Lord Chancellor Campbell, "as the member of a tribunal to decide a question of dogmatic theology—whether, that is, the Church of England teaches that there is absolutely spiritual regeneration by the act of Christian Baptism." And he rejoiced to find that the Court were able to come to the decision "so desirable for the peace of the Church—that neither liturgy nor Articles can be said exactly to define the mode of regeneration, and that the point on which the parties differ might be left an open question."[1]

We who can now look back on a whole series of Privy Council Decisions in Ecclesiastical affairs, are accustomed to draw distinctions between what the State Courts have pronounced and what the Church has in reality accepted. We know after this lapse of time that the Privy Council Decision on Baptismal Regeneration is practically as if it had never been. All the Catholic-minded in the Church of England view that Decision with imperturbable indifference. We continue serenely to say, as the Church directs at every Infant Baptism: "seeing now that this child *is* regenerate." Unless language is designed to mean the contrary of what it says, the Church is committed to the most definite possible affirmation of the spiritual reality involved when a child is baptised.

It would never occur to any Catholic-minded person to-day that the Gorham Judgment was an argument for secession from the English Church. To us it seems irresistibly clear that the actual language of the Baptismal Office is its unanswerable refutation. The Church of England is not ambiguous in that expression; on the

[1] Lord Campbell's *Life*, ii. 216, quoted by Spencer Holland, p. 41.

The History of the Anglo-Catholic Revival

contrary, it is so definite that men have complained of it on that very ground.

But the effect of this Privy Council decision in 1850 was to produce dismay and consternation in every Catholic-minded person—priest and layman alike. How deep that consternation was their words and actions display.

To William Dodsworth, for instance, Vicar of Christ Church, Albany Street, in S. Pancras, London, the devoted priest who with Pusey had been instrumental in forming the first Sisterhood in the Church of England since the Reformation, the fact seemed fatal that, although the Court which tried the matter first decided in favour of the Bishop of Exeter, that the Church of England allows no other doctrine than that of unconditional regeneration of Infants in Holy Baptism, the Final Court of Appeal reversed the judgment and allowed a priest to teach that regeneration is an open question in the Church of England. Dodsworth informed his people that this decision substantially altered the position of the English Church. He saw no way to evade that conclusion. He did not see how the Decision could be repudiated as a mere decision of the State. The only remedy he could see was an immediate revival of the Church's Synods and the enactment by the Church itself of terms which will admit no ambiguity.

Anderdon, Vicar of S. Margaret's, Leicester, appealed to the Church of England in the most impassioned terms to dissociate itself from the ambiguous position imposed upon it by the State.

"O my Mother, whose claims on the allegiance of thy sons and daughters are undiminished, nay endeared by

The Decisions of the Courts on Doctrine

thy cruel bondage, call upon us, we are thine! Command our obedience, not by human enactment, or policy of this world, or protection of any arm of flesh, but of thy divine undoubted prerogative, by the commission and promise of thy Lord, by the Gift of Pentecost.... Dare to lose all for Christ: and in thy sackcloth and tribulation thou shalt win back the hearts of thy children, distrustful of thee only amid the softnesses of this world, and the favour of potentates, and the golden chains whereby they pretend to honour, but in truth enslave thee."[1]

After this sermon the Vicar of S. Margaret's, Leicester, seceded. Charles Gutch, preaching to the desolated congregation, owned that humanly speaking this trouble could never have come upon them "had that most appalling sentence declaring our Regeneration in Baptism an open question" never been pronounced. And even after that sentence had done its miserable work, Anderdon would not have departed, "had the true doctrine then been plainly declared, authoritatively, or only reaffirmed by the collective voice, so earnestly besought, of the English Episcopate."[2]

A considerable number of secessions resulted. The Church of England lost Manning, Maskell, Dodsworth, Archdeacon Wilberforce, Allies, Hope Scott; nor were these by any means all. There were said to have been at least fourteen. Mercifully, others stood firm. A sober and deliberate estimate of the matter was pronounced from the University Pulpit at Cambridge by Professor W. H. Mill. Mill urged very strongly and deliberately that "it is far too evident to need proof to any one, that if the

[1] Anderdon, *Contending for the Faith*, 1850.
[2] Sermon by Charles Gutch, 1850, p. 15.

promulgation of new statements on matters of faith requires the sanction and cognisance of those in whom spiritual jurisdiction is lodged, no less so must the definition of the sense in which existing statements are received."[1]

But in spite of reassuring estimates the unsettlement and anxious fears created by the Gorham Judgment were profound. J. D., afterwards Lord, Coleridge, writing in 1850 to his father, said that "the whole Catholic feeling of the English Episcopate is centred in Exeter and Bangor (the latter too mild to move) and Exeter's right feeling is confined to one or two isolated points. What English Bishops, think you, would dare to advocate Sacramental Confession; the Sacrifice of the Eucharist; Prayers for the dead; due honour to the Blessed Virgin and the Saints; extreme unction, or half a hundred other points, of the one Catholic Faith?"[2]

How wide the unsettlement was among those who remained is shown in the same eminent lawyer's anxious words: "If we cease to have one Baptism, we may soon cease to have one Faith and one Lord, and then we *must* go whether we like it or not. But I think we ought to wait and see for a good long while."

On this Privy Council judgment in the Gorham case Dr. Pusey said: "The Judges knew nothing of Theology, and for fear of driving out of the Church a body, hardly any of whom agreed with Mr. Gorham, persuaded themselves that the most naked Zwinglianism was compatible with a Baptismal Service which thanks God for regenerat-

---

[1] W. H. Mill, *Human Policy and Divine Truth*, 1850, p. 17.
[2] *Life of Lord Coleridge, Lord Chief Justice of England*, 1904, i. 194.

The Decisions of the Courts on Doctrine

ing each baptised child, one by one. Almost all the Bishops reaffirmed the doctrine which the Judges had denied."[1]

Pusey said that what retained Keble and himself in the English Church after the Gorham Judgment was their conviction that the Church of England contradicted continually, and thus practically set aside for her members, that wrong teaching of the Privy Council: since at every Baptism of every child the Church expressed its thanksgiving that it had pleased God to regenerate the Infant. Had it not been for that conviction he must have left the Church of England, not to enter the Church of Rome, but either that of Scotland or America. The Gorham Judgment impaired the discipline of the English Church, but not its doctrine. That remained as distinct as before.[2]

II

In 1853 the Privy Council passed judgment on the Eucharist. Denison, Archdeacon of Taunton, taught in his sermons that "*it is not* true that the Consecrated Bread and Wine are changed in their natural substances, for they remain in their very natural substances, and therefore may not be adored. It *is* true that worship is due to the Real, though invisible and supernatural Presence of the Body and Blood of Christ, in the Holy Eucharist, under the form of Bread and Wine."[3]

The doctrine concerning the Real Presence which Denison, Archdeacon of Taunton, was accused before the Courts of holding included the following propositions:

[1] Pusey, *Unlaw*, 1881, p. 5.
[2] Ibid., pp. 3-4. [3] *Notes of My Life*, p. 251.

The History of the Anglo-Catholic Revival

"That the bread and wine became, by an act of consecration, the outward part or sign of the Lord's Supper; and, considered as objects of sense, are unchanged by the act of consecration, remaining still in their very natural substances; that the inward part or thing signified is the Body and Blood of Christ; that the Body and Blood of Christ being present naturally in Heaven, are, supernaturally and invisibly, but really, present in the Lord's Supper, through the elements, by virtue of the act of consecration; that worship is due to the Body and Blood of Christ, supernaturally and invisibly, but really, present in the Lord's Supper, under the form of bread and wine, by reason of that Godhead with which they are personally united. But that the elements through which the Body and Blood of Christ are given and received, may not be worshipped."

These doctrines which Archdeacon Denison was charged with holding and teaching were condemned in the first trial, then, on appeal to the Court of Arches, acquitted, and this sentence of acquittal was sustained by the Judicial Committee of the Privy Council.[1]

The condemnation of the doctrine of the Real Presence maintained by Archdeacon Denison pronounced by Archbishop Sumner in the first trial was the cause of Keble's writing his book on *Eucharistic Adoration*, which appeared in 1857.[2] His purpose was to give the evidence both in the English Church since the Reformation, and in the primitive Church itself for belief in the reality of the supernatural effect produced upon the elements by consecration. It should be remembered that in the

---
[1] Cf. Phillimore, *Ecclesiastical Law*, i. 532–533.
[2] Coleridge, *Life of Keble*, ii. 433–434.

The Decisions of the Courts on Doctrine

Christian Year, published years before, he had originally written about the Eucharistic gift the following lines:

> There, present in the heart,
> Not in the hands, the eternal Priest
> Will his true self impart.

Dr. Walter Lock remarks on these words that probably Keble would not have written this line in later life, for Keble stated in 1845 that when he wrote the *Christian Year* he did not fully understand the doctrine of the Eucharist. And he frequently refused to alter it because it seemed to him valuable as a protection against a notion of a gross carnal presence. But in 1866 "Bishops in Convocation quoted the lines as expressing Keble's opinion against a real objective Presence. And this weighed upon his mind so much that he decided to make the alteration" which on his deathbed he did. The later editions accordingly agree with his matured belief on the presence in the elements.[1]

While Evangelicals within the Church of England were protesting against the doctrine of the Real Presence connected with the consecrated elements in the Eucharist, it is interesting to note that an able critic outside the Church maintained that the Prayer Book did not support them. Dr. Martineau, the Unitarian, in a volume published in 1858, insisted that "the office of Communion contains even stronger marks of the same sacerdotal superstitions; and notwithstanding the Protestant horror entertained of the Mass, approaches it so nearly, that no ingenuity can exhibit them in contrast. Near doctrines, however, like near neighbours, are known to quarrel most."[2] Martineau

[1] Lock's *Life of Keble*, p. 56.   [2] Ibid., p. 51.

The History of the Anglo-Catholic Revival

notes that the significance of Consecrating the Elements is shown in the fact that "the sacredness thus imparted is represented as surviving the celebration of the Supper, and residing in the substances as a permanent quality: for in the disposal of the bread and wine that may remain at the close of the sacramental feast, a distinction is made between the consecrated and the unconsecrated portion of the elements: the former is not permitted to quit the Altar, but is to be reverently consumed by the priest and the communicants; the latter is given to the curate.[1] What the particular change may be which the prayer and manipulation of the minister are thought to induce it is by no means easy to determine; nor would the discovery, perhaps, reward our pains. It is certainly conceived that they cease to be any longer mere bread and wine, and that with them thenceforth coexist, really and substantially, the body and blood of Christ. Respecting this *Real Presence* with the elements, there is no dispute between the Romish and the English Church: both unequivocally maintain it: and the only question is, respecting the *Real Absence* of the original and culinary bread and wine: the Roman Catholic believing that these substantially vanish and are replaced by the body and blood of Christ, the English Protestant conceiving that they remain, but are united with the latter. Martineau's conclusion is that "However anxious, indeed, the clergy of the Evangelical School may be to disguise the fact, it cannot be doubted that their Church has always maintained a supernatural change in the elements themselves, as well as in the mind of the receiver." Consequently, Martineau cannot deny to the Oxford divines the merit

[1] Lock's *Life of Keble*, p. 52.

The Decisions of the Courts on Doctrine

(whatever it may be) of consenting with the theology of their Church.

Considering the period at which these reflections were published and the violent controversies on the Real Presence by which the Church of England was agitated, there is something deeply impressive in Martineau's recognition of doctrines which he could not appreciate, yet which he was convinced by its formularies that the English Church implied.

Bishop Thirlwall said that "apart from the express admission of Transubstantiation, or of the gross carnal notions to which it gave rise ... there can hardly be any description of the Real Presence ... that would not be found to be authorised by the language of eminent divines of our Church." Thirlwall was "not aware and did not believe, that our most advanced Ritualists have in fact overstepped these very ample bounds."[1]

III

The doctrine concerning the Eucharist was again brought before the Courts in 1869. Bennett, Vicar of Frome, had published various statements on sacramental doctrine, both in an Essay contributed to the volume on *The Church and the World*, and also in a letter to Pusey entitled *A Plea for Toleration in the Church of England*. In the course of these statements Bennett spoke of "the real, actual, and visible Presence of the Lord upon the Altars of our Churches."[2] He asserted further the doctrine that the Eucharist is a Sacrifice, offered by the Priest, and

[1] Quoted by MacColl, *Lawlessness*, p. 324.
[2] *Eccles. Judgments*, pp. 299, 331.

spoke of the Sacrificial character of the Altar. And, further, he declared that he himself adored and taught the people to adore "the consecrated elements, believing Christ to be in them."

The Church Association made these doctrinal statements the occasion for commencing a prosecution against their author in the Ecclesiastical Courts.

The terms in which Bennett represented the doctrine were unquestionably unguarded, and indeed seriously inaccurate. They were terms which no trained theologian could possibly defend. Pusey felt obliged to entreat the author to revise his sentences. Bennett consented. He cancelled the epithet "visible" as applied to the Presence of our Lord upon the Altar, and wrote in subsequent editions of his pamphlet "the real actual Presence of our Lord under the form of bread and wine, upon the altar." He corrected also the phrase about adoring the consecrated elements into adoring Christ present in the elements under the form of bread and wine.

When the case came before the Court of Arches (Dr. Phillimore) the Rev. W. J. E. Bennett was charged with committing an offence against the laws ecclesiastical by the publication of a work containing heretical doctrines. Bennett refused to appear or to recognise the Court's authority, with the result that the Court was obliged to hear arguments on one side only.

Three great Eucharistic subjects were considered. The Real objective Presence, the Eucharistic Sacrifice, and the Adoration of Christ as really present.

On the doctrine of the Real Objective Presence, Dr. Phillimore, referring to Bennett's original expression—the visible presence of our Lord upon the Altars of our

The Decisions of the Courts on Doctrine

Churches—criticised it with great severity. He said: "I have read these words with much surprise and sorrow." He insisted that the least that the Church has the right to expect from a clergyman who publishes his opinions to the world is "the knowledge and erudition of a theologian, and the use of the most careful and well-considered language." The expression "visible presence" was pronounced at variance with all the Formularies of the Church. The author's language was characterised as "lamentably loose and inaccurate." But as to the Reality of Christ's Presence Dr. Phillimore produced a large array of evidence showing that the actual presence of the Body and Blood in the consecrated Bread and Wine, a presence objective, external to the communicants, had been taught by accredited teachers in the English Church. Thus Bishop Andrewes could accept the statement that "the Elements are changed by the benediction, so that the consecrated bread is not that which nature has formed, but that which the benediction has consecrated." And Bishop Cosin could say that "the Bread and Wine by the power of God and a supernatural virtue, are set apart and fitted for a much nobler use, and raised to a higher dignity than their nature bears." And Bishop Moberly could teach that "the spiritual presence of the Lord is so brought down upon the elements of Bread and Wine, as that to the faithful they become verily and, indeed, however invisibly and mysteriously, the Body and Blood of Christ." "The ancient doctrine of the Church, and, as I read it, the unquestionable doctrine of the Church of England, is that the spiritual presence of the Body and Blood of our Lord in the Holy Communion is objective and real."

The History of the Anglo-Catholic Revival

The Court of Arches accordingly decided that the description of the Presence in the Holy Eucharist as actual and real does not contravene the formularies of the English Church.

The second doctrine complained of was that the Eucharist is a Sacrifice. The learned Judge, relying on the authority of a number of older eminent Anglican teachers such as Mede, Andrewes, Laud, and Bull—also the recent works of Pusey, Keble, Moberly, and Churton—was "led to the certain conclusion that it is lawful for a clergyman to speak in some sense of the Eucharistic Sacrifice, and therefore, in some sense, also of the Sacrifice offered by the priest, and the sacrificial character of the Holy Table." The language of Mr. Bennett did not conflict with the Articles of Religion, nor with the Anglican Liturgy.

On the third complaint against him—that of adoring the consecrated Elements—Dr. Phillimore pronounced that this expression is contrary to the mind of the English Church as expressed in the declaration about kneeling. But in the later editions of his pamphlet, Bennett had corrected this expression and replaced it by the words—adoring Christ present in the Sacrament under the form of Bread and Wine. In this corrected form the expression was not at variance with the declaration on kneeling, nor with the Twenty-Eighth Article of Religion, for that Article contains no declaration against adoring the Spiritual Presence of Christ in the Holy Eucharist.

The conclusion reached by the Court was pronounced in terms of considerable severity: reiterating the rebuke of the defendant for borrowing opinions which he had to some extent caricatured; regretting also that the im-

The Decisions of the Courts on Doctrine

portant alterations which Bennett had made in his doctrinal statements were "unaccompanied by any expression of regret or self-reproach for the mischief which his crude and rash expressions have caused"; explaining also that it was not the function of the Court to try the defendant for careless language, for feeble reasoning, or superficial knowledge; but declaring at the same time that if the Court were to condemn the statement as corrected, it would be passing sentence upon a long roll of illustrious divines. Accordingly, the judgment pronounced by Dr. Phillimore was that "the Objective, Actual, and Real Presence, or the Spiritual Real Presence, a Presence external to the act of the communicant, appears to me to be the doctrine which the Formularies of our Church, duly considered and constructed so as to be harmonious, intended to maintain." He did not lay down this as a position of law, nor did he say that what is called the Receptionist Doctrine is inadmissible, but only intended to pronounce that to describe the mode of Presence as Objective, Real, Actual, and Spiritual, is certainly not contrary to the law. This was in 1870.

From this masterly judgment in the Ecclesiastical Court of Arches the Church Association appealed to the Privy Council.

Pusey also wrote an important letter to Gladstone, calling the statesman's attention to the fact that, except for two careless expressions, retracted at Pusey's request, Bennett was actually indicted simply for approving the very doctrine which Pusey himself had taught; and that if the Privy Council condemned Bennett, then Pusey himself was condemned, for it would be Pusey's own words which would at the same time be condemned.

The History of the Anglo-Catholic Revival

Moreover, this was no mere individual or personal matter. For, said Pusey, "it is the existence of the whole High Church body which is aimed at, and which is at stake, and with them the possible existence of any future High Church party in England."[1]

In 1872 the Privy Council confirmed the previous decision.

The Privy Council, while pronouncing judgment in the Bennett case, laid down the principles on which it conceived itself required to act. It declared quite plainly that "this Court has no jurisdiction or authority to settle matters of faith, or to determine what ought to be the doctrine of the Church of England." It was no part of its duty to usurp the functions of a Synod or Council. Its duty was to ascertain whether certain statements are so far repugnant to or contradictory of the language of the Articles and formularies, construed in their plain meaning, that they should receive judicial condemnation.

Whatever theoretical distinction might be made between a legal decision as to the agreement of certain statements with the formularies of the Church, and an ecclesiastical decision of the Church itself as to what its formularies mean, the sequel proves that in practical results the distinction made no difference. The practical result of the Gorham judgment was that a priest pronounced heretical by the Ecclesiastical Court was allowed to contradict the Church's formularies on Baptism, and the practical result of the Bennett judgment was that a priest was allowed to teach the doctrine of the Real Presence and the Eucharistic Sacrifice and consequent adoration. The Authorities of the Church submitted to

[1] *Life of Pusey*, iv. 218.

The Decisions of the Courts on Doctrine

both decisions, neither of which decisions were pronounced by the Church, but only by the State. Whatever may be the reason, the fact remains that since 1872 the Privy Council has made no decisions on the doctrine of the Church.

An Episcopal estimate of Ritualism in the Diocese of Bath and Wells in 1873 characterised it as disobedience to the Prayer Book, sheer obstinacy, a plain act of immorality, and contrary to all principles of true Churchmanship.[1] It was an attempt to reimpose Popery upon the English people. "Shall the mighty Revolution of the sixteenth century be undone? Shall we have a restoration of the Popedom on British soil? A restoration of all those corruptions, those follies, those idolatries, those perversions of the truth, those wretched debasing superstitions, and that priestly tyranny, which for so many centuries almost quenched the light of Christianity, and annihilated the liberties of the laity?"

Behind these Episcopal denunciations lay a definite repudiation of the Catholic doctrine of the Eucharist. The Bishop held that "the Church's definition of a Sacrament is conclusive against her holding the notion of an objective Presence of the Body and Blood of Christ in the Bread and Wine, apart from reception."

Against this denunciation and this exclusion of the objective Presence Bennett of Frome openly protested with a formidable array of extracts from the great Fathers of the early centuries.

Sanderson, Headmaster of Lancing, replying in 1875 to the charge that in many Ritualistic churches you would hear Transubstantiation unequivocally taught,

[1] Wagner, 5, Pamphlets, vol. 5.

The History of the Anglo-Catholic Revival
quoted a significant passage from the *Dublin Review*, which, referring to Pusey's teaching on the reality of the Eucharistic Presence, observed that there was "a scrupulous avoidance of every word and sentence and illustration which supposes or implies a change of substance, which would be construed into sanction of the Doctrine of Trent, or come into collision with 'Twenty-Eighth Article of England.' "

CHAPTER IV

THE RISE OF RITUALISM

To estimate rightly the rise of Ritualism it is essential to bear in mind the condition of the Church of England at the time when the movement arose. This is a matter on which contemporaries of the Ritual Revival have recorded their own experiences. Gladstone, for instance, told the world in the *Contemporary Review* his recollections: "our services were probably without a parallel in the world for their debasement; and as they would have shocked a Brahmin or a Buddhist, so they hardly could have been endured in this country had not the faculty of taste, and the perception of the seemly or unseemly, been as dead as the spirit of devotion. There were exceptions, and the exceptions were beginning to grow in number: but I speak of the general state of things, such as I can myself recollect it."[1]

That is Gladstone's experience. And this experience is similar to many other witnesses. It seems generally agreed that the external appearance of Religion in the Church of England at the beginning of the nineteenth century was one of unparalleled slovenliness and neglect.

One of the most obvious facts about the Tractarians is their entire absorption in doctrine and their independence of Ritualism. Concentrated on the restoration of neglected Truth they paid no attention to its ceremonial expression. The movement aspired to teach the Faith,

[1] *Contemporary Review*, 1875.

The History of the Anglo-Catholic Revival

and to awaken thereby the devotional spirit. It inspired men and women with the spirit of self-sacrifice, and sent them out from the intellectual atmosphere of the University into the towns and great centres of the population, to devote themselves to life-long service among the uneducated and poor.

It was in contact with the Nation at large that the rise of Ritualism began. Many influences contributed to its advancement. Among other things there was at this time, quite independently of the Oxford Revival, an appreciation of the Beautiful in Art, and a longing to associate it somehow with Religion.

A well-known and very eloquent passage published in 1850 illustrates the reaction from Puritanism to Catholic Symbolism which was beginning to arise at that date. "My thoughts would wander from the parsimonious simplicity of their sacred edifices, from the obtrusive prominence of the leaders of their worship, and from their isolation in the great Christian commonwealth, to those august communions where the priesthoods of earth symbolise the hierarchies of heaven; where the successors, in unbroken lineage from the Apostles, yet minister at their altars; where the creeds and the collects of the first confessors of the faith still rise as incense at those venerable shrines, and where alone can thrive those severe but unobtrusive graces which have an exact subordination of ranks for their indispensable basis. From the long-drawn prayer, offered, in no blest cadence, beneath a roof raised as in utter scorn of architecture, fancy would allure me away to listen to the chant of some ancient liturgy, floating down the fretted aisles of some cruciform cathedral; and truth would extort from me

The Rise of Ritualism

the acknowledgement that the ascent of the human soul to the fountain of being, demanded other aids than are to be found among those who measure their approach to perfection by their distance from the models which during fifteen centuries had been reverenced throughout the Universal Church."[1]

What his Puritan forefathers would have thought of the author of that panegyric of Symbolical Religion is more easily imagined than expressed. But it illustrates the beginnings of a reaction which was destined to revolutionise the appearance of religion in England, not only within the Church but beyond it. When the disciples of the Oxford Movement went out to priestly work in the cities and among the people, it was inevitable that the problem of Religious Symbolism should become very urgent among them. How was the Catholic Religion to be presented to the generality of the population? The squalid surroundings of the slums, the monotony of inartistic, overcrowded dwellings, an atmosphere of sheer ugliness and repulsiveness, with simply nothing to uplift, to refine, to inspire, seemed one long reiterated appeal to present religion in forms of constraining dignity, beauty, and impressiveness. The clergy who carried the Revival into the cities were deeply convinced that something more and something different from instruction through the ear was essential to bring Catholic Religion home to thronging masses of average men and women. As Dolling said years later at Portsmouth, "if there is one place which needs a magnificent and impressive Church, it is a slum." That is exactly what the disciples

[1] Sir James Stephen, *Essays in Ecclesiastical Biography*, 1850, ii. 394–5.

of the first Tractarians felt. Exceeding magnifical was to replace the ideal of exceeding cheap.

The value of Symbolism and Artistic beauty to bring Religion home to the minds of the people was often recognised by men who were not themselves in the very least ritually disposed.

"Few occurrences have affected me more," said the Bishop of Exeter in his pastoral of 1851, "than the lamentations of the poorer worshippers in one of the districts of the metropolis, when they saw, or thought they saw, at the dictation of a riotous and lawless mob, the approaching surrender of the ritual which they loved, and which was their weekly—to many among them the daily—solace to that poverty to which the providence of God had consigned them."[1]

It was natural that lovers of Ritual should remind themselves and others of the wonderful pictures in the Revelation of S. John of the worship in Heaven. The robed singers, the censers and the incense, the heavenly harmonies, the figure of the Lamb as it had been slain, the Awe-inspiring presence, the angels who fell on their faces adoringly: all this Symbolism was employed to represent devotion at its highest. What else did the Symbolism of the Eucharist aspire to do than present an earthly counterpart to mortal eyes of this spirit of devotion?

Symbolism had always been a conspicuous characteristic of Catholic Religion. No sooner did the primitive Church emerge from the centuries of persecution, and acquire freedom from external repression, than it gave full and wonderful expression to its devotional spirit in elaborate and beautiful Symbolic ways. The magnificent

[1] Quoted by MacColl, p. 450.

The Rise of Ritualism

Cathedrals of the Middle Ages were not and never can be the appropriate surroundings of a bare and meagre ceremonial. The incongruousness of Puritanism in splendid Gothic sanctuaries has often been acutely felt. If Tractarianism developed into Ritual it followed the genius of the Catholic Religion.

Thus the Catholic Revival of external expression of devotion was supported by the Tradition of the ages. Moreover, and this was in the Movement a constant claim, room was allowed for it within the English Church by the Rubrics which had existed since ever the Reformation. That was the persistent contention of the younger generation of the Oxford Movement. They were doing nothing lawless. They were carrying out the Prayer Book spirit and intention, lamentably in the past ignored and neglected. So Ritualism arose.

Against any change whatever in the accustomed externals both Puritanism and Conservatism protested. To an observer like Gladstone their protest was at times singularly indiscriminating. In his retrospect[1] on the state of the Church before the Revival of Ritual of a Catholic nature, Gladstone recalled the time, about 1845, when "agitation in London and riot in Exeter were resorted to for the purpose, as was conscientiously believed, of preserving the purity of the Reformed Religion against the use of the Surplice in the pulpit, and of the Prayer for the Church Militant. In vain the bishops and the clergy concerned made their protests, and averred that they were advising, or acting, in simple obedience to the law. The appeal to that watchword, now so sacred, was utterly unavailing: Popery, and nothing less than

[1] Gladstone, *Contemporary Review*.

The History of the Anglo-Catholic Revival

Popery, it was insisted, must be the meaning of the changes. To me it appeared at the time that their introduction, however legal, was, if not effected with the full and intelligent concurrence of the flocks, decidedly unwise. But as to these particular usages themselves, I held then and hold now, that their tendency, when calmly viewed, must have been seen to be rather Protestant than Popish; that Popery would have led to the use of a different and lower garb in preaching, not to the use of the same vestment which was also to be used for the celebration of the Eucharist; and that no prayer in the Prayer Book bears so visibly the mark of the Reformation as the Prayer for the Church Militant. Be that as it may, I recollect with pain a particular case, which may serve as a sample of the feeling, and the occurrences, of that day. An able and devoted young clergyman had accepted the charge of a new district parish in one of our largest towns, with trifling emoluments and with large masses of neglected poor, whom he had begun steadily and successfully to gather in. Within a year or two an agitation was raised, not in his parish, but in the town at large; it had grown too hot to hold him; and he was morally compelled to retire from his benefice and from the place, for the offences of having preached the morning sermon in the Surplice, read the Prayer for the Church Militant, and opened his Church for Divine Service, not daily, but on all festivals."[1]

When the Eucharistic devotion resumed its long neglected form of Ritual expression then Puritanism broke out with revolt. The following are specimens of the language employed:

[1] Gladstone in *Contemporary Review*, pp. 670-1 (1875).

The Rise of Ritualism

"Pseudo-Romanism stalks unabashed through the land, fostered secretly by those who are solemnly pledged to resist it to the uttermost; while earnest Protestants look in vain to the dignitary, highest in place of power, for the bold hand that should check its pride."[1]

"Beware, ye most earnest and devoted sons of the Church," exclaimed a clergyman in 1859, "beware of stone altars, stone pulpits, lecterns, piscinæ, reredoses, credence tables, steps, images, priedieus, super-altars, crosses, banners, flowers, vestments, chasubles, dalmatics, tunics, copes, candles, bells, lace, fringes, paintings, illuminated Prayer Books, incense, early celebrations, midnight processions, bowings, genuflexions, processional crosses, *et id genus omne*, the toys of your dangerous and subtle foe."[2]

A Rector and Rural Dean, witnessing a funeral conducted by a Tractarian clergyman,[3] complained to the *Record* that the minister on that occasion "Wore a surplice and a black stole with an embroidered cross at the back of the neck and a cross similarly embroidered on either side." There was also a processional cross. The witness consoled himself as far as he could with the reflection that whatever his private opinions might be the responsibility of sanctioning the proceeding did not rest with him. A critic remarked that the fascinations of the basilisk are not easily resisted by those who are silly enough to play with the beast.[4]

To the original Tractarians the development of

---

[1] *Ingoldsby Letters*, i. 206.
[2] The author of this sentence published it in a book, *Ingoldsby Letters*, i. 263.
[3] 1859.
[4] *Ingoldsby Letters*, i. 262.

The History of the Anglo-Catholic Revival

Ritualism was entirely unanticipated. Pusey's earlier unconcern for Ritual presents a notable contrast, not only to the subsequent stages of the Movement, but also to his own attitude at a later time. He could not think that the particular position adopted at the Altar by the celebrant was so essential that if prohibited a priest should resign his work. He wore no Eucharistic vestments at Christ Church, and for years complied with the prevalent position at the Altar as celebrant; although in course of time he adopted the Eastward position. The intensity of his personal realisation of the Eucharistic Presence and Sacrificial nature made ceremonial expression for him comparatively indifferent.

Pusey witnessed with apprehension and regret the introduction of ritual observances by the younger clergy. Changes were certainly imposed at times on congregations half-instructed, unprepared, even reluctant, without due effort to prevent misunderstanding. He felt and said that the disgraceful riots of the mob at S. George's-in-the-East in 1860 would not have happened if the clergy had listened to his advice.

Six years later, however, in his first speech to the English Church Union, recalling the events of the previous thirty years, he said that the Tractarians had felt distinct fear with regard to Ritual lest the whole movement should become superficial. The Ritual Revival began at a time of extraordinary apathy and neglect. Neither Bishop Blomfield of London, nor Bishop Phillpotts of Exeter, had been able to induce their clergy to wear a surplice in the pulpit. And Pusey felt that the danger of superficiality was past. "Thirty years of suffering, thirty years of contempt, thirty years of trial, would

The Rise of Ritualism

prevent anything from being superficial."[1] In the very next year the Bishops in Convocation declared that Ritualism was in danger of favouring errors deliberately rejected by the Church of England. This declaration led Pusey to identify himself with the Ritualists in their Eucharistic observance. He saw that leaders in the Church were resisting the Ritual because they disbelieved the Eucharistic doctrine which it represented. Nevertheless, he reiterated his warning to the English Church Union against forcing Ritual on an unwilling Congregation. He felt and said that it was easier to change a garment than a heart. But the opponents of Ritualism made it plain that in their view doctrine and its outward expression were identified. The attempted suppression of the Symbolism drew the Tractarians and the Ritualists into closer unity. Their cause was the same.

The relation of Ritual to Doctrine was seriously forced by Tractarians in the second generation. Carter of Clewer[2] said that when the great mysteries of the Incarnation were first revived among them in the early days of the revival, doctrine alone fed and sustained them, without any ritual expression. But doctrine of necessity itself soon led to Ritual. It was so in the early centuries. Doctrine was at first the Church's life, and doctrine alone. But as the Church matured Symbolism arose. In fact doctrine depends on Ritual. When Symbolism ceases, doctrine declines. Puritanism turned out the Symbolism and the doctrine followed.

It really is profoundly true that ideas and their expression are intimately related. There are forms which are appropriate to the ideas, and forms which misrepresent them.

[1] *Life of Pusey*, iv. 213.   [2] Pamphlets, Purchas Judgment.

The History of the Anglo-Catholic Revival

Doctrine is not only conveyed by words, but also by signs and symbolic actions. It is not possible to deny that the Catholic Ritualism encircling the Eucharist conveys a general impression which Puritanism does not. Pusey said that the writers in the Tracts for the Times were so intent on bringing back in their vitality neglected truths of Revelation that they forewent any changes which might draw off attention from those truths. But he also said that the revival of ritual began with the Congregations. They often presented the Vestments to the priest. The clergy had taught them the doctrine and the people provided the symbolical expression.[1]

What made Pusey all the more convinced that practically Doctrine was not to be divorced from Ritual was the attempt of the Law Courts to allow the one and forbid the other. Protestants drew the same distinction. The Doctrine of the Anglo-Catholic about the Real Presence was protected by the Bennett Judgment. But the presentation of it before the eyes of the people in the Anglo-Catholic way was forbidden by the Purchas Judgment. You may teach the doctrine from the pulpit in whatever way you think edifying. But you must not, even if your congregation desire it, obey a Rubric which has been thought to express that doctrine. To that distinction Pusey felt constrained to reply that it makes the position of the celebrant almost a matter of principle.

Walter Ker Hamilton, Bishop of Salisbury, in his remarkable Charge to his clergy in 1867,[2] contemplating sympathetically the rise of Ritualism, set before his Diocese considerations against and in favour of Revived ceremonial. He said that he had always accepted the opinion

[1] Letter 3 to *The Times*, 1874. [2] Bishop Hamilton's Charge.

The Rise of Ritualism

of his venerated predecessor, Bishop Denison, as a guide for his own conduct. Bishop Denison, speaking on the Obligations of the Clergy, maintained that the doctrine of a virtual dispensation from positive rules, to be inferred from long and general desuetude, must be allowed as necessary in the existing state of the English Church; he held that the conscience of any individual clergyman need not be aggrieved at acquiescence in it, especially where there exists a superior power able to give effect to the dormant rule; and, therefore, in a manner having the responsibility of its neglect.

But on the other hand, Bishop Hamilton, assuming that the recent changes in ceremonial were lawful, represented what the Ritualists would plead. They would say that it is natural for external expression to correspond, however inadequately, with the doctrines held. Belief in the real Presence in the Eucharist cannot but tend to raise the standard of ceremonial accompaniments of that Sacrifice and Feast. Ritualists were enlisting the fine Arts on the side of Religion, making the same claim in behalf of Religion which Mill made for Education. Mill himself appreciated the influence of the great Italian artists on Religion. "Their Nativities and Crucifixions, their glorious Madonnas and Saints, were to their susceptible Southern countrymen the great school not only of the devotional but of all the elevated and all the imaginative feelings."

Bishop Hamilton added the further consideration that external ceremonial had been used for ages to confess the Mysteries of the Faith. He asked whether reflections such as these had met generally a fair consideration, or whether they had not uncommonly been treated scorn-

The History of the Anglo-Catholic Revival

fully, as the special pleadings of dishonest men, who with hearts disloyal to the Church of England are base enough to hold her offices and abuse their trust. The Bishop of Salisbury assured his Diocese that if Parliament interfered in this matter he would certainly not be a consenting party to such legislation. A sympathetic attitude such as this towards Ritualism was rare in 1867 on the part of the Fathers of the English Church.

Supporters of the Ritual Movement did not hesitate to deal faithfully with defects of character among its advocates. It was one of their own Journals which complained, as early as 1868, that "Modesty and humble-mindedness are graces which are distinguished by their absence from the Ritualist party—as a party." It said quite frankly that "a Catholic-minded priest is, on inquiry, found to be a gentleman of moderate abilities and limited information, who is distinguished for the fidelity of his adherence to the Roman sequence of colours, and to the correctness with which he wears and doffs his biretta."[1]

The same Journal said: "We have the profoundest respect for the judgment and opinions of habitual communicants in the Church of England. They are indeed, for the most part, what may be called the salt of the earth, and we believe, that as far as results are concerned, the matter might be safely trusted with them. We believe that the utmost deference to their feelings and wishes ought to be shown as regards all the accessories of divine worship. Perish the candles, the incense, and the vestments, rather than the souls of the devout should be scandalised." So wrote the *Christian Remembrancer* in 1868.

[1] *Christian Remembrancer*, 1868, pp. 204–5.

The Rise of Ritualism

It was sorrowfully admitted by leaders on the Catholic side that Ritual has been unadvisedly introduced in congregations habituated to the plainest of services, and introduced in cases quite suddenly, and without any adequate instruction about its meaning. There was no wonder that many were bewildered and disconcerted. Pusey had spoken strongly about this. But the recommendations of the Ritual Commission were naturally subjected to severe criticism. It was said, for instance, "It is scarcely possible to speak of the aggrieved parishioner, who has already become a household word, without raising a smile on the face of an educated Churchman, or provoking a sneer of contempt from the business-like man of the world."

Beresford Hope said that there were many "small questions in which the Ritualists have shown themselves deficient in tact, and careless in ascertaining the drift of popular feeling, even when that feeling may be prejudice." "A prejudice, if harmless, ought always to be enough respected at least to be taken into account by men whose duty and whose desire is to mould public opinion. At the risk of offending them, I must say that the tact of the ritualists has not been commensurate with their learning and devotion. They have erred both in what they have insisted upon as if essential, and in the manner in which they have worded their insistence."[1]

But whatever the defects of the promoters of this Ritual Revival, no defects in the agents could prevent the rise and ultimate dominance of a symbolism which is inherent in the principles of the Catholic Religion.[2]

"Ritualism is but part of a large movement, a branch

[1] Beresford Hope, *Worship*, p. 102.   [2] Pamphlets, 1880.

The History of the Anglo-Catholic Revival

of the Catholic reaction, which is itself but a stream of the general current of religious thought reflowing not only in Europe, but in Asia. . . . To quench a river of this nature by the aid of law is indeed a vain undertaking. A massacre such as that inflicted by the Chinese upon the unfortunate Mohammedan Panthays would be the only effective method of coercion."[1]

At the same time there are some weighty reflections of Fr. Benson of Cowley on the relation of Ritual to Religion.

"We must be careful not to let ourselves be carried away by the desire of ritual. I think one feels that the highest type of worship for us on earth is that plainness which S. Bernard would have inculcated. But even he allows that ritual beauty may be necessary—a necessary evil—for secular-minded people. The Religious ought to rise above it. So of course ought the religious-minded.

"We should always remember that ritual is not for the purpose of pleasing ourselves. It is the offering of wealth, in form, art, and substance to God for His glory, since all creation belongs to Him. If it is our fault that God is not glorified manifestly, we cannot look for the blessing of the worship. But if it is not our fault, the absence of outward beauty can make no sacramental difference in our service; and we ought not, therefore, to repine, if we are called to worship where things are distasteful. Outward beauty should not be despised, but our Lord's words call us to regard it as of very little practical concern. . . . Although it is a duty to make God's temporal house glorious for His honour, yet our hearts

---

[1] *Reflections on the P.W.R.A. and Ritualism*, by a Looker-on, 1875, p. 10.

The Rise of Ritualism

must be elsewhere, even with Himself in heaven. We must feel the nothingness of that which is so soon to pass away."[1]

As recently as 1906, Dr. Gore, at that time Bishop of Birmingham, felt it necessary before the Royal Commission on Ecclesiastical Discipline, to emphasise the relation between the Revival of Ritual and the vast æsthetic Movement characteristic of modern life.

"I think, if you ask me, I speak again out of the very depths of my own personal experience, that the ceremonial movement belongs to a great change in the minds of a great number of people. It is a real movement, I mean, of thought and feeling which was represented by a whole æsthetic revival which has strongly affected people outside the Church, and in a different way affected those inside the Church. While I have been ill I have been having read to me Sir Edward Burne-Jones's *Life*. Do you remember there the way in which the whole group of men round about Burne-Jones were affected by the ritual revival; and do you remember long after Sir Edward Burne-Jones had ceased himself to be, I suppose, a practising Churchman at all, the profound disgust with which he speaks of the service at Robert Browning's funeral, of the ceremony in the Abbey, and of what seemed to him to be the violent discord between the spirit of the Architecture and the spirit of the service? I am quite sure that that kind of feeling, as expressed in Burne-Jones's *Life*, represents a movement as deep and real as any movement of the human spirit in our time. I speak, of course, as one who feels with it profoundly. I love, as I hardly love anything in the world physically, except the

[1] *Letters of Fr. Benson* (written in 1879), p. 255.

The History of the Anglo-Catholic Revival

beauties of nature, that type and kind of ceremonial worship, which is called ritualistic by many people and Catholic by its maintainers. It appears to me personally to be the one kind of ceremonial worship which really expresses my feelings, and in which I feel really at home. And there are a very great number of people who experience the same kind of emotion and feeling. That is all that I wanted to say—that it really does represent a real movement and a widespread movement. You may call it æsthetic, or you may apply any term you wish to it, but it is a real change in public feeling."[1]

[1] Bishop Gore of Birmingham, to Royal Commissioners.

CHAPTER V

EUCHARISTIC VESTMENTS

THE general attitude of the Episcopate towards Eucharistic Vestments is seen in the discussion which was held in the Canterbury Convocation in 1866[1]—on Ritualism. Deep concern was expressed about an exhibition of Vestments, more or less gorgeous, made with a view to their being used by clergymen of the Church of England. One Bishop held that men might win through the eye what they failed to win through the ear. The value of æsthetic matters in education was being widely appreciated. If we stain the windows and decorate the walls of our Churches it is difficult to know where we are to stop. A low ritual has a tendency to make people desire to seek a higher ritual elsewhere if they cannot obtain it in our own Church. There ought to be freedom from restraint. Another Bishop was alarmed over what he held to be a Romeward tendency. Extreme Ritual would throw back the work of the Church in Wales a hundred years. The Bishops generally disapproved of the practices spoken of. A distinguished divine who witnessed these practices was so shocked that he felt unable to partake of the Lord's Supper from persons officiating in this Roman fashion. The evil will spread. Our Churches will be deserted. "There is not one of your Lordships who would venture to take part in the administration in some of the Churches where this extreme ritualism prevails." Ambiguous expressions in the present law should be as soon as pos-

[1] *Chronicle of Convocation*, 1866, p. 150 ff.

The History of the Anglo-Catholic Revival

sible rendered into intelligible language: meaning thereby that the Ornaments Rubric should be rewritten.

It so happened that precisely at this moment the Prolocutor of the Lower House appeared before the Bishops and presented the following Resolution just passed by the Clergy: "That this House recognising the evil which may arise from an excess of ritualism, deprecates nevertheless any attempt to avert these possible evils by the introduction of changes into the Book of Common Prayer. In coming to this resolution, the House by no means intends to express approval of deviations of any kind from Church order." The clergy asked the Bishops to adopt such measures as may seem fit, in conjunction with the Lower House, for clearing the doubts and allaying the anxiety that exists.

Whereupon the Bishops directed the Lower House to inquire into the matter and report to the Upper House.

Prolonged debates on Ritualism ensued in the Lower House of the Canterbury Convocation. The summary of the speeches occupied 180 pages of the official *Chronicle*. The subject of Vestments was dominant. The real question was the interpretation of the Ornaments Rubric. It was remembered that the Puritan Ministers at the Savoy Conference objected "forasmuch as this Rubric seemeth to bring back the cope, alb, etc.," they "desired it may be wholly left out."[1] It was observed that great credit was due to the foresight of these Puritans, for what they predicted in 1661 had certainly taken place in 1866. Various speakers explained that the use of Vestments was not their own practice, yet they strongly deprecated anything which would have the appearance of one-sided

[1] 1661, Cardwell, *Conferences*, p. 314.

Eucharistic Vestments

action. The innovators were among the most earnest and indefatigable members of the clergy in the Church of England. To certain members of Convocation the phrase of the Rubric "shall be retained and had in use" could not be taken as expressing less than a real desire and earnest hope on the part of our latest Revisers that the original Edwardian Vestments might really be used. Did not Cosin at Durham Cathedral wear a cope? Did he not say they were in use long before his time? Thus the cope and the surplice presented a divergency in practice about Vestments. Both alike were therefore in a fairly defensible position. On the Broad Church side it was urged that the various parties, Ritualist and Anti-Ritualist, ought to be tolerated, on the principle of inclusiveness, within the English Church. Things which quicken one man's devotion do not affect another. This reflection provoked the criticism: Gorgeous Ritual is attractive to the young and ardent, but is it Scriptural? Is it in accordance with the tone and spirit of our Church? To another mind these Ritual expressions were forms of doctrine. It was thought that the Ritualists had the law on their side. "These Ritualists are some of the most effective preachers of the doctrines of the Church." Let the Bishops tell us what is their view. That would be effective if all the Bishops were united. Refer the matter then to the collective Episcopate. "We do not desire to alter our Prayer Book but to keep it as it is." But "can any one point to a single instance for 200 years among all articles of inquiry that have been issued by English Bishops where these Vestments are required or even recommended?" Ritualists are dividing the Church into two parties, provoking Parliamentary interference, disturbing the Church's peace.

The History of the Anglo-Catholic Revival

From a different standpoint it was felt that the actual law of the Church should not be carried out. The law was perfectly clear and if men's feelings were not mixed up in this question, and if the idea of expediency were not entertained there would be no difficulty about our Ritual. Those who maintained the legality of the Vestments were neither young men carried away by the sanguine temperament of youth, nor men who have any sympathy whatever with the Church of Rome, though they have a large sympathy with the Church Universal. "And if any assembly of Bishops were to declare that such things are unlawful or superstitious, I must say that as long as I believe there is such a thing as Catholic authority, I must utterly repudiate such a judgment" (Dr. Jebb). The resumption of an ancient practice long disused is very unwise without the advice of our Bishops. But that is a very different thing from submitting to a Bishop who says such a practice is not law. The worship of God is far above external rites, but the latter do not hinder the former.

The spirit of caution suggested a fear that persons now accustomed to Ritual would secede from the English Church if they are deprived of the gratification of their tastes. On the other hand these unwonted manifestations may alienate. Would it not be better to leave such questions to be resolved by the Bishops in their own Diocesan Synods? Resistance to the opinion of the Bishops was reprehensible. "But we must remember this, that if a man believes the law of the Church, to which he has subscribed, imposes any particular observances upon him, he is bound to abide by that law."

When Convocation met again an elaborate Report on

Eucharistic Vestments

Ritual was presented. The Report declared that it was not enough to say that a practice is of very great antiquity, or of very general prevalence in other parts of Christendom. These are circumstances of great importance. And if the Church of England has retained the practice in question, these circumstances are doubtless among the reasons why the practice has been retained. But, after all, the question is whether the Church of England has really retained the practice in question, or by just implication has recognised it. If such retension or such implication of a particular practice by the Church of England can be made clear, then the probability is that the alarm which may have arisen from the adoption of a practice, when it was regarded as the act of individuals, will soon subside, when such practice is admitted to be agreeable to the mind of the Church.

It was further suggested that the Church possesses the powers of permitting differences of practice, such powers being necessary to the Church's free development. Consequently attempts to establish a uniformity of practice incompatible with such permissible power should be earnestly deprecated. When doubts arise about the limits of the permissible power, reference should be made to the Bishop.

It was remarked that although in the Privy Council judgment in the Liddell case an interpretation of the Ornaments Rubric was given which recognised the legality of Eucharistic Vestments, "yet it is right to observe that the question of Vestments was not before the Court, and therefore this remark of the Privy Council is not to be taken as a settlement of the question, and as excluding all doubts as to the actual state of the law."

The History of the Anglo-Catholic Revival

Resort to judicial proceedings was earnestly deprecated. If resorted to it would tend to promote rather than to allay dissension. Uniformity, which would be the necessary tendency of judicial proceedings, could only be obtained at the price of peace.

This Report was considered by the Lower House at great length in the Summer Session of 1866. To some of its members the general reflection commended itself that Ritual excess was the natural reaction from unseemly neglect. The opinion of four eminent Counsel recently issued was criticised as got up on behalf of some of their Lordships the Bishops. The Reformation was a great necessity, but no more to be gloried in than a sickness from which a man recovers. Various corrections were proposed to the phrases in the Report. It was not strong enough: it was far too strong. Much was said on approximating to the doctrines and practices of the Church of Rome. The mode of celebrating the Holy Communion was made to resemble that of the Romish Mass. It was asked, if we are not to go to law how are we to get the law defined? Others had no conscientious objection to ministering in any Vestment, only they would be glad to know what Vestment they ought to wear. They would gladly submit themselves to legally constituted authority. But they objected to disintering practices which never had any existence in the Reformed Church of England. The Vestments question was the root of all the rest. It affected the population more than any other, because it appeals the most decidedly to the eye. The Reformation was not a fit of sickness, but a fact to glory in. The right course toward Ritualistic practices was to discourage their continuance. The proper Vestment for the pulpit is the

Eucharistic Vestments

gown. A Broad Church observation was that Vestments were not worth half of what is said about them. They are perfectly unmeaning, and really no more sacerdotal than they are anything else. They are void of all meaning, except that they are very gorgeous and are descended from the Roman Empire. They do not convey any special doctrine. If they are legal, they are extremely unusual. Yet what to do with the Ritualists was a perplexity. "Suppose these men are driven out, they still exist. They cannot be burned. They cannot be exterminated. If, then, they are driven out they must either exist as a nonjuring sect, or as Roman Catholics." Our prime duty is to keep them. From a very different standpoint it was urged that the Bishops in 1662 retained the Ornaments Rubric as it had stood ever since the Prayer Book had been brought back under Queen Elizabeth, "not with the intention of restoring the use which that Rubric presented, but because they were determined not to lower the standard which had existed all along." "What is to be above all things dreaded or deprecated in this great matter is a resort to legal proceedings. When will the Church of England learn that you cannot ostracise enthusiasm?" "Do but consider the possible consequences of going to law. . . . If ever Parliament should pass a law to alter, in any particular, even a Rubric of the Prayer Book without the consent of Convocation, we know for certain that the clergy would not recognise it." Other speakers deprecated tendencies towards Rome. Opinion was hopelessly divided whether Eucharistic Vestments signified doctrine or had no doctrinal significance. It was further suggested from a different quarter that whether Convocation had any judicial power or not, it certainly had the power to supply lawyers with ecclesiastical information. Counsel's opinion lately supplied to the Bishops consisted of the opinion of four men who were learned in the secular law of the land, but as for being learned in the spiritual law, the law of the Church, it was no disparagement to them to say that they cannot be expected to have such qualifications. If the Vestments were declared by the law of the land to be legal the speaker would be perfectly prepared to wear them. If the highest court in the land declared them to be legal he could reply to complainers that he was obedient to the law of the Church. In reply to the oft-repeated criticism that the tendencies of Ritualism were towards Rome, it was suggested that every movement is a tendency in one direction or another. If we walk out of the Western door of the Abbey here, we proceed in the direction of the West Indies. But it does not follow that you will really reach such places. What had happened was only part of a great movement which had been going on for nearly a century. It may have its excesses. All movements have. Another voice informed the House, apropos of Counsel's opinion obtained by certain Bishops, that Counsel's opinion was also being sought by others. What if the two sets of opinions conflicted? "There never was a greater fallacy in the world than to say that by going to law you can ascertain the mind of the Church." The counsel of the wise old Pharisee Gamaliel ought not to be neglected. On the other hand, the necessity of a Judicial decision was strongly urged, and was repeated. A very different advocate insisted that an attempt to sever practices and doctrines would be unwise. The whole question resolved itself into the maintenance of

Eucharistic Vestments

the doctrine of the Real Presence. This was declared to be the intention of all who adopted the Eucharistic Vestments. By this statement some were bewildered and scared. If in the ritual movement Vestments are regarded as emblems of doctrine their introduction becomes alarming. But then the speaker admitted that he could not understand what is meant by the worship of the real spiritual presence in the Holy Communion. He thought the Church of England was rocking on its foundations. Objection was raised to the introduction into the Sacrament of any obsolete practices such as acts of adoration.

After further prolonged discussion it was ultimately resolved in the Lower House: (1) that the use in Parish Churches of the surplice is a sufficient compliance with the directions of the Church; (2) that without pronouncing on the legality of the Vestments . . . prescribed in the First Book of King Edward VI, the House considers that they should not be introduced into any parish Church without reference to the Bishop.[1]

Archbishop Tait was determined to alter the Ornaments Rubric. Bishop Wilberforce opposed him. "It would be a total readjustment of our system, and involve us in unspeakable difficulties."[2] Wilberforce also opposed the Archbishop's idea of a collective address of the Bishops on the Ritual question. He did not think it was according to the constitution of the Church that the Bishops, out of Synod, should thus assume any aggregate authority.

The Archbishop thought he would have no difficulty in securing a unanimous consent among the Bishops to the discarding of Vestments and adhering to the surplice.

[1] *Chronicle of Convocation*, 1866, p. 562.
[2] *Life of Bishop Wilberforce.*

The History of the Anglo-Catholic Revival

But in 1866 at Lambeth he found this was impossible. The Bishop of Exeter warned the Episcopate: If you try to enforce the rubric you will have a rebellion; try to alter it, and you will cause a shipwreck. Consequently the scheme collapsed for lack of unanimity.

The Ritual Commission produced their first Report in 1867. It was confined to the subject of Eucharistic Vestments. "We find that whilst these Vestments are regarded by some witnesses as symbolic of doctrine, and by others as a distinctive vesture whereby they desire to do honour to the Holy Communion as the highest act of Christian worship, they are by none regarded as essential, and they give grave offence to many. We are of opinion that it is expedient to restrain in the public services of the United Church of England and Ireland all variations in respect of vesture from that which has long been the established usage in the said United Church, and we think that this may be best secured by providing aggrieved parishioners with an easy and effectual process for complaint and redress." This conclusion was issued under the presidency of Archbishop Tait.

The phrase "restrain" the use of Vestments, instead of abolish or prohibit, was it appears subtly designed to leave a loophole for their regulated use. It is said that the main body of the Ritual Commission "failed to perceive the elasticity of this word." It must be owned that if the Commission failed to perceive the ambiguity, neither did Pusey perceive it. He took a completely pessimistic view of the Ritual Commission. It seemed to him a complete extirpation of the Vestments; an absolute and complete defeat. He said, "It would have been far better to have had all Shaftesbury's Bill and let him do

Eucharistic Vestments

his worst." Wilberforce, in private letters, endeavoured confidentially to explain the subtlety of the expression. At any rate he thought that the Commission prevented parliamentary interference, which would have been still more disastrous.

The difficulty experienced by Anglo-Catholics in securing recognition of Eucharistic Vestments is illustrated by Dr. Littledale's letter to the *Church Times* in 1867, in which he proposed as a reasonable compromise retention of Vestments wherever in use; permission to use them in all Churches hereafter built, when its founder and first incumbent are so minded; permission to employ them at extra services in old Churches, when both Churchwardens and not less than one-third of the Communicants of the congregation shall agree to petition for their use; permission to employ them at the regular services, when not less than three-fourths of the Communicants, together with the Churchwardens desire it. Prohibition in other cases.

The literature on Vestments at this period became enormous. In justification of the use of Eucharistic Vestments it was argued that in spite of assertions that the Ornaments Rubric was ambiguous, its meaning was acknowledged by certain great lawyers to be perfectly plain. Elizabeth's Act of Uniformity was not intended to destroy Vestments, but as Sandys, afterwards Archbishop of York, represented the matter to Archbishop Parker, "that we shall not be forced to use them, but that others in the meantime shall not convey them away, but that they shall remain for the Queen." On this interpretation a very natural comment was made in 1873: "A most incomprehensible provision if it was intended to abolish

The History of the Anglo-Catholic Revival

them altogether. What on earth was the Queen to do with them? Was she to convert them into dresses for herself or for her courtiers? Did she purpose to replenish her exchequer by a public sale of them?" "The words of Bishop Sandys proves that the contemporaneous interpretation put by the Puritans on the Rubric of Elizabeth's Prayer Book and on the Act of Uniformity was, that they legalised the Eucharistic Vestments as a maximum of ritual, but promised a minimum by way of relaxation to the Puritans, who meanwhile should not be forced to use them."

To the objection that if the Ornaments Rubric had intended the use of Eucharistic Vestments their disappearance from the Altars of the Church of England is inexplicable, Pusey replied that those who think it strange that a Rubric should have been inserted, which lay unused so long, and so doubt whether it could have been intended to be used at all, do not bear in mind the difficulties under which the Church laboured, after the iron rule of Cromwell had ceased; the inadequate number of the clergy who survived it, the hostility of the Nonconformists, whom it was a duty to win if possible, yet whose leaders held it contrary to the Word of God to require the use of the surplice; ... Pusey appealed to Bishop Forbes's account of the ceremonial which had actually existed in the Church of England at the beginning of the seventeenth century.[1]

That Vestments symbolised Doctrine was a matter on which many men were convinced, and indeed this was the ground of their objection. Fraser, Bishop of Manchester, told his Diocesan Synod in 1873 that "the

[1] *Unlaw*, p. 27.

Eucharistic Vestments

symbolism of Eucharistic Vestments, lighted candles, the eastward position, indicate the doctrine that the minister is offering a propitiatory sacrifice, and this is not the doctrine of our Church."[1]

The Royal Commission on Ritual was followed by a message from the Crown directing Convocation to revise the Rubrics of the Book of Common Prayer. Archbishop Tait obviously expected by that means to get the Ornaments Rubric changed. But at this very time, it was early in 1874, the Archbishop was busily engaged in securing in Parliament the scheme for Public Worship Regulation. And in promoting this Act of Parliament he had deliberately avoided consulting Convocation. His theory was that Convocation had no inherent right to veto or delay Parliamentary action on the part of the Bishops, at least in a matter of this kind. He regarded it as a matter of legal procedure. He considered that the affair would be interminable if it had to be submitted to the Lower House of Convocation. Acting on the principle he refused to give Convocation the opportunity for full discussion on the subject. As the Archbishop's biographer says: "Convocation, as might have been naturally expected, took a different view, and the complaints of undue haste were loud and deep." "The Lower House was not to be appeased. And the measure and its authors were denounced with increasing vehemence as the week's debates went on." The Lower House declined to be coerced. Members of either School were apprehensive that any alteration of the Rubric in question might imperil their respective positions. Accordingly, the Lower House resolved in 1875 to leave the Ornaments Rubric unchanged.

[1] *Life of Bishop Fraser*, by Hughes, p. 226.

The History of the Anglo-Catholic Revival

How deeply the Archbishop's arbitrary procedure was felt in the Lower House is shown by the fact that echoes of resentment were still to be heard two years later at the beginning of the discussions in 1877. It was complained by a speaker in the Lower House that the Report which they had sent to the Upper House was received in a very high-handed way; but that the Upper House since then had had a serious lesson, and will probably never deal with us with such high-handedness again.

By this time, however, the Ridsdale Judgment had been given in which the Eucharistic Vestments were forbidden. On the authority of this Privy Council decision, Archbishop Tait made another attempt to get the Ornaments Rubric altered.[1] The Lower House debated the subject once again.[2]

In behalf of the Ritualists who wore Vestments it was now pleaded that when they adopted these Vestments they were under the full belief that they were not only permitted, but that priests were bound to wear them. They will not obey this new law until they are obliged. With regard to a distinctive dress for the Holy Communion it was suggested that no amount of splendour could be out of place in that administration. And for this purpose the chasuble is very suitable. Whereas the cope, because it embarrasses the arms, is not. It was asserted that the chasuble was not necessarily expressive of any unsound doctrine. There is nothing unsound involved in the use of Vestments. It was agreed that the Eucharist was, in some sense or other, a Sacrifice. If it be a sacrifice of any sort, that is a sufficient reason for wearing a sacrificial

---

[1] *Chronicle of Convocation*, 1877, p. 71.
[2] Ibid., p. 269 ff.

Eucharistic Vestments

Vestment. But the speaker declared that it was not sacrificial dress.

Bewildering want of acquaintance with the Vestments was betrayed in the course of debate. An Archdeacon asked a Dean whether he wore a cope, and received for answer: "I do not even know what a cope is." Another speaker deprecated the use of any distinctive dress in celebrating the Sacrament: appealing to the opinion of Bishop Guest, that if we should use another garment herein, it should seem to teach us that higher and better things be given by it than by the other service, which we must not believe. "I would ask the House to take notice of the words—which we must not believe." He asked: "Should not great care be taken how we lead persons to suppose, by assigning a distinctive dress to the minister in the Holy Communion, that when they receive Christ's Body and Blood in that holy Ordinance, they receive higher and better things than when they put on Christ, and receive the Holy spirit of Christ in the Divine Ordinance of Baptism and the Divine Ordinance of Prayer?"

Other speakers held it inexpedient to frame a new Ornaments Rubric to meet a present difficulty. It was bad to retain the existing Ornaments Rubric, and append a regulation which in one chief particular sets that Rubric aside.

Other speakers urged that no persecuting law was good. The use of Vestments had become so widely prevalent (this was in 1877) that prohibition would be unsuccessful unless persecution were very thorough. It was quite certain that in England persecution never could be very thorough. The country is impatient of anything like

The History of the Anglo-Catholic Revival

persecution. The wisest course was to tolerate the Vestments in places where they are already in use, and to put hindrances to their use elsewhere. Who could prophesy, in these days of love of display and dignity, what will be the state of public feeling as regards Vestments twenty or thirty years hence?

Another speaker was astonished at the indecency of Convocation setting itself up as a kind of court to review the judgment of the Privy Council. Vestments were not part of a growing taste for Art and Beauty, but of sympathy with Romish doctrines about the Holy Eucharist. An unscriptural doctrine lies at the bottom of this matter of Vestments. The Vestments and the Doctrine cannot be separated.

Another urged that the Church of England was right in sustaining the ancient majesty through all its services. Vestments should be used at every service, not only at the Eucharist. Convocation was more than a Club or a Conference, and was not bound by judicial decisions which contradicted themselves. Since it appeared that in fact everybody was disobeying the law in some respect or other, the epithet "rebel" ought not to be used so glibly. The Church of England was not at peace. The Judgment of the Privy Council was not accepted by all. Are there to be more of these lamentable and intolerable prosecutions?

Then it was proposed to keep in the word "Cope" and leave out the words "or Vestment," thus getting rid of the Chasuble as an alternative. This idea of excluding what was called the one indefinite word pleased many.

What then, inquired another, about Norway and

Eucharistic Vestments

Sweden, where both Cope and Chasuble are in use? A Cope is worn, added another, by the Vice-Chancellor of the University of Cambridge.

But the Ritualists who wear a Chasuble will not be satisfied to be relegated back to a Cope. After the elasticity which has been allowed to doctrine, it is inconsistent to refuse the same to ritual.

The final decision was permission to wear a Cope in celebrating Holy Communion, no mention being made of the Chasuble.

This decision, which was a singular departure from the previous resolve of the clergy to maintain the Ornaments Rubric unchanged, is generally known as the Cope Compromise. The Bishops did not discuss it.

In 1879 Archbishop Tait[1] made yet another endeavour to have the Ornaments Rubric reconsidered. The Cope Compromise satisfied nobody. Tait's "argument was that the Ornaments Rubric, taken by itself, seemed to enjoin the Vestments as compulsory, but that as nobody now regarded the enactment in that light, it was absurd to re-enact it, as had been suggested, precisely as it stood, with an addendum enjoining something quite different. He therefore proposed to limit the Rubric until further order shall be taken by a Canon of the Church." The Archbishop's proposal was decisively rejected by the Lower House. Tait, however, insisted in spite of the opposition. He called a conference of both Houses, and made a new proposal. The new proposal was to order the surplice as the ordinary Eucharistic dress, but to allow that other Vestments might be introduced in particular cases, provided that the Bishop of the Diocese gave no

[1] *Life*, ii. 415.

monition to the contrary. Under this pressure a majority of the Lower House gave way.

The Rubric as altered under the Archbishop's influence became as follows: "And here is to be noted that such ornaments of the Church and of the ministers thereof, at all times of their ministration, shall be retained, and be in use, as were in this Church of England, by the authority of Parliament in the second year of the reign of King Edward the Sixth (until further order be taken by lawful authority. In saying Public Prayers and administering the Sacraments and other rites of the Church, every priest and deacon shall wear a surplice with a stole or scarf, and the hood of his degree, or, if he thinks fit, a gown with hood and scarf; and no other ornament shall at any time of his ministrations be used by him contrary to the monition of the Bishop of the Diocese).

The paragraph in brackets followed on the Ornaments Rubric as given in the Authorised Book.

That alteration was accepted by the Southern Convocation. It must, however, be carefully observed that the Northern Convocation insisted on the Ornaments Rubric being retained unaltered. It is obvious that the action of the Southern Province, when in conflict with that of the North, is not the action of Convocation, and can in no way commit the English Church. The two provinces disagreed, and no united resolution was reached. However, Archbishop Tait made the most of the concession of the Southern Province.[1]

After this achievement Dr. Tait recorded in his Diary "henceforth no consistent High Churchman will be able

---

[1] Cf. Archbishop Davidson in *Report Royal Commission Eccles. Discipline*, ii. 355.

Eucharistic Vestments

to plead even a shadow of ecclesiastical authority when he disobeys the order of his Bishop, given in accordance with the law. Thank God for what we have been able to do."

Archbishop Tait then attempted to persuade the Government to let him introduce into Parliament a Bill to give legislative force to this vote in Convocation. But Gladstone decisively discouraged it. Beaconsfield pronounced that ecclesiastical legislation was out of the question. Lord Salisbury replied that "the Bishops would do wisely to shield the incumbent from litigation, at least if he did not go further than to act upon the apparently literal interpretation of the Ornaments Rubric." Salisbury added that Ritualism is too strong to be put down: a serious attempt to do so would simply shatter the Church. All that Tait was able to secure was the Government's consent to the appointment of a Royal Commission.

The Bishop of London (Dr. Jackson)[1] insisted in his Charge that the Ornaments Rubric had been twice investigated by the Final Court of Appeal; that to accuse such a Court or suspect it of partiality would be to strike a blow at all confidence in the judicial integrity which has long and deservedly been our country's boast; that their decision made wearing the Chasuble an offence against the law ecclesiastical. He thought it would have been more logical and perhaps more prudent not to have left the Ornaments Rubric unaltered, but to have omitted from it all mention of the Ornaments of the ministers of the Church. A conservative unwillingness had prevailed.

In Convocation, 1881, Bishop Fraser moved that "the

[1] Primary Charge, 1879.

The History of the Anglo-Catholic Revival

present Ornaments Rubric be expunged, and that, by Rubric or Canon, a clear rule be established in conformity with the usage which has prevailed for two hundred years in the Church of England." This motion was carried unanimously in the Upper House, but defeated in the Lower by two votes, twenty-eight to twenty-six.[1]

In Convocation in 1881, Canon Gregory[2] moved that the Bishops should be asked "to forbear to interfere by authority with such diversities of ceremonial as are consistent with a literal interpretation of the Rubrics." He urged that three courses lay open to them. "First we might persevere in the policy of coercion; or we might temporise; or lastly, we might try a policy of conciliation." "If the policy of coercion is to be continued, if every one who determines to use Vestments ... is to be prosecuted, we shall have to deal with no inconsiderable numbers of our brother clergy. It is manifest that those who sympathise with these persons form no small portion of the ranks of the clergy of the Church of England. It is quite clear that there are thousands—certainly there are many hundreds—who sympathise with them; men who do not practise the ritual themselves, but who, if those who do are to be put in prison will feel that the position is intolerable, and will consider themselves called upon to stand by their suffering brethren. If we are to stamp out ritualism to the extent that would be necessary in order to eliminate it from the borders of the Church of England, it will require a very formidable amount of persecution indeed."

In 1906, when Bishop of Birmingham, Bishop Gore

[1] *Life of Bishop Fraser*, p. 316.
[2] *Autobiography of Robert Gregory*, p. 96.

Eucharistic Vestments

informed the Royal Commission that there were forty Churches in his Diocese where Vestments are used, and he urged upon the Commission the necessity of tolerating two uses.[1]

The persistent efforts to modify or efface the Ornaments Rubric, and with it the sanction of Eucharistic Vestments, constitute a singular chapter in the History of English Liturgical development. No one who admires perseverance and determination can fail to appreciate the labours exhausted in attempts at removal of this Reformation ruling. Meanwhile, the significant fact is the gradual, steady, and persistent revival of the Vestments, so that their use has become not only tolerated but recognised and, in spite of various efforts of authority to prevent their increase, has become not only quite impossible to abolish, but has gone on extending more and more widely.

The impossibility of suppressing Eucharistic Vestments had become self-evident to every party in the Church by the time that the Revision of the Prayer Book was undertaken. The Ornaments Rubric was accordingly reconsidered in a very different spirit from that which had prevailed in the nineteenth century. The result appeared in 1927.

While the Ornaments Rubric remains in the Authorised Book unchanged, the Prayer Book as revised contains the following:

"For the avoidance of all controversy and doubtfulness, it is hereby prescribed that, notwithstanding anything that is elsewhere enjoined in any Rubric or Canon, the Priest, in celebrating the Holy Communion, shall wear

[1] *Eccles. Discipline*, ii. 501.

The History of the Anglo-Catholic Revival

either a surplice with stole or with scarf and hood, or a white alb plain with a vestment or cope."

Although the Revised Book failed to receive approval from the State, and did not receive the final technical endorsement from the Church, still it represents the Church's considered decisions, and expresses the mind of the Church in its Synodical deliberations. It is, as usual in the Church of England, a compromise, a compromise no doubt more or less created by the Church's own divisions, and by the impossibility of securing agreement between the Evangelical and the Catholic.

CHAPTER VI

CONFESSION AND ABSOLUTION

THE practice of Confession, which has existed in the Church of England ever since the Reformation, was systematically and extensively revived by the Oxford Movement. As early as 1850 Pusey published his book, *The Church of England leaves her Children free to whom to open their Griefs.*

In 1858 the Reverend Alfred Poole, curate at S. Barnabas, Pimlico, who was accustomed to hear Confessions, was accused of asking his penitents indelicate questions, an accusation which he solemnly denied, and also of encouraging habitual Confession, which he frankly acknowledged to be true. Complaint was made to Dr. Tait, at that time Bishop of London. The Bishop, after a private interview with his priest, withdrew his licence and deprived him of his curacy. Appeal was made from the Bishop of London to the Archbishop of Canterbury, Dr. Sumner, who, without hearing the case or interviewing the priest, endorsed the action of Bishop Tait. Liddell, Vicar of S. Paul's, Knightsbridge, a well-known name in Ritual procedure, thereupon wrote to the Bishop of London complaining that his assistant priest had asked for a public hearing as the most effectual means of clearing his personal character from the cruel aspersions cast upon him. That request had been refused. Liddell further protested that if the Bishop of London and the Archbishop of Canterbury intended to condemn a priest of the Church of England simply for systematic hearing of private confessions from such of his people, be they many or few, who come with burdened consciences, and desire of their own accord to open their grief, he identified himself with the cause for which his curate had been deprived. "Neither do I wish," added Liddell, "to shelter myself behind the protection which the law, on mere secular grounds, affords to a beneficed clergyman, beyond which it does to a stipendiary curate: but I am ready to defend my principles and my practice in the courts of law, and to abide by the consequences, be they what they may."

What answer Bishop Tait gave to that protest we cannot say. But in his primary Charge to the Diocese of London in that same year, he made the following emphatic declaration: "If what I deem a dangerous systematic invitation and admission of their people to confession is endeavoured to be maintained by any clergyman in this Diocese, I shall feel myself bound to watch his proceedings very carefully, and shall hold him most deeply responsible for any evils that ensue."

Such was an ordinary mid-Victorian episcopal attitude toward auricular Confession. There were, of course, exceptions. But frequently the impression was left that Confession itself was repudiated, and not only the abuses to which, like all things human, it was liable. The full and definite acknowledgment that a priest possessed absolving power, and that the penitent had the right to resort to it when they felt the need, was frequently, to say the very least, evaded. The authorities did not definitely deny that Confession to a priest might be on very rare occasions tolerated, but they reduced the privilege to such narrow limits, imposed upon it such

Confession and Absolution

restrictions, and surrounded it with such suspicions, that they rendered resort to it something to be deprecated and avoided rather than to be sought. This attitude naturally raised a doubt whether some of the Bishops had ever heard a confession in their lives, or were even aware of the existence of any Englishmen in the nineteenth century who had cause to be uneasy in conscience and for whom such practice might be exceedingly beneficial.

The dismissal of the Rev. Alfred Poole by his Diocesan, endorsed by the Primate, aroused determined protest. The Guild of S. Alban's, Liverpool, sent the deprived priest an ardent expression of sympathy entirely approving his conduct, and declaring that if he had refrained from inviting to Confession those for whose benefit the office was laid upon him, he would have failed to discharge the trust which the Church had given him. Poole became for a while Curate to Keble, author of the *Christian Year*, and was subsequently made Vicar in another Diocese, and, at a later date, preached before the University of Oxford, defending the benefits of Sacramental Confession, and advocating the importance of the study of moral theology, in order to qualify a priest for this difficult and momentous ministry.

It was impossible that the ministry of Absolution could be suppressed.

Pusey, in his letter to *The Times* in 1866, said that he had been asked to receive Confessions "from persons in every rank, of every age, old as well as young, in every profession, even those which you would think least accessible to it—army, navy, medicine, law."

Bishop Moberly of Salisbury, in his Bampton Lectures

The History of the Anglo-Catholic Revival

on the Administration of the Holy Spirit in the Body of Christ, lectures delivered in 1868, strongly commended the obligation of conferring Absolution on the sick and dying after Confession to a priest.

"And in the time of heavy and dangerous sickness, in the time when death seems to be impending, when the conscience is likely to be burthened with weighty matters lightly regarded, perhaps hardly remembered at all in the days of health and strength, when bodily and mental powers are enfeebled, and the heart is tempted to sink down and despair under the prospect of appearing immediately in the presence of the most Holy God with all its sins upon it—in the blessed comfort of the solemn confession to God in the presence of His priest, and the tender administration of God's Holy Words and promise, crowned by the audible words of authorised and express absolution, not to be refused to the afflicted and dying sinner, humbly and heartily, O let no shrinking from the honest and faithful use of the divinely descended powers that come to the Church and to her priest from the holy words and breath of Christ—let no base fears of worldly objection or scorn lead a priest of God to grudge to his dying brother the clear, outspoken, ringing words of holy absolution, which the Church has put into his mouth, which the sad sinner humbly and heartily craves, which his faithful full confession has earned. Do not mock the dying patient by reminding him that he, too, is a physician. Do not cheat the broken-hearted penitent by telling him that he is a priest himself. God has provided an express comfort for him in his extremity of distress. God has given to you, and to none but you, the very anodyne for his poor soul's pain. You are cruel, you are faithless,

Confession and Absolution

you are untrue to your holy calling and duty, if, out of fear of man, you shrink from using it."[1]

During the agitation to secure a Revision of the Prayer Book by which the formula of Absolution in the visitation of the Sick should be cancelled, *The Times*,[2] while urging revision, declared that "those who stand outside the pale of the Establishment may be allowed to expatiate upon the immoral tendency of Confession; but no such privilege can be accorded to those who have avowed their unfeigned assent and consent to all that is contained in the Prayer Book, unless they first demonstrate that the authoritative standards of the Church lend no sanction to the offensive practice. Evangelical combatants ... when defeated in the Prayer Book, commonly sound a retreat upon the Bible. But the manœuvre won't do. If the Bible and the Prayer Book teach the same thing, it is unnecessary to shift the ground of argument; if they do not, then one or the other must be abandoned.... The question is, how far does the ritual of the Church of England lend its sanction to the practice of Confession? This is not a theological point at all, but simply one of interpretation, of which any man of sound sense, who understands the English language, may set himself up without presumption as a competent judge. What is the meaning of those words in the Ordination Service: 'Whose sins thou dost forgive, they are forgiven; and whose sins thou dost retain, they are retained?' It will not do to say merely that those are scriptural expressions: we are entitled to know why they occur in that particular service, and what rational interpretation can be assigned to them. It is open for a controversialist to allege that they may

[1] Moberly, *Lect.* vii, p. 213. [2] 1855.

The History of the Anglo-Catholic Revival

apply literally to the twelve Apostles, without having been intended to apply to every young man who kneels before a Bishop in the ceremony of ordination. The use of these words in the ordination service implies certain theological views, certain canons of interpretation—what are they? When A.B. and M.N. are respectively told that the sins of the people which they forgive are forgiven, and that the sins they retain are retained, what are they to understand by it? Are they to infer that the Church holds it a sin for a layman to confess himself before any tribunal but the highest, and that no erring man has the prerogative of receiving confession and pronouncing pardon? If so, it is time to renounce our faith in the use of language. Again, in the service for the Visitation of the Sick the priest is directed to proceed as follows: . . ." *The Times* declared that it was impossible to deny that the language there employed lends a sort of sanction to the practice "unless we altogether falsify its plain and obvious meaning." *The Times* went on to refer to a letter from a correspondent in which the writer (a clergyman) said that he had been in orders forty years and had never once used the form of absolution prescribed in the Order for the Visitation of the Sick, although he had knelt by the bedside of many dying persons. On this the comment of *The Times* was very frank. "How a Country Vicar can reconcile this deliberate repudiation of one of the Church's formularies with his call to minister on the doctrine and sacraments as this Church and the realm hath received the same, may well perplex the brains of an orthodox Churchman."

The Times was by no means advocating a restoration of the practice of Sacramental Confession.[1] Its motive

[1] Quoted in *Suggestions for Revision*, 1859, pp. 12–14.

Confession and Absolution

was to show that the principles and directions of the Prayer Book were discordant with the popular belief and practice. It desired to revise the Rubrics into agreement with the popular belief. But the drift of the argument is that so long as the Rubrics stand unchanged it is not the Evangelical who refuses to repeat the words, but the Catholic who repeats them, who is in harmony with the Church's rule.

The *Edinburgh Review* took up the subject of Liturgical Revision in 1861, and discussed both the formula of ordination of priests and the formula of Absolution. With regard to the first it said, after quoting the words: "that these words, identical (but for some amplification) with the Saviour's authoritative benediction of the disciples after the Resurrection, should be arrogated by mortal man on any occasion, however solemn, does indeed seem monstrous to ordinary apprehensions, and would go beyond the pretensions (one should think) of those who have the loftiest views of priestly dignity and apostolical succession. Nothing, in our opinion, but the positive permission or command of Christ Himself would justify their use."

The Edinburgh Reviewer, in this remarkable passage, is acutely sensitive of the "lofty priestly dignity" which this use of our Lord's "authoritative benediction" involves. The curious thing, however, is that he passes in silence over the fact that a Church which deliberately identifies itself with this use of Christ's Words has thereby in a very impressive way revealed its own ideas about the supernatural nature of the authority which it possesses and of the powers with which its ministry is endowed.

The History of the Anglo-Catholic Revival

Yet in spite of pronouncing this ordination use of Christ's words as "monstrous to ordinary apprehension," the *Edinburgh Review* was cautious about suggesting their removal. The Reviewer seemed to feel instinctively that the operation would be dangerous. Accordingly, the suggestion was made—leave it to the Bishops. "It concerns them chiefly. Let them decide it. If they really think such language becoming and right—if by any interpretation they have been used to give to the words, they can justify their retention, and are content to employ them, it may be the wiser course to let this matter alone, and not to alarm the susceptibilities of that portion of the Church who think most reverently of the grace of ordination. And yet let it be remembered what a prolific source of scandal these words have proved, and will always prove to be so long as they continue in the Ordinal."

Thus the formula of Ordination was made a question of expediency. If the words could be interpreted in a sense which can justify their retention let the formula be retained. But the Reviewer had grave misgivings about the possibility, for he predicted that the words will always prove to be a source of scandal so long as they continue in the Ordinal. But why? Plainly because there will always be people who are convinced that the words, if so employed, lend themselves almost inevitably to a supremely authoritative interpretation. The *Edinburgh Review* recommends a diplomatic policy.

One insuperable reason why sacramental Confession could not be suppressed is that it was recognised and directed in the Book of Common Prayer. The more thoughtful opponents of the whole practice clearly saw that so long as the present directions of the Church of

Confession and Absolution

England remained it was impossible that such confession could be prevented. Hence a movement began to get the Prayer Book directions changed. In 1857 J. C. Fisher, a lawyer, published a work on Liturgical Purity, in which he declared that the Evangelical Party in the Church of England anxiously desired that the formula of ordination and the formula of Absolution in the Visitation of the Sick should be materially altered. The writer insisted that the future maintenance of our National Protestantism required some modification of these present forms of liturgical expression. Quoting the formula by which a priest is ordained, he made the following comments:

"Such is the language—rash, surely, and presumptuous in the extreme—of that most important of all the offices of the Anglican Ritual. And such the stupendous powers which one frail man assumes the right to confer upon another when called upon to invest him with the unpretending, though responsible duties of the Pastoral office. One is almost ready, indeed, in such a case as this to pass by in silent astonishment at the almost unparalleled assumption that must have dictated them, a form of words so little suited to the occasion, and so utterly repugnant, in their present application to the true sense of Holy Scripture."

The writer acutely realised the stupendous nature of the priestly claim. He did not, however, dwell on the fact that this claim is on his own admirably clear exposition that to which the Church of England is committed. Nor did he pause to reflect whether if the Church gave up that claim it would not cease to be the Church which the State had accepted as Established. But he clearly saw that this claim depended on the principle of Apostolic

The History of the Anglo-Catholic Revival

transmission, in which, of course, he did not for a moment believe. And he frankly added that "if upon an occasion so solemn, men have Apostolical gifts and authority ostensibly committed to them; it is no wonder surely that they should assume to themselves Apostolical dignity, and the right to exercise apostolical power."

But what caused the writer still more perplexity was that the formula of Ordination was not the only expression of priestly power which the Prayer Book contained. There was also that formula of Absolution of the Sick.

"Had this passage (the formula of Ordaining a priest) stood alone its withdrawal would still in times like these have been imperative. Unfortunately, however, it does not stand alone. The power to remit and retain sins, conferred upon the clergyman at his ordination, is authenticated beyond a doubt, by the very terms of the forms prescribed for his direction, when afterwards called upon to exercise it. 'I absolve thee from all thy sins' is most appropriate language in the mouth of one to whom it has been said, as upon Divine Warrant, 'whose sins thou dost forgive they are forgiven.' Nay, how could such an one fail to use it and yet be faithful to his solemn trust?"

His legal mind was keenly conscious of the consistency of these utterances. And that is precisely why he resented them. He felt that nothing short of their obliteration can set the Evangelical-minded free from what to him were priestly pretensions. He explains exactly what he felt to be the danger of their principle. If this power were really vested in Christian ministers, then he complains that the lay members of the Church are delivered over body and

Confession and Absolution

soul absolutely and for ever into the power of a class of men no less frail and fallible than themselves. What then becomes of the freedom wherein we are enjoined to stand? Accordingly, he attempts to prove that this doctrine of the Church of England is all wrong. But that it is the doctrine of the Church of England he fully acknowledges. That, indeed, was his complaint.

And then he uttered these memorable words: "I absolve thee: So long as language thus clearly indicative of the loftiest pretensions even of Papal assumption is deliberately retained, not in *one* alone, but in *two* of the most significant, and in every other respect most admirable services which the Prayer Book contains, it is, indeed, the height of infatuation to suppose that we can either destroy or weaken Tractarianism."

He therefore demands "that the principle of a mediatorial priesthood, which is the essential element, must be eradicated from the Book of Common Prayer."

In 1863 the Rev. Edmund Clay,[1] Minister at Brighton, addressed an appeal to the Lord Chancellor, in which he complained that the formula of Ordination of Priests is regarded by many as an offence against Scripture. Its expressions were, he urged, contrary to sound doctrine. When our Lord employed those words, "whose sins thou dost forgive they are forgiven," He used them in what the writer calls a donative sense; whereas the Prayer Book undoubtedly, so he said, uses them only in an optative sense, expressive only of a pious wish and prayer. Why then employ the Words of Christ, when our meaning is not the same? Whereas, it seems as if it were the same, and thereby many are misled and their consciences

[1] Wagner, Pamphlets, vol. 5, p. 5.

offended. Similarly with the formula of Absolution in the Visitation of the Sick it is urged that a minister using such words must be, and is in most cases, understood as using them in a literal and absolute sense. But that trenches upon the Divine prerogative.

Now, urged the Brighton Minister, the law compels the use of these formularies and even insists upon a profession of unreserved adherence to them on the part of the ministers of the Church; while, at the same time, the Church Tribunals authorise, and custom encourages, those ministers to evade the plain meaning of those formularies. Does not such a state of things, said the Minister, addressing the Lord Chancellor of England, involve a glaring inconsistency?

He therefore proposed that the Liturgy should be adapted to what he called a larger comprehensiveness, which he asserted to be required by the best interests of the country, demanded by public opinion, and solemnly sanctioned by the Ecclesiastical Courts. He urged accordingly that the Prayer Book should be revised with this intention. He was quite aware that not so long ago a most important declaration, signed by many thousands of the clergy, appeared, deprecating the present time as unfitted for any alteration or revision of the Prayer Book. But he agreed with a Bishop who thought that the existence of this strong conservative feeling was a security against dangerous innovations.

This appeal to the Lord Chancellor is significant as an acknowledgment that the official language of the Church of England, in its formula of Ordination to Priesthood and in its formula of Absolution in the Office for the Visitation of the Sick, was essentially Catholic, and as

Confession and Absolution

such repugnant to those who repudiated the Catholic conception of the priestly commission.

There were, however, Evangelicals who endeavoured to interpret these formulas in a Protestant sense. An example of this endeavour was Canon McNeile.

It is an interesting feature of the controversy that Dr. McNeile's interpretation of the priestly formula of the Church of England failed entirely to carry conviction in certain circles of English Nonconformity. The Congregationalist Minister, Dr. Mellor, well known at a later period for his Congregational Union Lectures, published, in 1867, reflections on the interpretation placed on Anglican formulas of priestly absolution by Dr. Pusey and by Dr. McNeile. "The acknowledgment of Dr. Pusey that for twenty-eight years he has been in the habit of receiving auricular confession and of administering private absolution may startle many who may have been unsuspicious that such a procedure was at all possible in the Protestant Church of England.... But ought it to be a matter of astonishment to us that such a practice has sprung up in such a quarter? Does not Dr. Pusey, and with reason, claim that the teaching of the Prayer Book is unambiguously on his side? Whatever may be said in reply to him when he seeks to shield under the same authority auricular confession, we believe him to be impregnable when he points to it in defence of sacerdotal absolution...."[1]

Dr. Mellor here quotes the various Prayer Book passages, and adds, "With words like these, uttered in a solemn service in the presence of the great God who searcheth all hearts, and will not be mocked, can any

[1] Mellor, *Ritualism*, 1867, pp. 165–8.

The History of the Anglo-Catholic Revival

thoughtful man, whom system and customs have not blunted and blinded, wonder that Dr. Pusey, and hundreds and thousands ministering in the same Church, should regard themselves as possessing plenary authority to forgive or retain sins? The wonder is that there is a clergyman within its pale who can hold any other opinion. And it is a greater wonder still that an eminent canon of the Church" (Dr. McNeile) "in a recent lecture on the priesthood, should, in order to escape the pressure of the words in the Ordination Service, have betaken himself to a subterfuge unworthy of him, both as a scholar and a minister of Christ. He, though a priest in the Church of England, in maintaining the same position as that defended in our first lecture, that there are no sacerdotal offices in the Church of Christ, was confronted with the words of the Bishop in the Ordination of Priests, 'Receive the Holy Ghost, etc. . . . Whosesoever sins ye remit they are remitted unto them.' And how does he deal with them? He says: 'If you accept them in the form of a prayer, and under limitation, then those words may be applied to your office?' Is this candid? Did not the worthy Canon see that they are not in the form of a prayer—that the prayer was finished—and that the Bishop, having completed the petition, then draws near to the candidate and lays his hands upon his head, employing the most direct imperative language, which he follows up with words which are neither imperative nor precatory, but declarative, and that in the plainest manner, of the power the priest has received. Did he not see that . . . there is not one expression which without even the most violent and licentious exegesis can be regarded as having the form or force of a prayer? '*If* you accept them in

Confession and Absolution

the form of a prayer'—this is his supposition. But if we may play what tricks we choose with words, we may make any word mean anything." The Congregationalist goes on to criticise the Evangelical who is severe enough on the Tractarians when they take liberties with the language of the Prayer Book.

Reynolds, President of the Nonconformist Cheshunt College in 1870, wrote on the priestly absolution in the Visitation of the Sick, "the form of this absolution follows closely in the spirit of that which had been in use throughout the Churches of the West; it is as old as the Sacramentary of Gelasius, 490; it reveals clearly the sacerdotal basis which Anglican Catholics can discover for their profession in the structure of the Book of Common Prayer."[1]

In the Congregational Union Lectures for 1874, Dr. Mellor repeated his conviction that "No words can more emphatically teach it (Absolution) than those which are found in the Service for the Visitation of the Sick: 'By His authority committed to me, I absolve thee from all thy sins.' ... The inference in favour of priestly absolution seems to us inevitable, and the sacerdotalists have here an entrenchment from which they can never be dislodged."

In 1873 Archbishop Tait read in Convocation a petition, signed by 483 priests of the Church of England, suggesting among many other matters the advisability of licensing duly qualified confessors. Considering that comparatively few of the Bishops tolerated Confession at all, and that many were strongly opposed to its habitual use, and that Tait himself as Bishop of London in his primary Charge

[1] Reynolds, *Eccles.*, 1870, pp. 309, 310.

The History of the Anglo-Catholic Revival

had scarcely left room for its exercise, it was certainly a bold move of the 483 to make this suggestion, however intrinsically desirable, and to base it, as they did, on "the widespread and increasing use of sacramental confession."[1] The Archbishop, after reading the petition to the Bishops, declared that every member of the House of Bishops present altogether repudiated the practice of habitual Confession, and all considered the sacramental view of Confession a most serious error.

The petition naturally roused the Protestant opposition, which Lord Shaftesbury voiced in vigorous terms: away with this pollution of the red one of Babylon. Shaftesbury's emphatic language was more effective than the Archbishop's remark that strength of language is not always perhaps proof of a strong cause. The Bishops issued a declaration that the Church of England knew no such words as Sacramental Confession, but for the relief of troubled consciences had made special provision in two exceptional cases. But this does not authorise the clergy to encourage any practice of habitual Confession to a priest.

Into this atmosphere of strain and suspicion was publicly introduced the privately printed book called *The Priest in Absolution*.[2] Written by a member of the Society of the Holy Cross under a deep sense of the necessity for priests to be instructed in Moral Theology, this volume was never published at all, but only circulated, as a medical book might be, intended only for members of that profession. It dealt with moral diseases. On its compiler's death the remaining copies were offered by the executor for sale to the Holy Cross Society which,

[1] Cf. *Life of Tait*, ii. 163.   [2] 1877.

Confession and Absolution

in order to avoid publicity, purchased them. But a copy of the book fell into hostile hands. Extracts were read in the House of Lords, rousing the whole Protestant feeling of the Nation. The Bishops were in panic, and from any point of view the incident was calamitous.

Bishop Jackson of London was much more guarded in his Charge in 1879 than Bishop Tait had been in 1858. But he restricted Confession to a priest as at most exceptional and under special circumstances. Indeed, he went so far as to say that: "It can hardly be denied that the Church of England, judged by her formularies, treats confession to a clergyman with a view to absolution, only as a remedy, or at most, as an exceptional duty, under special circumstances." But he held that "the Saviour's redeeming merits, God's pardoning love, embraced and held fast by a penitent faith, leave neither need nor room for private absolution and auricular confession."[1]

Bishop Jackson went so far as to interrupt the examination of his Candidates for Priesthood by a severe criticism and warning against the danger of auricular Confession; and this in the presence of certain young men who, of course, unknown to himself, had recently made their Confession, and were in that peace of mind which follows on a serene assurance that their sins were all forgiven. How painfully the warnings of the Bishop contrasted with and jarred upon the absolution pronounced by the priest may be better imagined than described.

Canon Carter of Clewer felt constrained to make a public appeal to Archbishop Tait on Freedom of Confession in the Church of England.[2] He submitted to his

[1] Bishop Jackson of London, Charge, 1879, pp. 60, 67.
[2] 1877.

The History of the Anglo-Catholic Revival

Grace the results of an experience of many years, explained that with the approval of Bishop Wilberforce Confession to a priest had entered largely into the pastoral work in the House of Mercy. He could not conceive such work being carried on without such aid as Confession supplies. He had carefully studied the leading Divines of the Church of England since the Reformation on this subject, and proceeded to quote the advice given by those whom all Churchmen had been led to regard as among the most devout and learned teachers. Then followed the teaching of George Herbert, Hooker, Bishop Jeremy Taylor, *The Whole Duty of Man*, Archbishop Wake, and others. It seemed inconceivable to Canon Carter that these men, who were in their day the most earnest and powerful advocates of our position in the controversy with Rome, could have used the language which they employed about Confession to a priest if they regarded it as untrue to the principles of the English Church. "One would have trusted," wrote Carter, "that the revival of Confession would be a cause of rejoicing and thankfulness to your Grace and the rest of our chief pastors: for certainly its rise and progress have been coincident with the more active ministry, the growing conviction of sin, the deepening and advancing of spiritual life, which have been the blessing of our later years."

Edward King, afterwards Bishop of Lincoln, published in the same year as Bishop Jackson's Charge (1879) the sentence that "the Church of Rome compels her children to make Confessions; the Church of England compels her priests to hear them." [1]

Over against the whole of these discussions and

---

[1] Edward King, *Reply to Rev. C. J. Elliott*, 1879, p. 9.

Confession and Absolution

arguments and interpretations of Rubrics it may suffice to set the one simple but conclusive fact, that the practice of Confession steadily grew, in spite of protests whether in Parliament or out of it, and has established itself in the religious experience of tens of thousands in every diocese and has deeply rooted itself into the life of the English Church. It has evidently met a profound spiritual need. And one of the saddest features of recent years is that where this relief from the burden of conscience has been refused, men and women have been known to seek in the Roman Church an absolution which was denied them among ourselves.

CHAPTER VII

THE TREATMENT OF RITUALISM

THE treatment of Ritualism in the Church of England falls naturally into four successive periods. First came its treatment by the Privy Council. Secondly, its treatment under the Public Worship Regulation Act (1874). Thirdly, its treatment in the Archbishops' Court (1890), in the case of the Bishop of Lincoln. And finally the Lambeth Hearings (1897).

I

Period one is the treatment of Ritualism by the Privy Council. The erection of a Privy Council Committee into a first Court of Appeal in cases affecting the Church synchronised with the beginnings of the Oxford Movement. Both are dated in 1833. It is frequently said that the Privy Council never contemplated that purely ecclesiastical subjects would come within its jurisdiction. But it was created by an Act of Parliament without consulting the Synods of the Church. Indeed, Convocation could not have been consulted since it had been practically silenced since 1717.

The general attitude of the State towards the Church at this period may be illustrated by the following examples.

It was the autumn of 1850. The Pope had just nominated Dr. Wiseman Archbishop of Westminster and raised him to the dignity of Cardinal in the Roman Church. This action was followed by a pastoral letter which ignored the existence of the English Church. Nothing was more

The Treatment of Ritualism

certain to set on fire the Protestant feeling of the nation, always ready to burst forth in fury at any much slighter provocation. This hour of intense excitement was chosen by the Premier, Lord John Russell, to write his famous letter to the Bishop of Durham.

The Durham Letter, nominally a protest against what was called the Papal Aggression, included a vigorous protest against the Anglo-Catholic Revival. It said that "Clergymen of our own Church who have subscribed the Thirty-nine Articles, and acknowledged in explicit terms the Queen's supremacy, have been the most forward in leading their flocks step by step to the very verge of the precipice." "The superstitious use of the sign of the Cross, the muttering of the Liturgy so as to disguise the language in which it is written, the recommendation of auricular confession, and the administration of penance and absolution—all these things are pointed out by clergymen of the Church of England as worthy of adoption, and are now openly reprehended by the Bishop of London in his charge to the clergy of his diocese."

"What then," the Statesman asked, "is the danger to be apprehended from a foreign prince of no great power, compared to the danger within the gates from the unworthy sons of the Church of England herself?" The writer concluded with an impassioned appeal. "I rely with confidence on the people of England, and I will not bate a jot of heart or hope so long as the glorious principles and the immortal martyrs of the Reformation shall be held in reverence by the great mass of a nation which looks with contempt on the mummeries of superstition, and with scorn at the laborious endeavours which are now making to confine the intellect and enslave the soul."

The History of the Anglo-Catholic Revival

This public letter, issued from Downing Street on November 9, 1850, roused the whole country. Papal aggression and Puseyite insidiousness were coupled together in public esteem. Anglo-Catholic contemporaries considered the Durham Letter as the inflammatory cause of the furious outburst of violence which ensued against the leading Churches of the Revival.

The controversial style of the Prime Minister was broadly adopted. If the Chief Minister of State represented Ritualism as "the mummeries of superstition," others denounced "the gaudy trappings of theatrical Ritualism" and popular lectures pronounced that "Anglican Sacerdotalists and Roman Catholic Priests" were "equally impious," and predicted that it would be "more tolerable for the worshippers of Juggernaut in the day of judgment than for these."[1]

The future Lord Shaftesbury determined to see for himself what was actually happening in the Ritualistic Churches. Accordingly, he attended S. Alban's, Holborn.[2] His comment was that "in outward form and ritual, it is the worship of Jupiter and Juno."[3] At the same time he admitted that "it may be Heaven itself in the inward sense, which none but God can penetrate." But Shaftesbury denounced in public meetings the "histrionic arrangements, adapted only to the theatre, and impeding all worship in spirit and in truth." He called Ritualism "symptom of a deep-seated corruption of faith and doctrine, enticing, and intended to entice, the people from the simplicity of the Gospel, and to lead them to submit to the sacerdotal forgery of a sacrificing priesthood,

---

[1] Beeman, *Ritualism*, p. 144.
[2] 1866.   [3] *Life of Shaftesbury*, ii. 333; iii. 213.

The Treatment of Ritualism

and the necessary and inevitable train of abominable superstitions." "I speak," continued the orator, "the sentiments of thousands in this realm, that if we be driven to this necessity (which God in His mercy avert!), I had rather worship with Lydia on the bank by the river side than with a hundred surpliced priests in the temple of S. Barnabas" (Pimlico). The effect of this enthusiastic fervour was electric. "Here the whole assembly enthusiastically rose to their feet—vociferous cheering succeeded." Yet Shaftesbury was out of heart. The Puseyites were a source of great anxiety. Their unity of purpose, systematised action, vigilance, penetration, zeal, perseverance, was, he confessed, "a match for a discipline ten times greater than Evangelicals could show."

During the disgraceful riots at S. George's-in-the-East,[1] Dr. Tait, Bishop of London, answered a letter from the Vestry that with regard to the use of unaccustomed vestments by the officiating clergy he had announced his "determination of putting a stop to such follies" where his jurisdiction enabled him. He spoke of the "childish mimicry of antiquated garments," and the clergyman "dressing himself up that he may resemble as much as possible a Roman Catholic priest." The Bishop regarded prosecutions for Vestments in a court of law inexpedient, and, indeed, derogatory to the character of our Church. At the same time, if the parishioners deliberately desired to prosecute the Rector for wearing garments which not unnaturally offend them, the Bishop would be ready to afford them all due facilities for the commencement of their lawsuit so far as his authority extended. Meanwhile he prohibited all unusual vestments.

[1] 1850.

The History of the Anglo-Catholic Revival

The powerful influences in State and Church opposed to the Oxford Movement rendered united action on the part of its adherents the natural, almost instinctive, course in self-defence. The English Church Union was formed in 1860. The first numbers of the Journal, which has always been the representative organ of Anglo-Catholicism, the *Church Times*, appeared on February 7, 1863. On the Evangelical and Protestant behalf, the Church Association came into existence in 1865. The function of the one Society was to secure toleration for Catholic principles and ceremonial: of the other to secure their suppression. The method of the one was prosecution; of the other passive resistance. Coercion was the distinction of the one, endurance of the other. Hence the fact that, in controversial sarcasm of the day, the Church Association acquired the name of the Persecution Company Limited.

The course of the Ritual controversy was marked by the action of these two Societies. Certainly every effort that influence and money could produce was exerted to crush the revival of Ritual in the English Church on the one side, and to secure its freedom of expression on the other. The powers of the Crown, of the Law Courts, of the larger number of the Episcopate, were resources on which the Church Association could as a rule rely. It succeeded in harassing the minds and ruining the earthly prospects of a number of priests. But it was utterly powerless to suppress the great movement itself. The Revival went on until it covered the land.

For half a century and more since 1868 the English Church Union, under the Presidency of Lord Halifax, has effectively promoted Anglo-Catholic principles. It has sustained, defended, and advanced them, by its counsel

The Treatment of Ritualism

and support, and many an unfortunate incident would have been averted if its advice had been sought first before any action was taken. The remark of an historian[1] of the nineteenth century that the English Church Union "has long ceased to be insignificant," cannot be accused of exaggeration. In the same cautious strain Lord Halifax is described as "able, courteous, but uncompromising." This estimate may fairly be supplemented by that of Pusey, who described him as "one of singular moderation as well as wisdom, who can discriminate with singular sagacity what is essential from what is not essential";[2] and who expressed his own faith on deep subjects with a precision which reminded Pusey of Hooker's wonderful enunciation of the doctrine of the Holy Trinity. Pusey predicted that as President of the English Church Union Lord Halifax would be the sense and moderation of it.

In 1866 both the English Church Union and the Church Association were in active opposition. This expressed itself in Deputations to the Archbishop of Canterbury, Archbishop Longley. The Anti-Ritualists appealed to the Bishops to repress the Ritual changes as illegal, and to secure that measure of uniformity which is involved in the idea of a National Church. The English Church Union objected to any alteration being made in the Prayer Book directions. To the former the Archbishop replied that the first step was to ascertain what the law allows. To the latter that no alteration should be made in the Prayer Book without the full concurrence of Convocation. The motive which prompted this action of the English Church Union was the well-founded apprehension that an effort would be made in Parliament to pass a Bill

[1] Warre Cornish, *History C. of E.*, ii. 3. [2] *Life of Pusey*, iv. 325.

The History of the Anglo-Catholic Revival

prohibiting Ritual advances. Keble's criticism on the situation was that the opponents of Ritual were adopting the line that these Ritual advances, which in their private judgment were wrong and mischievous, had the direct sanction of the law and were becoming popular. Parliament was, therefore, to be requested to be so kind as to pass an act to put them down.

The next move of the Bishops was to get Counsel's opinion. Four lawyers were consulted. Roundell Palmer, Hugh Cairns, and others. Their opinion was that Vestments, Altar Lights, Incense, mixed Chalice, and Wafers were all illegal.

Then the English Church Union arose and obtained Counsel's opinion. Against the four selected by the Bishops nine eminent lawyers were consulted. They included Phillimore, Hanna, Deane, Prideaux, James, and Coleridge. These pronounced the legality of Vestments, and generally the disputed Ritual, excepting incense.

The Ritual Commission of 1867[1] drew up a series of recommendations whose observance it was thought would remedy the ceremonial disorders in the Church. It suggested that the rule of the Church of England with regard to Ritual should be that which had prevailed for the last three hundred years. If any variation from the established use was made, either by the Introduction of Vestments, Altar Lights, or Incense, in the public Service of the Church, parishioners might complain to the Bishop, who could forthwith order the discontinuance of the same. Complaint might be made to the Bishop either by the Churchwardens or by five resident parishioners,

[1] *Christian Remembrancer*, 1868.

The Treatment of Ritualism

who shall declare themselves to be members of the Church. The purpose of these recommendations was to provide for aggrieved parishioners. The Commissioners agreed that the National Church ought to be comprehensive, but no novel practices should be introduced which are welcome only to some and offensive to others.

These recommendations of the Ritual Commission were severely criticised in journals on the Catholic side. Their principal quarterly, the *Christian Remembrancer*, insisted that these proposals amounted to a repeal of the Ornaments Rubric, since it was well known that funds were forthcoming to subsidise from three to five aggrieved parishioners in every parish.

Moreover, the Commission itself was divided. A minority of one-third opposed the recommendations of the majority.[1] Much criticism also was poured on the reference to "the Church's usage for three hundred years." It was asked what sort of consistency or uniformity could the Ritual Commissioners venture to claim for the practices of the Church of England during the century that elapsed between the death of Queen Mary and the Restoration of Charles II? Is there any imaginable abomination that was not practised in the Parish Churches of this country at some period or other of those one hundred years? Had not all kinds of irreverence taken place both as regards the administration and reception of the Holy Communion? The author added, "we forbear from publishing our own disgrace." The Commissioners' appeal to three hundred years of usage seemed a flimsy argument on which to base an "expediency of restraint." The Commissioners did not venture to propose that the

[1] *Christian Remembrancer*, p. 190 ff., 1868.

The History of the Anglo-Catholic Revival

Ornaments Rubric should be repealed, or taken clean out of the Book of Common Prayer. The further remark was made that they cannot put down the doctrine, but they desire to stop its exhibition in practice.

Among the facts which irretrievably damaged the opponents of Ritualism was the method employed to secure the required quota of aggrieved parishioners. Dr. Liddon said that "the pettiest resentment of a social or even of a commercial origin, sufficed to create the aggrieved parishioner, who forthwith became constant in his attendance at the Parish Church, not simply with a view to worshipping Almighty God, but in order to collect materials for a law-suit."[1]

It is not possible in a limited space to describe the experiences which many a priest endured in the revival of Eucharistic Ritual. One example may be selected—that of Mackonochie. It is a significant example both for the length of its duration and for the sacrifices it involved. In 1868 the Privy Council condemned Mackonochie for kneeling or prostrating himself during the Prayer of Consecration, and for having during the celebration two lights upon the Altar.

On this condemnation followed Queen Victoria's celebrated letter to Mackonochie, in January 1869, ordering him, in accordance with the judgment pronounced against him by the Privy Council, to cease the Ritual Acts therein prohibited. "We do . . . hereby command you, the said Reverend Alexander Heriot Mackonochie, to abstain for the future from the elevation of the Cup and Paten during the Administration of the Holy Communion, and from the use of Incense, and from

[1] Preface to Keble's *Tracts*, 1877, p. xiii.

The Treatment of Ritualism

the mixing of Water with the Wine during the Administration of the said Holy Communion, and from kneeling or prostrating yourself before the Consecrated Elements during the Prayer of Consecration, and also from using in the said Church Lighted Candles on the Communion Table during the Celebration of the Holy Communion at times when such lighted candles are not wanted for the purpose of giving light. And hereof fail not."

Tait, as Bishop of London, said that he had no better man in his Diocese than Mackonochie, but he also warned Stanton that if he became his curate he would lose all prospect of promotion.

In November 1870 the Privy Council suspended Mackonochie for three months from the discharge and execution of all the functions of his clerical office, on the ground that he had not obeyed the ruling given. Mackonochie pleaded that he had literally obeyed.[1] The Church-wardens gave their word in Court that this was true. "The Court, however, decided upon the sworn evidence of three paid informers—paid as stated in the Bill of Costs, at the rate of two guineas per diem—that the officiating clergyman unconsciously and unintentionally elevated the Wafer and the Cup to the extent mentioned in the affidavits; that the posture assumed and maintained for some seconds by Mr. Mackonochie was a humble prostration of the body in reverence and adoration."

In December 1874 Mackonochie was prosecuted again for other Ritual Acts on which no judicial sentence had as yet been pronounced. Again he was condemned and suspended from his priestly functions for some weeks, and ordered to pay the costs of the trial. On this sentence

[1] Bayfield Roberts, *History of E.C.U.*, p. 129 ff.

The History of the Anglo-Catholic Revival

Bishop Jackson of London sent for Fr. Stanton and forbade the use of vestments, wafers, and even of a stole. "In consequence of this order, celebrations of the Holy Communion ceased, and the congregation attended celebrations at S. Vedast, Foster Lane." When the six weeks were over Mackonochie resumed his priestly functions and the use of Vestments and Wafers. That was in August 1875. Peace reigned until 1878, when Lord Penzance decreed that Mackonochie was suspended from his office and benefice for a period of three years. Application was, therefore, made on behalf of Mackonochie to the Court of Queen's Bench, which declared that the decree of suspension pronounced by Lord Penzance was illegal. Lord Penzance, holding this decision to be an invasion of his own judicial independence, "endeavoured to obtain a reversal of the Judgment." In 1879 the judgment of the Queen's Bench was reversed. This reversal of judgment was made at the public expense. Lord Penzance thought it wise at the moment to decline to proceed to compulsory measures. But at the end of the same year he reissued his decree of suspension. Mackonochie, however, persisted in his priestly function. This rendered him liable to imprisonment. But the promoter of the case was unwilling to incur the odium of a priest's imprisonment. The opponents of Ritual thereupon made application for a new case against Mackonochie in 1880. Lord Penzance held it but refused to pronounce a decree of deprivation. Mackonochie's opponent then announced to the Bishop of London that he would not appear any more as a prosecutor. Thereupon the Bishop of London sequestered the benefice of S. Alban's, Holborn. In 1882 appeal was made to the Privy Council against the refusal

The Treatment of Ritualism

of Lord Penzance to deprive Mackonochie of his position as incumbent of S. Alban's. The Privy Council declined to pronounce as requested by the prosecutor an immediate sentence of Deprivation, and left it to the inferior Court to determine what punishment would be most proper. So the affair lingered another year. Lord Penzance was applied to once again to pronounce a sentence of deprivation. Meanwhile the Archbishop of Canterbury, Dr. Tait, within a month of his death, wrote to Mackonochie asking him to minimise the difficulties by resigning the benefice of S. Alban's, Holborn. Mackonochie did so. Then the Bishop of London arranged to institute Mackonochie to S. Peter's, London Docks, and Suckling to S. Alban's, Holborn. But the Church Association thwarted this arrangement. In July 1883 Lord Penzance deprived Mackonochie of all his ecclesiastical preferment in the Province of Canterbury. Mackonochie, therefore, withdrew from S. Peter's, London Docks. And the Bishop of London appointed Fr. Wainwright in his place. Thus the Church Association triumphed, so far as the individual priest was concerned. It drove out from his people one whole-heartedly devoted and deeply beloved. But the congregation and the Ritual remained. The English Church Union raised a special Mackonochie Fund to provide the exiled priest with an income of not less than £300 a year until he should receive suitable preferment.

Four years of life remained to him. In December 1887 he lost his life in a snowstorm in a Scottish forest.

What is popularly known as the Eastward Position came before the Courts in 1870. The charge was that the Rev. John Purchas and the assistant clergy on several occasions "stood before the Holy Table with their backs to the people." The Court held that this was contrary to the Rubric, whose apparent meaning was the north side of the holy table. The Judicial Committee of the Privy Council in 1871 (Purchas Judgment) declared the Eastward Position illegal: "The Eastward Position of the officiating clergyman which had thus been declared to be illegal and penal, was by widespread consent very closely connected in the popular apprehension with the maintenance of Eucharistic Truth, and certainly was most in accordance with the prevailing practice of Christendom. It was practically identified in the eyes of those congregations who had been accustomed to it, with a belief in the Sacrificial aspect of the Holy Eucharist."

Pusey, in his letter to Liddon,[1] complained that the Privy Council, which in the case of Essays and Reviews had sanctioned the greatest laxity of doctrine, was now enforcing the most rigid stringency in matters of Ritual.

After the decision of the Privy Council in the Purchas case the Bishop of Gloucester (Ellicott) wrote to Randall, Vicar of All Saints', Clifton, insisting very earnestly and solemnly that alterations should be made in the mode of conducting services in that Church in obedience to the Privy Council judgment.[2] In particular that Vestments should not be worn. Randall replied in "a respectful remonstrance," reminding the Bishop that Vestments had been pronounced lawful in the Court of Arches. He was convinced that in wearing Vestments he was obeying the law of the Church. Of the ten persons who had complained of the Ritual at All Saints', only one ever attended the Church, and some of the others were Dissenters.

---

[1] *Life of Pusey*, iv. 222.
[2] Randall, *Respectful Remonstrance*, 1874, pp. 5 ff.

The Treatment of Ritualism

Upon this reply the Bishop refused to ordain any clergy for work at All Saints'. A series of letters followed with further refusals to license any curate at all.

More influential was the Letter[1] addressed to the Bishop of London after the Purchas Judgment by the two Senior Canons of S. Paul's Cathedral, Liddon and Gregory, pointing out the indulgence with which the Evangelical neglect of the Rubrics was treated by him, and asking him to extend to those of his clergy and laity who were aggrieved and distressed by the recent decision of the Privy Council the indulgence which he had not hesitated to extend so liberally to others. The two Senior Canons declared that the Final Civil Court was not a Synod of the Church; its jurisdiction had never been formally recognised by the collective Church, and its original purpose was to hear appeals in Admiralty and Colonial cases. It was the decision of the Privy Council, and not any judgment of the English Episcopate, which the Bishop of London was recommending his clergy to obey. They urged that while it was very difficult in practice to determine the point at which the conscience of an individual presbyter cannot safely acquiesce in an episcopal decision, still they were well assured that the Bishop of London would admit that the canonical obedience which the clergy owe their Bishops has its limits *in foro conscientiae*. "Had you been a presbyter of this Diocese in the days of your predecessor, Bishop Bonner, you would have counselled and practised disobedience to his injunctions," "nor would you condemn the learned and intrepid Dr. Döllinger for his present attitude towards his diocesan, the Archbishop of

[1] Pamphlets, Purchas Judgment.

The History of the Anglo-Catholic Revival

Munich." The two Canons informed their Diocesan that they both proposed to continue to say the Prayer of Consecration while standing before the Table, and requested that they might both be included in any proceedings which in the exercise of his coercive jurisdiction the Bishop of London might think it his duty to sanction.[1]

The *British Quarterly Review* (April 1871), edited by Congregationalists, and certainly with no prejudice in favour of Ritualism, commenting on Privy Council judgments affecting the Church of England, remarked that "considerations of public policy have affected the decisions, and the strict letter of the law has been disregarded in a fashion which would find little favour in Westminster Hall."[2]

On the Privy Council itself as a Judge in affairs of the Church, Dr. Pusey said "such a Court of Appeal in religious matters had not existed anywhere, since our Lord founded His Church on earth."[3]

II

The second period of the Treatment of Ritualism by the Authorities of Church and State was during the primacy of Archbishop Tait. If Liddon characterised Dr. Tait's elevation as a miserable appointment, it should be remembered that Tait as Bishop of London had already displayed his Broad Church preference by selecting Arthur Stanley as his examining chaplain. The appointment was just as repulsive to that staunch Evangelical

[1] Letter of the two Senior Canons, 1871.
[2] Quoted in Liddon's Letter to Coleridge, 1871, p. 52.
[3] *Unlaw.*, p. 14.

The Treatment of Ritualism

Lord Shaftesbury as it was for the Catholic-minded preacher. Shaftesbury said: "I like much that he has written, but as for examining chaplain, avert it for heaven's sake."[1] "The Bishop knows not the gulf that he is opening for himself, the distrust, the suspicion, the covert, the manifest opposition, I fear, that he is preparing for himself among his clergy, aye and his laity." Tait, however, succeeded in persuading Shaftesbury that all was well. Nothing that was in Tait's power to say could have persuaded Liddon. The Archbishop and Shaftesbury soon combined on the Protestant side.

It was a time when Protestant antagonism was intensely roused by various long since forgotten publications on the subject of Confession. The opponents of Ritualism presented to the two Archbishops, through the Church Association, a Memorial signed by 60,000 persons, urging the entire suppression of ceremonies and practices adjudged to be illegal. Archbishop Tait replied expressing sympathy, and spoke of the danger caused by a considerable minority who "desired to subvert the principles of the Reformation." He then proceeded to introduce into Parliament the scheme for Public Worship regulation.

The Archbishops of Canterbury and York, in 1873–75, called on High Churchmen to separate from the Ritualists. The Appeal entirely failed. High Churchmen as a body felt acutely that the attacks on Ritualism involved theological principles which were their own vital convictions. The Archbishop of Canterbury himself publicly rebuked such men as Dean Church and Dr. Liddon, both of whom were Tractarians rather than Ritualists.

[1] *Life of Tait*, i. 208.

The History of the Anglo-Catholic Revival

The state of party feeling in the Church in 1873 may be seen in the following facts. In that year the two Archbishops of Canterbury and York received at Lambeth a deputation and a protest composed by the Church Association, which recommended them in the distribution of patronage to exclude the whole High Church party.[1] The Archbishops returned a written reply declaring that the danger of a considerable minority both of clergy and laity desiring to subvert the principles of the Reformation was real. Four hundred clergy had presented to the Convocation of the Province of Canterbury a petition "in favour of what they designate as Sacramental Confession." The Archbishops said, "we take this opportunity of expressing our entire disapproval of any such innovation, and our firm determination to do all in our power to discourage it." On the receipt of this reply the Church Association drew up resolutions embodying the Primate's opinion, and quite naturally gave them a wide circulation.

This led quite as naturally to the following forcible comments on the High Church side. "The Church Association has been the real prosecutor in all the so-called Ritualistic suits, and the two Archbishops are among the most eminent members of the Final Court of Appeal. That is to say, two of the Judges in the Court of last resort receive a visit from the prosecutor, listen to his wholesale accusations, express their entire approval of them, denounce the defendant, suggest means of worrying him, and virtually pass judgment beforehand on every point likely to come before them in their judicial capacity. And yet people wonder that the Ritualists treat with scant respect the decisions of a Court, two of whose members

[1] MacColl.

The Treatment of Ritualism

set at nought not merely the substance, but even the outward forms and decencies of justice."

This illustrates how fierce were the passions roused.

The same year (1873) witnessed the appearance of another Petition to the Archbishop of Canterbury from the Catholic side. It contained the plea, "We the undersigned clergy and lay communicants of the Church of England, being members of the University of Oxford, humbly entreat your Right Reverend House not to pass the New Rubric proposed by the Lower House of the Convocation of Canterbury, to discourage the attendance throughout the Communion Office of worshippers who do not then intend to communicate, because such a Rubric would be an inroad on the liberties of the faithful laity, and would interfere with their devotions without being necessary to afford relief for a grievance to any other persons." Among the signatories to that Petition were Pusey, Bright, Liddon, and King.

On this Petition the Archbishop commented in the House of Lords. His comment was: "When I see men whose duty it is to teach the doctrines of the Reformed Church to young men who are to be her ministers encourage such a petition as that, I am led to ask who is responsible for the appointment of those Professors?" His Grace went on to express a hope that in future more thought would be given to such selections by her Majesty's advisers.

His Grace went on to rebuke the Dean and Chapter of S. Paul's Cathedral. "I consider it is also a misfortune that the central Cathedral of this Metropolis should exhibit violations of the law of the Church." The reference was to Canon Gregory, Canon Liddon, and Dean

The History of the Anglo-Catholic Revival

Church, and their adopting the Eastward position at the Altar.

The credit of the ill-fated Public Worship Regulation Act of 1874 is generally given to Archbishop Tait. But the letters (published in 1926)[1] show how vigorously he was driven on by Queen Victoria. She wrote to him in January 1874, insisting that "the defiance shown by the Clergy of the High Church and Ritualistic party is so great that something must be done to check it and prevent its continuation." Tait replied that the Bishops had agreed that he should bring a Bill into Parliament empowering the Bishop of each Diocese, assisted by certain of the clergy and laity, carefully selected, to control the services of the several Churches within their respective jurisdictions. The Queen also addressed Gladstone on "the progress of these alarming Romanising tendencies" which had become so serious of late, the younger clergy seem so tainted with these totally anti-Protestant doctrines. The Queen went on to describe herself as "Protestant to the very heart's core," and shocked and grieved to see England forgetting her position. She felt she must speak openly, especially to Mr. Gladstone, "who is supposed to have rather a bias towards High Church views himself, but the danger of which she feels sure he cannot fail to recognise." Gladstone, in a powerful and dignified reply, remarked that he was from time to time denounced as a Ritualist, a Papist, and a Rationalist, but that he bore in silence the ascription to himself of these and other names. He had never at any time admitted any party designation in Religion, because he felt that the voluntary assumption of such designations would compromise what he cherished

[1] *Letters*, ii. 300 ff.

The Treatment of Ritualism

as the first of earthly blessings—his mental freedom. With regard to the Ritual excesses, he did not doubt the legal and moral inconsistency of a considerable number of clergy whose doings had brought them most before the public eye. But he reminded her Majesty that there were others whose mischievous excesses, while less apparent, were more subtle. "There is not a doubt that a certain number of clergymen not only deny the authority of Holy Scriptures and of the Church whose Ministers they are, but disbelieve the deity of our Saviour, His Incarnation, and His Resurrection. Mr. Gladstone reserves his judgment as to the wisdom of searching out all these classes of persons, to expel them from their places; but he holds them all to be altogether beyond the limits, from within which alone it is his duty to recommend to your Majesty with a view to ecclesiastical preferment."

What the Queen thought of Gladstone's letter is not told. There is no trace of a reply. But she wrote about the same time, quite accurately, to the German Emperor, that "notwithstanding an active and restless Catholic minority, the English Nation, as a whole, is essentially Protestant." But she refused to admit advanced High Churchmen into her Household unless they undertook not to take a prominent part in Church politics. On the other hand, she congratulated Dean Stanley in his support of Bishop Colenso.

Lord Selborne's opinion of the Public Worship Regulation Bill was uncompromising. He declared that from first to last the business was mismanaged. "In the course of its progress through the House of Lords it was suffered to fall into the hands of Lord Cairns and Lord Shaftesbury; excellent men, but in their religious views representing the lowest churchmanship of the Evangelical party."

As soon as this new Parliamentary legislation was proposed, Pusey intervened with three important letters to *The Times*, in which he urged that if the Public Worship Regulation Bill were passed, the Bishops, since they held themselves bound by the decisions of the Privy Council, could not be exponents of the Law of the Church. He insisted that the main object of this new plan was to give the Bishops power to enforce by sequestration or other penalties the recent decisions of the Privy Council. He predicted that this proposed coercive power would be more difficult for the Bishops to enforce than for the Tractarians to endure. He reminded the Bishops that much forbearance had been exercised by High Churchmen towards their Low Church brethren. It had often been suggested that in order to check the prosecuting zeal of the Church Association, some counter prosecutions of Low Church irregularities might be effectively undertaken. But High Churchmen refrained from such measures in order to avoid aggravating exasperation. The new scheme was simply intended to enforce a certain interpretation of rubrics. "This wrong judgment on Ritual," said Pusey, "has notoriously increased Ritualists." "The Vestments are used in more Churches than before they were forbidden."

Archbishop Tait was not likely to be influenced by Pusey's warnings. He exerted every means to secure for his regulations of worship the approval of Parliament. In these efforts he was opposed by Gladstone and supported by Disraeli. Disraeli shrewdly appreciated "the unexpected fervour with which the House of Commons

The Treatment of Ritualism

received the Bill,"[1] and supported it as a determination to put down Ritualism. In phrases which were unforgettable, Disraeli went on to say that the Church of England could include men of the most various opinions, but not Ritualism, because that led to Rome. He could respect the convictions of Catholics, but he could not tolerate a Protestant minister playing the part of a Catholic priest; nor the Mass reduced to a farce and masquerade. Other orators insisted on the complete subordination of the Church to the State. Sir William Harcourt contended that the authority of the Bishops was not divine, but purely human. Under these auspices the Public Worship Regulation Bill became the law of the land. Soon after it was passed nearly nine thousand clergy petitioned that Eucharistic Vestments should be allowed, and five thousand that they should be forbidden.

The first case which came before Lord Penzance under the Public Worship Regulation Act was that of Ridsdale, of S. Peter's, Folkestone. On appeal to Privy Council, the Vestments were forbidden and Eastward Position allowed. Ridsdale consented to obey if the Archbishop would dispense him from obeying the Ornaments Rubric. The Archbishop gave him dispensation.

A series of other cases followed. In the next year Arthur Tooth was imprisoned in Horsemonger Lane Gaol for refusal to recognise the authority of the Court, and then released by order of the Court on the request of the complainants in the suit. In the case of Charles Lowder the Bishop imposed his veto on the case. In the Enraght case a consecrated Wafer was produced in Court. Religious feeling was affronted and scandalised. Sidney Faithorn

[1] *Life of Tait*, ii. 213.

The History of the Anglo-Catholic Revival

Green, of S. John's, Miles Platting, was prosecuted by the Church Association and imprisoned in Lancaster Castle (1881). To these must be added the cases of Pelham Dale, and of Mackonochie, than whom Tait himself had confessed there was not a better man in his Diocese.

Liddon predicted that the day would come when the desire to obey a Supreme Court of Appeal, formed in accordance with our Lord's will respecting the discipline of His Church, will no longer be regarded as a mere fancy, worthy only of the unpractical and dreamy temper of some recluse ecclesiastics.

The Public Worship Regulation Act in 1874 added to the previously existing troubles of the Church of England.[1] The Act was, said Liddon, the creation of a panic, and many of those who took part in its enactment had already (three years afterwards) lived to regret that they did so. It was doubtless intended and expected by some of its authors to promote peace in the Church. It produced exasperation. Avowedly introduced not to secure equal justice to all the subjects of the Crown, but, as the Prime Minister explained, to put down an unpopular religious School, it had from the first corresponded to the programme thus traced.

What most Catholic-minded persons felt, and many declared, is that the Court set up by the Public Worship Regulation Act was established by the sole authority of Parliament, without consent of the Church and against resolutions of the Lower Houses of both Convocations.

In the great meeting held by the English Church Union in 1874 Pusey declared that this invoking the

---

[1] Preface to Keble's *Tracts*. Written in 1877.

The Treatment of Ritualism

Imperial Parliament to crush the Catholic Movement was an impressive testimony to the Movement's strength. People do not destroy a gnat with a sledge-hammer. Dr. Liddon maintained that whatever might be said for Hooker's theory, which represented Church and State as two different aspects or phases of a body which is substantially one, circumstances had changed so fundamentally that it was absolutely impossible to quote him, or any of the precedents on which he relied, as applicable to our own time.[1] Protestant Dissenters, then Roman Catholics, then Jews, then any sort of persons had been allowed, as a matter of political justice, to take their seats in the National Parliament. "By this self-enlargement Parliament had doubtless increased its claims upon the loyalty of the English people; but obviously, in precisely the same proportion, it had diminished its capacity for dealing with strictly theological questions."

Phillimore reminded his hearers that the Lord Chancellor, who was chief of the Judicial Committee in the case of Martin v. Mackonochie, whom no one would accuse of partiality for Ritualists, declared in the House of Lords that the Judgments of the Privy Council in the case of Mackonochie and in the case of Purchas, were irreconcilable and could not stand together.[2]

The Bishop of London (Jackson, 1879 Charge) instructed his Diocese that "the ambiguous rubric which directs the position of the minister while saying the Prayer of Consecration has ... received an authoritative interpretation by the Judicial Committee of the Privy Council. There is no specific direction, it is held, that during this prayer the minister is to stand on the west

[1] *Report*, p. 20.   [2] Ibid., p. 52.

side, or that he is to stand on the north side. But he must stand so that he may in good faith enable the communicants present, or the bulk of them, being properly placed, to see if they wish it, the breaking of the bread, and the performance of the other manual acts mentioned. The rubric must henceforth be read with this interpretation. The position carries with it no doctrinal significance."

The well-known but singular story how the failure of his proceedings against Ritualism by the Public Worship Regulation Act was ultimately realised by Archbishop Tait himself is impressive. Its singularity culminated in the case of the imprisoned priest, Sidney Faithorn Green. Tait supported a Bill in Parliament to secure the prisoner's release, but failed to get it passed.[1] Then he sent for the leaders of the Church Association and attempted to induce them to move for Green's release—and failed again. Then he made overtures to Green himself—and failed once more. Then the Archbishop again introduced a Bill to release the imprisoned priest, passed it in the House of Lords, but failed to pass it in the Commons. Then finally, afflicted by fatal illness, the Archbishop of Canterbury appealed to the Archbishop of York and to Green's Diocesan, the Bishop of Manchester, who, after considerably hesitation, consented to apply for Green's release, and succeeded. Thus the dying Primate endeavoured to neutralise the results of his own achievements.

As to the Public Worship Regulation Act the Bishop of London (Jackson) said: "I must now admit that hitherto it has failed." It had brought about a result which had been generally overlooked, namely, that the penalty for

[1] *Life of Tait*, ii. 455 ff.

The Treatment of Ritualism

disobedience to monitions issuing from the Court was imprisonment. The consequence of this result has been, the Bishop owned, that "public feeling receives a shock, and sympathy is enlisted on the side of the sufferer. Imprisonment as the result of an ecclesiastical suit *looks* like persecution for religious opinions, and there is at least an apparent incongruity, when a more severe and degrading penalty is the consequence of a broken rubric, than would have followed on a moral offence." The Bishop therefore felt obliged by facts to confess that "so far the endeavours to restrain the excesses of unauthorised ritual by the coercive action of the Courts have not proved successful."

The effect of the imprisonment of Ritualist clergy was that public opinion, which had violently opposed them, came to sympathise with them. The *Record* in 1884 admitted: "We believe that ecclesiastical litigation, whether against Bishops or clergy, is at the present time not only undesirable, but extremely likely to do mischief to the cause of Protestant Evangelical truth in the Church of England."

Not only was it true, as Bishop Jackson of London said, that public sympathy was on the side of the sufferers. The same thing was also true of a considerable section of the Evangelical opponents of the Revival. Dr. Liddon reminded the religious world that Evangelicals of the previous generation had contrasted Evangelical Religion with popery on the ground that the latter relied on force for the propagation of its tenets, while the former trusted entirely to the converting influence of the Holy Spirit.[1] The Rev. S. Garratt, of Ipswich, publicly expressed his

[1] *Church Troubles*, p. xxxi.

The History of the Anglo-Catholic Revival

distress that the controversial enterprises of the party, to which he had been accustomed fondly and always to give the tender and sacred name of Evangelical, were now associated with the names of Horsemonger, Holloway, and Warwick gaols. There were in the Evangelical School many who felt it a duty to discourage proceedings and a temper which are, said Dr. Liddon, ruinous to whatever is best in Evangelicalism itself.

After the Royal Commission on Ecclesiastical Courts,[1] Lord Penzance, in a separate report, advised against resorting to law. "I would only appeal to the Law and the Courts of Law in the last resort. If an appeal to a Court of Law could be avoided, it would be no longer necessary to send solicitors' clerks to attend Divine service in order to obtain definite and legal evidence of the way in which the service is conducted."

Moreover, what increased the public dislike of the imprisonment of the clergy for asserted excess in ritual was its unmistakable one-sidedness and lack of impartiality. The fact, which at a later date Bishop Stubbs impressed on the Diocese of Oxford, that the Judicial Committee of the Privy Council had "never been asked to deal out impartial justice to the anti-ritual side,"[2] was dawning on the public mind in 1880. The justice of Dr. Liddon's plea was felt that "if the Rubrical Law of the Church, or some recent interpretation of it, is to be enforced rigidly on one section of the clergy, it surely should be enforced on all. If creeds may be omitted, and the plainest Rubrical directions deliberately set at nought without any rebuke on the part of authority, it cannot be right to visit certain ceremonial excesses,

[1] 1883.   [2] *Visitation Charges*, p. 106.

The Treatment of Ritualism

if they be excesses, with imprisonment and deprivation."[1]

Bishop Stubbs reminded the Diocese of Oxford in 1890 that, with regard to ritual and rubrical observance, the simplest efforts to improve the arrangement of divine service had been attacked as insidiously designed to lead congregations to Rome. Men had been persecuted within the previous forty years "for doing things which an honest interpretation of simple words has now vindicated as legal, and made customary also."[2]

A penetrating reflection on the results of Ritual prosecutions was made in 1900. The results were "a defeat which those involved in it will not easily forgive; a victory which the victorious will find to have been so costly as to count for little, if anything, better than an overthrow."[3]

As a solution of the problems which distracted the Church, subsequent judgment has pronounced the Public Worship Regulation Act an utter failure from first to last. It has been called the most unpopular and unworkable of modern Acts of Parliament. Pusey, alluding to Dr. Tait's Presbyterian antecedents, remarked that "the Archbishop had naturally an hereditary antipathy to ritual."[4] His Grace "did not seem to have any glimpse of the soul of Ritualism. He sees it only as an outward thing, as outward as the Vestments themselves." Perhaps hardly any estimate is more severe than that of Warre Cornish: "His temperament and manner of thinking were those of a layman rather than a Churchman."[5]

Lord Selborne's estimate of Archbishop Tait is weighty:

[1] *Church Troubles*, p. xxviii. [2] Stubbs *Charges*, p. 103.
[3] Bowen, *ut supra*, p. 234. [4] *Unlaw.*, pp. 44, 57.
[5] Warre Cornish, *History*, ii. 347.

The History of the Anglo-Catholic Revival

"His intellect was of a type frequent among his countrymen: dry and strong, cautious without timidity, tenacious and practical. His Theology, a mixture of Evangelical and Broad, reflected his character. The Tractarian Movement found no favour with him: when a tutor at Oxford he was active in opposing its developments. . . . He bestowed his confidence and his patronage on some who went much further in a Latitudinarian direction than he did himself. If, when Primate, he did not succeed better than others in the government of the Church, it was only because he was not in sympathy with the prevailing current of opinion among the more active clergy, and they were not in sympathy with him. The greatest mistake which he made was when in 1874 he was induced, by the extravagance of some Ritualists, and a clamour against the Bishops for not putting them down, to propose an ill-considered measure of legislation, and to accept in lieu of it, from Lord Shaftesbury and Lord Cairns, another still more open to objection."[1]

When Pusey died[2] Lord Selborne said of him that "he was a power in the Church of England greater than Archbishop or Bishop, for almost half a century; and for sixteen years before his death he was the sole leader of his party. To the cause which that party represented he devoted with unswerving sacrifice many great gifts: birth, high station in the University, unwearied industry, solid learning. His zeal was apostolic, his life saintly. . . ."

The impression which Pusey as a preacher made on Fr. Benson was of "a man coming forth from ascetic retirement, bearing the traces of mental and bodily austerity, with a face marred beyond his years by self-

[1] *Memorials*, ii. 80-1.   [2] 1882.

The Treatment of Ritualism

discipline and external opposition and manifold anxiety, and speaking in the calm power of the Holy Ghost, not as the head of a party, but as the somewhat saddened but irrepressible instrument of the Divine Will."[1]

III

The third period in the treatment of Ritualism was the erection of the Archbishops' Court at Lambeth by Archbishop Benson in 1890. The Primate, earnestly bent on securing harmony in the Church on Ritual disputes, introduced a novel method of solution: or, rather, he endeavoured to put in practice what he conceived to be the intention of the direction in the Book of Common Prayer concerning the Services of the Church. The direction, of course, is that "forasmuch as nothing can be so plainly set forth, but doubts may arise in the use and practice of the same; to appease all such diversity (if any arise) and for the resolution of all doubts, concerning the manner how to understand, do, and execute, the things contained in this Book; the parties that so doubt, or diversely take anything, shall alway resort to the Bishop of the diocese, who by his discretion shall take order for the quieting and appeasing of the same; so that the same order be not contrary to anything contained in this Book. And if the Bishop of the diocese be in doubt, then he may send for the resolution thereof to the Archbishop."

The Catholic-minded were concerned with misgivings as to the value of the Archbishop's claim, and also with anxieties as to the use which he would make of it. It is well known what Bishop Stubbs thought of the Primate's

[1] *Letters*, i. 73 (1893).

position in the matter. The Bishop of Oxford's comment, that it was not as Court but as Archbishop in his Study, has become historic. That criticism implied a conception of the relation between a Bishop and the provincial Synod which the action of the Archbishop appeared to contravene. Is an Archbishop alone the constitutional judge of a Suffragan's orthodoxy? or does the decision rest with the Synod of the Province?

The case which Archbishop Benson undertook to decide was not only concerned with one of Episcopal dignity. Archiepiscopal judicial Authority, supposing it to exist over a Suffragan, could not have been exerted in a nobler case than the saintly Bishop of Lincoln. Opposition to Ritual now passed away from the ranks of the Priesthood to that of the Successors of the Apostles. The advance was, from any standpoint, critical.

Lord Selborne considered the Bishop of Lincoln's case "in every point of view a great misfortune and full of dangers to the Church." He felt that it was the Archbishop of Canterbury's official duty to hear and determine the case upon its merits if he accepted the Order in Council as settling the question of his jurisdiction over Suffragans accused of offences against the ecclesiastical law.[1] But the ultimate ground of the Lord Chancellor's apprehension was that the prosecutors of the Bishop of Lincoln would be very likely to appeal to the Privy Council, if anything was decided against them. And a reversal of the Archbishop's judgment by the Privy Council would be a very serious matter. Happily no such conflict between the Archbishop of Canterbury and the Privy Council took place. The Editor of the Selborne

[1] *Memorials*, ii. 399–400.

The Treatment of Ritualism

Memorials notes that "those who were with Lord Selborne at this time can never forget his anxiety before the decision of the Privy Council; nor his overflowing thankfulness at the confirmation by the Privy Council of the Archbishop's Judgment."

"This horrid Lambeth trial haunts me," wrote Dean Church; "the only hope I have is that the Archbishop may have sagacity enough and courage enough to see that the safest course is the boldest, and dare to revise the Privy Council rulings."[1]

Of the series of complaints against the Bishop of Lincoln the most important was that before the Consecration Prayer he stood in what is called the Eastward Position. This Charge was dismissed.[2]

The Lambeth judgment was indeed courageous, since it reversed the judgment of the Privy Council, which in 1871 declared the Eastward Position illegal.

When the Lambeth Judgment had been pronounced, Dean Church's opinion was: "It is the most courageous thing that has come from Lambeth for the last two hundred years."[3]

IV

The last of the four periods in the treatment of Ritualism was that of the Lambeth Hearing. It was held in the closing year of the nineteenth century. The subject being the use of Incense.

Bishop Creighton, in a letter written in 1899, related

[1] *Life and Letters of Dean Church*, p. 349.
[2] *In the Court of the Archbishop of Canterbury*, 1890, p. 45.
[3] *Life*, p. 349.

The History of the Anglo-Catholic Revival

that he had succeeded in inducing several Churches which were contemplating the introduction of incense to abstain; and several Churches to abandon perpetual Reservation; and to cease carrying lighted candles in procession. He had found disinclination to obey with regard to ceremonial use of incense, and introduction of lights at the Gospel. These two subjects were referred to the Archbishop of Canterbury in the Lambeth Hearing.[1]

In 1899, in his Annual Address to the English Church Union on the Agitation against the Oxford Movement, Lord Halifax complained of the timidity of the Bishops and their lack of impartiality in their treatment of Evangelicals and Anglo-Catholics. "Why is it when the more unpopular portions of the Church's teaching, say the doctrine of Confession and Absolution, are attacked in Parliament and elsewhere, the Heads of the Church, with few exceptions, seem so incapable of standing up for their clergy, and of vindicating in plain terms without compromise or apology, the teaching and practice of the Church? Why is it that an agitation like the present is sufficient to induce Bishops to take proceedings against clergy and congregations who have endeavoured to restore some of its ancient dignity and splendour to the service of God's House, on assumptions of illegality impossible to prove, but that nothing similar is ever threatened against those whose whole teaching and practice contradicts in the plainest manner what the Church enjoins?"

The subject of Reservation became most prominent in the opening of the twentieth century. Its development seems to have followed a parallel course with that of other features of the Oxford Movement.

[1] *Life*, ii. 359.

The Treatment of Ritualism

At the beginning of 1899, just when the Lambeth Hearings were approaching, 220 Incumbents under the Chairmanship of Montague Villiers of S. Paul's, Knightsbridge, drew up some important resolutions, which were sent to the Bishops. The Resolutions declared: (1) That "by Canonical Obedience is meant obedience to the Canons, and to the Bishop of the diocese calling on any individual to obey the Canons and to conform to the law, usages, customs, and rites of the Church which has canonical authority. (2) That the clergy owe it to the whole Catholic Church of Christ faithfully to refuse to obey any demands, even though they come in the name of Authority, which conflict with the laws, usages, customs, and rites of the Church, whether ecumenical or provincial, which have canonical authority. (3) That the Reservation of the Blessed Sacrament in parish Churches, for the *bona fide* purpose of communicating the sick and dying, and ceremonial use of incense being laudable practices of the whole Catholic Church of Christ, and both being included in the directions contained in the Ornaments Rubric, the right to such reservation and ceremonial use of incense cannot and must not be abandoned."

The redoubtable champion of Protestantism, Sir William Harcourt, wrote to *The Times* on these Resolutions the following comment: "I have witnessed not a few impudent transactions in my life, but for sheer downright insolent folly I think that cartel to the Bishops has never been surpassed. It is not the isolated outbreak of some single crack-brained, self-conceited parson. It is the well-considered, deliberate defiance of the law and of the authorities of the Church of England by that conspiracy

The History of the Anglo-Catholic Revival

of faithless priests who are and have long been compassing the betrayal of the Church to which they profess to belong."[1]

This "conspiracy of faithless priests" included such clergy as Brooke of S. John the Divine, Kennington, R. J. Suckling of S. Alban's, Holborn, C. N. Gray, Vicar of Helmsley, and W. B. Trevelyan, Vicar of S. Matthew's, Westminster.

The Archbishops, in their Lambeth Hearing in 1899, expressed the opinion that neither the liturgical use of incense nor the carrying of lights in procession was lawful in the Church of England. Accordingly, they requested the clergy to discontinue such use.

Dr. Sanday thereupon published his reflections. He complained that English people found it extremely difficult to separate in thought what is Catholic from what is Roman. For more than sixty years "the High Church party" had been insisting on the difference. But the habit of confusion was so inveterate that the distinction had not even yet been successfully brought home to the popular mind. He thought that there were some High Churchmen who had not quite brought the distinction home even to themselves. For himself he was convinced that the High Church party does aim at making the Church of England Catholic, and does not aim at making it Roman. Or, rather, to put it more accurately, an instructed High Churchman would not allow that he was trying to make the Church of England more Catholic, but only that he was trying to assert those elements of Catholicity which were inherent, though perhaps latent, in its Constitution. Our Church is Catholic in the same

[1] Quoted in Bowen, *Crisis*, p. 219.

The Treatment of Ritualism

sense in which the Church of Rome and the Churches of the East are Catholic. Sanday added that if the High Churchman thinks it right to emphasise what he has in common with these other great Churches, he did not see where he can be gainsaid. The question really is, How far does the common ground extend?

The Archbishops, however, instead of facing this question, confined themselves to the smaller issue: What is in accordance with, and what is opposed to, the law of the Church of England? They could not have decided that the use of Incense was uncatholic; since it is common both to the East and to the West. It is in any case early, if not primitive.

The Archbishops' decision thus brings into relief the possibility that there may be some practices which, though Catholic in themselves, are not consistent with the law of the Church of England. They took their stand on the Act of Uniformity of 1559. They passed by the Ornaments Rubric. Sanday greatly doubted whether this treatment of the Ornaments Rubric would in any respect give permanent satisfaction. In any case the Archbishops base their decision on an argument from silence. Sanday doubted whether that could be justified. Sanday gave instances to show that incense was in use and well established by A.D. 385. He suggested that since there existed a strong desire in the minds of many for better relations with the great Communions from which we are parted, one would think that the rulers of the Church would abstain from doing anything that would emphasise the insular character of our Church at the expense of its Catholicity. If the Law of the Church of England were clear and precise there would, of course, be no choice;

The History of the Anglo-Catholic Revival

but the legal case against incense was by no means clear and precise. The decision of the Archbishops was disappointing, all the more because their action was "thoroughly statesmanlike and well considered." Yet it ought to be obeyed.

In a paper read at Sion College in the same year (1899) Sanday owned that "as a matter of fact, looking back over the history of the Catholicising party, its greatest gains have been won really by disobedience. The most effective weapon in the hands of the party has been the willingness of its members to go to prison." Sanday did not hesitate to say that "From the time of Queen Anne onwards, through courses largely political, the Bishops have been taken from the party opposed to revival." And while he "cannot forget that obedience to Bishops is also a Catholic principle," he could not see "how it is possible for the Primates of England . . . to think only of a clause in the Act of Queen Elizabeth."

CHAPTER VIII

THREE REPRESENTATIVE DOCUMENTS OF THE REVIVAL

THREE principal manifestoes of the Catholic Faith have been produced by the Anglo-Catholic Movement in the course of the century. First came the *Tracts for the Times*, of which the last appeared in 1841. The second was *Lux Mundi*, published in 1889. The third was *Essays Catholic and Critical*, issued in 1926. Much light is thrown on the intellectual side of the Movement by a comparison of these three.

I

The *Tracts* were concerned to revive neglected or forgotten elements of the Anglican position. There was, as Dean Church said, "absolutely nothing in them but had the indisputable sanction of the Prayer Book, and of the most authoritative Anglican divines."[1] Nothing was more characteristic of them than their appeal to what the Prayer Book contains. Two series of quotations accompanied them: quotations from the Anglican theologians of the seventeenth century; quotations from the early Fathers of the Church. This was at once a double claim to identity: identity with their Anglican predecessors; and identity with the great teachers of the Universal Church. The *Tracts* were circulating in brief what was afterwards extended into the two great series of the library of Anglo-Catholic Theology

[1] *History Oxford Movement*, p. 106.

The History of the Anglo-Catholic Revival
and the library of the Fathers of the Church. The nature of the Church, the Apostolic Succession, the Sacraments, the principle of Tradition, priesthood—these subjects and such as these dominated the series of which the first collected volume appeared in 1834. These illustrate alike its interests and its limits.

It has been the fate of the *Tracts for the Times* that the general teaching of the whole series has been largely eclipsed owing to the sensation created by the final pamphlet on the interpretation of the Articles. But, as the introduction to the series declares, the purpose of the *Tracts* was to contribute towards the revival of doctrines which, although they were principles of action for our predecessors in the seventeenth century, had become obsolete with the majority of the members of the Church of England. Among these principles special mention was given to the Apostolic Succession, and the Holy Catholic Church. The very first of all the *Tracts* was concerned with the Apostolic Succession, because on that doctrine rested the ministerial commission. Quoting the formula of Ordination to Priesthood, the *Tract* inquired, Whence comes the ordainer's right to confer these powers? "Has he any right, except as having received the power from those who consecrated him to be a Bishop? He could not give what he had never received. It is plain then that he but *transmits*; and that the Christian Ministry is a *succession*. And if we trace back the power of ordination from hand to hand, of course we shall come to the Apostles at last.... And therefore all we who have been ordained clergy, in the very form of our ordination acknowledged the doctrine of the Apostolical Succession." "The Lord Jesus Christ gave His Spirit to His Apostles; they in turn

Three Representative Documents of the Revival

laid their hands on those who should succeed them; and these again on others; and so the sacred gift has been handed down to our present Bishops, who have appointed us as their assistants, and in some sense representatives."

"Why," asked the writer of this *Tract*,[1] "should we talk so much of an Establishment, and so little of an Apostolical Succession?" The Tractarians claimed that in the seventeenth century the doctrine was definitely held. It was no Tractarian invention. They only rendered prominent what had become obscured.

II

More than half a century elapsed between the publication of the *Tracts* and the publication of the second important Manifesto of the Oxford Movement. *Lux Mundi* appeared in 1889. During the interval the Darwinian theory of Evolution had been published. Biblical criticism had come across from Germany and become impressive. Rationalistic or agnostic theories were influential. By all these the religious atmosphere was deeply affected. An exposition of Anglo-Catholic principles in relation to these recent developments was imperatively required. *Lux Mundi* was a systematic endeavour to meet this need. According to Fairbairn, Principal of Mansfield College, there was an impressive contrast between the tone of the *Tracts* and of *Lux Mundi*. "In 1833 the first issue of the *Tracts* began, breathing the courage, defiance, and furious despair of a forlorn hope; in 1890, the men who have replaced the old leaders are within the citadel, victorious, proposing their own terms of peace."

[1] No. 4, p. 5.

The History of the Anglo-Catholic Revival

The writers of *Lux Mundi* were a remarkable group. A series of Essayists, which included Scott Holland, Aubrey Moore, Illingworth, Talbot, Moberly, and Walter Lock, beside the Editor, was bound in every way to be exceptional.

The sensation which the volume created was immense, its circulation astonishingly rapid and wide. In the preface to the tenth edition the Editor complained, and not without reason, that disproportionate attention had been given to some twenty pages on the subject of inspiration of Holy Scripture. The purpose of the Essayists had been "to succour a distressed faith by endeavouring to bring the Christian Creed into its right relation to the modern growth of knowledge."

The fact is that *Lux Mundi* should first be considered as a whole, as a general exposition of the Catholic principles with which it deals, and then afterwards the special section which roused so much criticism and was so keenly debated.

Most significantly the whole volume is on the Religion of the Incarnation. That is the basis: not the Atonement. Aubrey Moore's brilliant essay on the Christian Doctrine of God reproduces Origen's argument that "if God had ever existed alone in simple unity and solitary grandeur, apart from some object upon which from all eternity to pour forth His love, He could not have been always God. His Love, His Fatherhood would have been added in time, and there would then have been a time when He was imperfect." Elsewhere it is maintained that an eternally living God, knowing and loving, must be a God Whose Being involves eternal relationships. To make love possible there must be a lover and a loved.

Three Representative Documents of the Revival

Then on the Atonement much importance is attributed to the idea of Sacrifice and priestly mediation. "The propitiatory sacrifice which is to effect our reunion must, for we are powerless to effect it, come from without." The wrath of God represents the fixed and necessary hostility of the Divine Nature to sin. Hence it is God Who needs to be reconciled to man, as well as man to God. "The reconciliation to be effected is not merely the reconciliation of man to God by the change wrought in man's rebellious nature, but it is also the propitiation of God Himself, whose wrath unappeased and whose justice unsatisfied are the barriers thrown across the sinner's path to restoration." And if the propitiatory character of Christ's Death appears to be rested rather on the idea of an external infliction than on the sorrow of the Sinless Sufferer self-identified with the sinful, yet very great stress is laid on the doctrine of the priesthood of Christ.

In the Essay on the Church it was maintained that life is stunted so long as it is lived in individual isolation; that knowledge of truth comes through the mediation of others; and that worship is essentially corporate. The principle of co-operation for spiritual life, of association for the propagation of ideas, and of union for the purpose of worship, are all consummated in the Church. "Dogma is authoritatively taught, that the individual may be kept safe from mere individual caprice and fancifulness, but also that he himself may come to a rational understanding of his belief." The Church carries on the priestly work of Christ on earth. Milligan's sentence is approvingly quoted. "Sacerdotalism, priesthood, is the prime element of her being." The Church is the source of blessing to mankind: she pleads and intercedes and gives herself for all mankind. "As the teaching function of the whole Church does not militate against the special order of teachers, so the priestly function of the whole does not militate against a special order of priests." Moreover, in this Church there is a ministerial Apostolic Succession. Historical continuity of the Church is secured that way.

"No one will dispute that Jesus died upon the Cross. If He did not, on the third day, rise again from that death to life—*cadit quaestio*—all Christian dogma, all Christian faith, is at an end."[1]

This conservative exposition of Catholic Tradition was largely overlooked at the time; attention being arrested by the section of Biblical Criticism contained in some twenty pages out of more than 530. The theory of Evolution in the *Origin of Species* raised at once and acutely the problem of the value of the account of the origin of the human race in the Book of Genesis. Historical criticism was claiming to have overthrown many of the accepted opinions about the Old Testament. The Essayist's object was to reassure the distressed by showing that the Christian Faith is not vitally affected by the conclusions at which criticism seemed to have arrived. That involved discussion of Inspiration. The Question had to be faced, What Inspiration is. Does the inspiration of the recorder guarantee the exact historical truth of what he records? It was urged that the Church cannot insist upon the historical character of the earliest records of the Old Testament as it can on the historical character of the Gospels or the Acts of the Apostles. Very little of the early record could be securely traced to a period near

[1] *Lux Mundi.*

Three Representative Documents of the Revival

the events. "What we are asked to admit is not conscious perversion, but unconscious idealizing of history." Inspiration certainly meant the illumination of the judgment of the recorder. "The possibility and reality of miracles has to be vindicated first of all in the field of the New Testament; and one who admits them there cannot reasonably exclude their possibility in the earlier history." Especially was it to be remembered that the Church is not committed to any dogmatic definitions of the meaning of Inspiration. Mythology and allegory are the earliest modes in which the mind of man apprehended truth.

And, further, it was maintained that there was nothing in our Lord's use of the Old Testament which really constituted an argument against these concessions.

Then followed the famous sentences about the limitations involved in Incarnation. "The Incarnation was a self-emptying of God to reveal Himself under conditions of human nature and from the human point of view." That involved limitation in knowledge. It was, however, expressly guarded by the reflection that "this limitation of knowledge must not be confused with fallibility or liability to human delusion, because it was doubtless guarded by the Divine purpose which led Jesus Christ to take it upon Himself."

These pages on Inspiration and the limitation of our Lord's human knowledge produced exactly the contrary effect to that which their author intended. If in one direction they succoured a faith distressed, they caused profound distress among Anglo-Catholics. It has, of course, often been said that neither Keble nor Pusey would have endorsed them. But the fact is that large numbers of the Catholic-minded at the time when *Lux Mundi* appeared were profoundly disconcerted. Liddon preached his celebrated sermon on the inspiration of inveracity.

The protest introduced into Convocation by Denison, Archdeacon of Taunton, in 1891, was carried to the Bishops assembled in the Upper House by the Prolocutor of the Lower. The Declaration on the Truth of Holy Scripture, lamenting the growth of impressions that Holy Scripture had been discovered not to be worthy of unquestioning belief, was signed by a number of leading clergy of Catholic convictions, including Berdmore Compton, Canon Carter of Clewer, Canon Randall, Canon Churton, Dean Butler of Lincoln, Wagner of Brighton, and Kirkpatrick of S. Augustine's, Kilburn.

Bishop Stubbs, in his first Visitation Charge to the Diocese of Oxford, delivered in the very next year after *Lux Mundi* was published, expressed himself very vigorously about the Higher Criticism. The Old Testament, he said, was going through a process of analytical criticism "which had no parallel for acuteness of investigation, carefulness of method, and completeness of apparatus." This process was producing very startling results, "seeing that they interfere seriously with the literary and religious beliefs of two thousand years, modify all definite theories of prophecy and revelation, and demand a readjustment, to say the least, of all existing religious theories of inspiration.

"And further than this, when our Lord quotes a passage from the Old Testament, and argues from it, on an acceptance of authorship which is now assumed to be disproved, His own credibility, and with it the divine

Three Representative Documents of the Revival

and perfect knowledge which in His one personality He must, as we have been taught, have possessed, becomes a matter of doubt; and therewith the doctrine of the Incarnation, the complete union of perfect godhead and perfect manhood in the one person of the Son. Such a result is a very terrible one...."

Bishop Stubbs went on to add: "I have stated matters, of course, as you will understand, in the most extreme way." And after this pessimistic view he adopted an optimistic tone. "We have often been told, when some startling novelty has been broached, especially in relation to religious theory, that opinion goes through three phases: first, the new truth is said to be destructive of the old; second, it does not make any difference; third, it is absolutely confirmative of the truth that it seemed at first to contradict. The formula is a cynical one, but there is this much of truth in it—it is the novelty that alarms, it is the amount of proved truth that confirms. So far we may accept it. It will pretty certainly be the result now, if we will wait, and not let our impatience, by cutting knots that may and will be untied, spoil the opportunity, and encumber the faith of God with new difficulties and embittered relations."

As Bishop Stubbs most truly observed, "We are not all of us so well read in patristic theology as to be able to determine the exact bearing of the several theories that prevailed in the days nearest the days of the Son of Man, as to the relation between the divine knowledge which He possessed as God, and the measure of it which the human faculties which He possessed as the perfect man, were capable of realising and using; but we do know enough about patristic divinity to be aware that the theories of the Fathers were not all the same." Consequently he encouraged his hearers not to pass judgment, but to wait. It is unfortunate that it cannot be said that the Bishop's subsequent reflections on the Higher Criticism at his second Visitation Charge, delivered in 1893, were as conducive to patience and delay in judgment. And the attitude of this great and profoundly learned man illustrates the embarrassment which the advanced criticism of the period had produced in the generality of religious-minded people.

III

The third exposition and defence of the Faith by the Anglo-Catholic School is, of course, *Essays Catholic and Critical*, which appeared in 1926. Once more the circumstances had greatly changed. Just as *Lux Mundi* was required to meet a Biblical criticism which was not taken into account by the authors of the *Tracts*, so the *Essays Catholic and Critical* had to deal with fresh advances of the same. *Lux Mundi* deliberately omitted the subject of the Authority of the Church, whereas *Essays Catholic* devoted marked attention to the subject of religious Authority in general, and to that of the Church in particular.

Alike in *Lux Mundi* and in *Essays Catholic* there is the same insistence on the Christian conception of God as essentially Trinitarian. It is worked out more fully, as might be expected, in the latter by reflections on the idea of unity and on that of fellowship. But in both it is substantially the same.

So also the Catholic conception of Incarnation is

Three Representative Documents of the Revival

maintained firmly in the *Essays Catholic and Critical*, as well as in *Lux Mundi*. We are reminded in the *Essays* that whereas disparagement of the doctrine of two Natures in Christ has become almost conventional in some writings, the fact is that "if the doctrine of the Incarnation is true, we cannot escape from a psychological puzzle." The problem of Incarnation could only be escaped either by explaining away the Divine element or else the human.

The exposition of the doctrine of Atonement in the *Essays Catholic and Critical* is an effective proof of the inadequacy of Rashdall's reduction of Christ's Passion to a manward appeal. The moral value of our Lord's Death as an example, an appeal to love, and incentive to imitation, is true as far as it goes. But it is only an appeal by way of imagination; and imagination is weak, feeble, and inactive. If we are to depend for our Salvation on the impression which the Passion of Christ makes on our imagination, our chances are tenuous at best. The Passion as a mere example gives little hope to the ordinary man. Those would benefit by it most who are most highly endowed with the capacity for emotional or imaginative quickening. What has to be added is that sin requires Reparation. That word is frequently repeated. What needs then to be emphasised is the inadequacy of the offender's acts of Reparation. "If A has no appropriate sacrifice of his own that he can bring to the altar, he can avail himself of, associate himself with, B's offering; if he is, for any reason, tongue-tied, another can speak the necessary words for him, provided only that he signifies his assent." This conception of vicarious reparation has profoundly important bearing on the Christian

The History of the Anglo-Catholic Revival

theology of Atonement. "That the sacrifice of Christ is appropriate for this purpose need hardly be argued; that it is adequate will scarcely be doubted by anyone who sees in Jesus the Son of God, of the essence of the Godhead, incarnate for the salvation of the world." "Similarly there can be no doubt as to the description vicarious: the death was offered by the divine Victim on man's behalf, and as we have argued is available for man to identify himself therewith."

This strong insistence on Redemption as a godward offering, a reparation presented to the Holiness of the Father, identifies the Essayists with the Catholic Tradition, and, indeed, with the Apostolic conception of the value of our Lord's Death. It is peculiarly valuable at the present time when the subjective aspect of the Passion has been rendered popular and forcibly commended, and when so much indefiniteness prevails about the Atonement in the Evangelical School of thought.

There is a very impressive difference between *Lux Mundi* and the *Essays Catholic* in the fact that whereas the former does not attempt to discuss and determine questions of biblical criticism, the latter freely criticises the biblical critics, questions their assumptions, indicates their arbitrariness, and shows the inadequacy and inconclusiveness of some of their inferences. This carrying the controversy into the opposing camp is a characteristic feature of the *Essays Catholic*. It is most effectively performed with regard to the Synoptic portrait of Christ, and again with regard to Christ's Institution of the Sacraments.

It is, perhaps, on the subject of our Lord's Resurrection that the sharpest difference exists between the attitude of

Three Representative Documents of the Revival

Lux Mundi and that of *Essays Catholic and Critical*. The memorable sentence in *Lux Mundi* must be before us: "If He did not, on the third day, rise again from that death to life—*cadit quaestio*—all Christian dogma, all Christian faith, is at an end." Taken by itself this sentence, it might be urged, does not necessarily involve the Empty Grave. But when the same writer goes on to add: "Now given, first the certain condition that no miracle occurred; and secondly, a working hypothesis as to the growth of the Christian Scriptures, which not only enables, but requires, you to set aside, on grounds of subjective criticism, all such evidence as seems to you to be improbable; and it follows that, if you are still of a very religious mind, you will probably have to take refuge in what may yet be to you the beautiful story of a Resurrection exclusively spiritual. You must, of course, deal very violently with the direct evidence.... Tolerating these things, however, you may admit the truth of the Resurrection (as you may admit every proposition of the Creed) in words; only in a sense so refined, so exclusively spiritual, that no bodily reality of Resurrection is left. There is no resurrection in your creed correlative to the dying. There is no resurrection more, or more demonstrable, than what we believe to be true of men in general. ... The question raised is not whether correct imaginations of the Resurrection may possibly be more or less exaggerated in the way of materialism, but whether there was any corporeal reality of Resurrection at all. And the question is settled in the negative. The foundation of the Creed is etherealised away; and all the rest, with it, becomes together impalpable and subjective."

The change between this conception of Christ's

Resurrection in *Lux Mundi* and that propounded in the *Essays Catholic and Critical* is very considerable indeed. In the latter the whole treatment of the subject is dominated by psychological influences. Thus whereas the Gospel account sets first the evidence of the Empty Tomb and subsequently the evidence of the Appearances, this order is reversed in *Essays Catholic*, which places the appearances of the Risen Master first, discussing them in twenty-four pages, and then the question of the Empty Tomb, which is dismissed in three pages.

Heiler, impressed by the decided influence of German Protestant criticism of the Bible, and also of the Roman Catholic Modernism on the younger generation of Anglo-Catholics, both in Oxford and Cambridge, remarks that the Dean (Inge) of S. Paul's must revise his former opinion that Anglo-Catholicism was not on a level with the theology of to-day (*Um. Ringen*, p. 421).

It is interesting to compare the treatment of the Thirty-nine Articles in the *Tracts for the Times* with their treatment in *Essays Catholic and Critical*. In the former everybody remembers Tract 90. In the latter it is said "the formulæ of doctrine which emerged from the settlement were couched in studiously ambiguous terms. Only a special pleader will argue that the Thirty-nine Articles say one thing and mean another; but their compilers, where points were in dispute, succeeded in saying two things in one breath with remarkable adroitness."

CHAPTER IX

THE REVIVAL OF CONVOCATION

AT the time when the Catholic Revival began the English Church was deprived af all Synodical self-expression. For more than a hundred years Convocation had been silenced by the State. When the Nonjuring Bishops were deprived, their places were largely filled by men of latitude. In 1689 a Royal Commission prepared a series of Alterations in the Prayer Book in the latitudinarian interests, and attempted to secure their approval by Convocation. But Convocation resisted. Whereupon the King refused to allow the clergy to proceed and dissolved the Convocation. For ten years the clergy never met. The Crown continued its policy of nominating Broad Churchmen to the Episcopate, with the natural result that when Convocation was permitted to resume its functions after 1700, conflicts arose between the House of Bishops and the House of Clergy. These discords reached their height in the notorious controversy when Hoadley, Bishop of Bangor, published theological opinions which the Lower House of Convocation was determined to condemn. This condemnation of latitude was only prevented by the arbitrary silencing of Convocation by the Crown in 1717. It may well be that this silencing, which lasted for 135 years, saved the English Church from Synodical utterances on the part of the Episcopate which might have placed almost insuperable obstructions in the way of self-recovery. But it accustomed the Church to an unconstitutional condition, to a chronic incapacity

The History of the Anglo-Catholic Revival

to express its corporate requirements, or to protect itself in any normal way against assumptions and encroachments on the part of the State. The Church was reduced to impotence. The spiritual independence of the Church, which had ceased to exist in fact, ceased also for many of its members to exist in principle. The Church inevitably sank in the National esteem.

During the 135 years between 1717 and 1852 the usual practice was that Convocation was summoned by the Crown, as a matter of form, to meet at the beginning of a new Parliament. A few members accordingly appeared, elected a Prolocutor for the Lower House, sat for a brief space for what Burke called "the purpose of making some polite ecclesiastical compliments to the King," then dispersed, and was heard of no more until another Parliament was elected.

This subjection of Convocation was based on a legal interpretation of the Act of Submission of the clergy in the reign of Henry VIII. The Act of Submission decreed that the clergy should not enact any Canons without the King's licence to make, promulge, or execute such canons. The Judges informed the House of Lords that according to this Act Convocation not only cannot assemble without the King's assent, but also when assembled cannot confer without the leave of the King. Consequently, Convocation was always assembled by the King's direction, but never permitted to confer or deliberate on any affairs of the Church. The Historian Hallam, recording in his *Constitutional History* the fact that Convocation had been practically suppressed, characterised the event in the following famous terms: "In the ferment of that age, it was expedient for the State to scatter a little dust over

The Revival of Convocation

the angry insects; the Convocation was accordingly prorogued in 1717, and has never sat again for any business." This amazing criticism illustrates the popular view and shows how utterly incapable English people had become to realise the significance or use of the Church's Synodical constitution. And this was a widely prevalent idea when the Historian wrote in 1850.

The commonly prevalent idea of State and Church was clearly, if somewhat apologetically, formulated by the *Quarterly Review* in 1843:

"It does certainly appear something worse than absurd, that assemblies forming integral parts of the Constitution —necessary, as it would seem, to good ecclesiastical government—indeed essential to the very idea of a Church —and expressly sanctioned by law—should be ... periodically convoked for no other purpose than to be instantly dissolved. It is therefore very natural that, whenever any such difficulties as those we are now discussing occur in Church matters, there should revive amongst the clergy (and in many of the laity also) a feeling of dissatisfaction at so violent an inconsistency between the theory and practice of the constitution, and a strong desire that Convocation, at least, should be allowed to perform its natural and legal functions. This feeling, however, generally dies away with the crisis that prompts it, and a more sober consideration satisfies men's minds, that, like many other anomalies of our constitution and condition, the practical result is the wise one. Instead of an occasional crisis, which produces temporary regret at the absence of the Convocation, we should inevitably have, if Convocation were to be restored to the actual exercise of its theoretical powers, a constant agitation in

The History of the Anglo-Catholic Revival

the Church—a more intermitting fever of feud and faction, more intense, more uncontrollable, and more passionate, than that which parliamentary elections and debates create in the political world; and a development, we fear, of individual vanity, paradox, and ambition, which could not fail to multiply sects, schisms and contentions, and, within no long period, to scatter the Church, and religion itself, to the winds—not of heaven!

"The situation of our clergy, and particularly of our Bishops, in regard to Church Government, appears in the existing relations of Church and State, rather anomalous, and does afford at first sight some countenance to, or at least some palliation for, the complaints too warmly and too resentfully made by some of the Tractarians—and more soberly by cooler heads—of the want of sufficient authority within the Church for her own direction and guidance."

The *Quarterly Review* suggested that separate utterances of each individual Bishop were preferable to their united action, since each Bishop was thereby thrown on his independent abilities and debarred from the convenient shelter which want of learning or of judgment can so easily find under the collective impunity of an assembly. But the *Quarterly Review* was embarrassed by the inconvenient practical results of its own paradox; for the stubborn fact confronted it that the Bishops could not agree. The *Quarterly* was obliged to confess that if a certain learned prelate had discussed the topics with some of his brethren his decisions might not have appeared in their present state, and certainly it was "not seemly that a preacher should be enjoined to wear a white gown at one end of London Bridge, and a black one at the other

The Revival of Convocation

—which must be the case till the Bishop of Winchester shall have adopted the Bishop of London's views, or which we rather hope, the Bishop of London may reconsider the case." Accordingly, the *Quarterly* advised that the Bishops should meet together, on the one condition that the meeting must be in private.

The disastrous effect of this suppression may be illustrated in the Gorham Judgment in 1850. The State usurped the function of interpreting the Creed. As Gladstone said, the Primate instituted a Priest rejected by his Bishop for false doctrine.[1] And while individual Bishops and clergy made separate protests against the Privy Council decision, the Church, as a corporate Institution, had no power whatever to declare its mind. It was this powerlessness of the Church to resist which compelled Churchmen to agitate for the revival of Convocation. The Movement was begun by High Churchmen. Bishop Wilberforce of Oxford, under Gladstone's influence, led the way in the House of Lords in 1851. But the Archbishop of Canterbury opposed. Apprehensive of the controversies which would be certain to arise, he strongly discouraged it in the interests of peace. Wilberforce, however, was not daunted. He renewed the movement in Convocation itself.

At this critical time members of the Church began to dispute the interpretation which the Judges had placed on the Act of Submission. The theory that according to this Act Convocation, even when directed by the King to assemble, could not confer without express royal permission, was the work of that eminent lawyer, Lord Chief Justice Coke. It has been accepted ever since the

[1] *Life of Wilberforce*, ii. 134.

time of James the First. Nevertheless, the discovery was now made that neither the word "confer" nor any corresponding expression could be found in the Act at all. This discovery is attributed to a fellow of Magdalene College, Cambridge, the Rev. Edward Dodd, who instructed Bishop Wilberforce, and Henry Hoare, the munificent promoter of the Church House, on the true meaning of the Act of Submission. Hoare declared publicly that lawyers, Divines, and Statesmen had been misled by Coke. Convocation had perfect right of discussion, and needed no royal permission to do so.

It seemed a sufficiently audacious thing for men outside the legal profession to challenge the accepted legal opinion. Henry Hoare persisted. His contention was that Lord Chancellor Coke, anxious to satisfy his royal master King James the First, had stretched the wording of the Act beyond its proper meaning.

The attitude of the State to the Church towards the end of the seventeenth century was remembered and appealed to. Cardwell, writing with distinguished Authority on the Synods of the Church, reminded his age that "in the year 1662, when changes made by Convocation in the Book of Common Prayer were debated in the House of Commons, it was decided, though only by a small majority, to adopt them without examination, and with a still greater deference to authority of the Church in the year 1689, when the Bill of Comprehension was before the Commons, they petitioned the King to summon a Convocation as the more proper Assembly for discussing ecclesiastical questions. In this statement the Lords afterwards concurred, and a joint address was

The Revival of Convocation

presented to the throne, praying that, according to the ancient practice and usage of this Kingdom and of Parliament, his Majesty would be graciously pleased to issue forth his writs, as soon as conveniently might be, for calling a Convocation of the Clergy of this Kingdom to be advised with in ecclesiastical matters.[1]

To the apprehension and misgivings of those who argued against the freedom of Convocation to debate, the following popular reply was given:

"But the Convocation claimed too much. Be it so. Did the Commons never claim too much? There were great disturbances, and unseemly disputings between the Upper and Lower Houses. Granted. Did the Commons never interfere in the Lords in any way, even to denying, yes, and destroying, their constitutional position and rights, and of the Crown too? Yet such disputings were never put forward as any reason for doing away with the due balance of those two Estates. . . . And Convocation, let us remember, is not destroyed. Churchmen are not pleading for its revival, but for its action. It cannot be abolished."[2]

To these remarks another writer added the following severe reflection: "At the meetings of Convocation, right reverend and revered divines are assembled, as if it discharges momentous business; they are required to offer up prayers for divine assistance in their deliberations; yet if they presume to do business or to deliberate, they are cut short by a sentence of prorogation. What wonder, then, if this mocking of sacred things should extend

---

[1] Cardwell, *Synodalia*, Preface, p. 20.
[2] W. Fraser, *The Constitutional Nature of the Convocation of the Church of England*, 1852, pp. 25, 26.

The History of the Anglo-Catholic Revival

itself to holy ordinances in general, and even to the Sacraments themselves."[1]

Protests of Churchmen increased in volume without diminishing in vigour and, supported by Gladstone and Wilberforce, prevailed over opposition, whether ecclesiastical or secular.

The *Christian Remembrancer*[2] of 1852 gave its readers a singular account of the circumstances in which Convocation recovered its right to deliberate. This first occasion of debate since it was silenced over the case of Bishop Hoadley was naturally pronounced to be "the ecclesiastical fact of the year."

"No notice had been given of the intention of the Archbishop of Canterbury to hold a meeting of Convocation on February 3rd. But as much interest was felt among the clergy in consequence of what had passed last year ... inquiry was made as to the day and hour. ... The Bishops of London, Winchester, Exeter, Chichester, Oxford, Lichfield and S. Asaph attended at 12 o'clock. The Archbishop had appointed a Meeting of all the Bishops at the Bounty Board at half-past twelve, in order to consider the provisions of a new Clergy Offences Bill. ... Petitions were presented from 19 of the 21 Dioceses of the Province of Canterbury, praying the House to address a Petition to her Majesty to sanction the Meeting of Convocation for real synodal action. It could not be said that the matter came by surprise on the Archbishop, for a Petition had been entrusted to his Grace to present to the House—which Petition he had requested another Bishop to introduce."

[1] Caswall, Synodal Action Necessary to the Church, Letter to Gladstone, 1852.   [2] P. 490 ff.

The Revival of Convocation

In presenting the Petitions entrusted to himself, the Bishop of Oxford declared his intention of moving that the House consider the Petitions. Upon this the Queen's Advocate (Sir J. Dodson) interposed, saying that he felt it his duty, as legal adviser of the Archbishop, to declare that such a proceeding was without precedent; that for 135 years the Crown had called Convocation to meet merely as a form, and had not permitted it to perform any business. He quoted the Statute of 25 Hen. VIII, c. 19, as forbidding Convocation to do any business whatsoever without the express permission of the Crown.

"Upon this, the Bishop of Exeter said that though he had not lately looked into that Statute, yet his recollection of its import was clear, that the learned Queen's Advocate had ascribed to it inadvertently much larger words than it really contained. He had cited the word *business*, as used by the statute: whereas his (the Bishop's) recollection was clear (speaking with due deference in contradiction to so high a legal authority) that the prohibition in the 25 Hen. VIII was not against Convocation doing any business whatever without the Royal licence, but against making Canons, or conferring together for the making of Canons, when assembled under such licence. (The Queen's Advocate assented.) The Bishop recognised the right of the Archbishop to prorogue the Convocation at pleasure—to stop him, if he thought fit, while he was speaking. But as to the fitness of his Grace being advised to do so, on the ground of no precedent having occurred of Convocations doing more than meeting and bowing, and being dismissed, during nearly a century and a half, he must be permitted to express his astonishment at such a reason being given for such advice. Why, the disuse of all action on the part of Convocation, for so long a period, was the very matter of complaint—the grievance which was to be remedied: to make the existence of that very grievance to be a reason for its continuance was nothing short of mockery. . . . If precedent was to be cited, let them look to the precedent set by that Sovereign who died a martyr to his fidelity to the Church. His declaration prefixed to the Articles, and reprinted as often as the Book of Common Prayer was printed, contained a solemn promise that the Sovereign would do, as often as Convocation should ask him to do, that which it was the prayer of all these Petitions that we should beseech her Majesty to do.

"The Bishop of Oxford said that . . . there was notice of the intention to introduce a new Clergy Discipline Bill—a matter in which the Clergy at large were immediately interested, and on which the Bishops all knew that the greatest dissatisfaction was felt and expressed by the clergy, that they were not consulted. He, therefore, deemed it his duty to move that this House do present an humble Address to her Majesty, praying her Majesty to issue her Royal Licence for Convocation to meet and consult together respecting the fittest provisions to be introduced into the intended Bill."

The Bishops of London, Exeter, and Chichester expressed their warm assent to this motion: after which the Bishops of Winchester, Lichfield, and S. Asaph declared themselves against it. ". . . His Grace declared that he thought it most unfit that the Church should be placed in opposition to her Majesty's Government, and announced his purpose to prorogue to the 19th of August next. Upon this, the Bishop of Oxford gave notice that

The Revival of Convocation

he should repeat the motion which he had this day made.

"The Lower House was then sent for, in order to the prorogation. On their arrival, the Prolocutor, holding a paper in his hand, stated that he had to present an address to the Upper House, which, with his Grace's permission, he would read.

"His Grace said that they had been sent for, in order that the Convocation be prorogued. Sir John Dodson, the Queen's Advocate, declared that it was contrary to all precedent, that, under such circumstances, an Address from the Lower House should be received. The Bishop of Exeter saying that he much doubted the accuracy of the Queen's Advocate's statement, or at least its relevancy, the Lower House was desired to retire to their chamber, while this question was considered.

"After they had retired (the Bishop of Exeter again intervened and) His Grace declared his willingness to receive the Address. Accordingly the Lower House was recalled, their address was read, received, and entered as part of the proceedings of the day. After which his Grace declared the prorogation to the 19th of August next.

". . . The immediate result was the courteous conduct of the Bishop of London, who at once signified his purpose to abandon the Clergy Discipline Bill, against which the Clergy had in their petitions so strongly protested, until in some way the opinions of the Church could be formally taken upon it."

Thus, says the *Christian Remembrancer*, the principle was established that no measure deeply affecting the interests and sympathies of the Church will henceforth be submitted to Parliament without the formal intervention and consultation of some deliberative ecclesiastical body.

CHAPTER X

THE SPIRITUAL INDEPENDENCE OF THE CHURCH

THE conflict between Anglo-Catholicism and the State in the nineteenth century was in reality due to a rising claim to independence on the part of the Church, and refusal on the part of the State to allow it. The right of a spiritual Institution to self-expression within its own sphere was asserted on the one side, and denied on the other. The Church, through the influence of the Catholic Revival, was awakening to a consciousness of its real nature, whereas the State regarded itself as the one and only power. This view of the State was inherited from the eighteenth century. All through that century there had been a gradual encroachment of the State over the Church.

In legislation the Church as a body was not consulted. The State was not only dominant, but was regarded as the one and only real power. The Church was not only subordinate, but controlled. Many leading politicians came to regard the Church as little else than a department of the State. The notion that the Church could have a mind of its own, an authority which the State did not give, had become for the generality of Englishmen incredible; that the Church could venture to differ from the decisions of the State was judged audacious and scandalous. The powers that be were ordained of God. But the only corporate Institution which was divinely ordained was in public opinion the State.

The Spiritual Independence of the Church

Ecclesiastics themselves contracted a servile mentality. Even the language of the prayer for the King "duly considering whose authority he hath," unbalanced by any corresponding recognition of the Authority of the Church, lent itself in the public mind to a one-sided estimate of the supremacy of the State. It was natural that a generation which inherited this general outlook should see nothing incongruous in the erection of a Judicial Committee of the Privy Council to be the final Court of Appeal in matters which concerned the Church.

Many leaders in the State, and indeed in the Church, were quite unable to understand how the Catholic Movement could justify its resistance to the judicial decisions of the Privy Council. The lawlessness of the Puseyites was to a large number of law-abiding Englishmen perfectly unintelligible. What possible right had these strange innovators to resist? They that resist shall receive to themselves damnation. Queen Victoria complained that her Supreme Headship had been called in question. She wrote to the chiefs in her Government to demand an explanation. Archbishop Tait held that the Established Church had been regulated in many matters by the authority of Parliament. He could not conceive why the supreme authority in the realm should not decide in ecclesiastical disputes.

On the side of the Catholic Revival a quite unexpected array of arguments and authorities was produced. The great lawyer Coke was effectively brought forward as a witness.

"Certain it is that this Kingdom hath been best governed, and peace and quiet preserved, when both parties, when the Justices of the Temporal Courts and the Ecclesiastical judges, have kept themselves within their proper jurisdiction, without encroaching or usurping one upon another; and where such encroachments or usurpations have been made they have been the seeds of great trouble and inconvenience."[1]

The great authority of Bishop Gibson on canonical matters was repeated. "When the laws relating to the Royal Supremacy, which were made in the reigns of Henry the Eighth, Edward the Sixth, and Queen Elizabeth, say that all ecclesiastical authority is in the Crown, and derived from thence, or use any expressions of the like import; it is to be remembered that the principal intent of all such laws and expressions was to exclude the usurped powers of the Pope, and that they must be interpreted consistently with that other Authority which our constitution acknowledges to belong to every Bishop by the Word of God."[2]

The learned Oxford student, Sewell, insisted that "in temporal matters it would be impossible to select a tribunal more authoritative, for its own intrinsic claims to respect, than the judicial committee of the Privy Council; but the submitting of ecclesiastical matters to temporal Judges, sacrifices a great principle, on which depends the very existence of the Church. If we once admit laymen to adjudication over things spiritual, if they are made Judges in matters of faith and doctrine, it is not unlikely that there will be as many heresies as there are Judges; at all events their decisions will be equally as unsatis-

[1] Coke, *Fourth Inst.*, p. 321.
[2] Gibson, *Codex*, 1761, vol. i, p. xviii. Introductory Discourse. Repeated by Sewell, *Vindiciae Ecelesiasticae*, 1839, p. 67.

The Spiritual Independence of the Church

factory to the clergy, as the judgments of the bench of Bishops would be to a lawyer, on a difficult question of real property or a disputed point of pleading and evidence."[1]

Writing in 1843, Robert Phillimore[2] insisted that "Perhaps, if, during the last twenty years, the Corpus Juris Canonici, and still more, if the Provincial Constitutions of our own country, as given in Lyndewode, had been more thoroughly known and more deeply studied, the Church might have escaped some of those impediments which have been thrown in the way of her discipline and development by Acts of Parliament framed with the best intentions for the support of her interests. It is sad to think how often a deeper acquaintance with her jurisprudence would have prevented this hasty and crude legislation; how frequently the positive enactment of to-day has been found to mar the wisdom of her ancient law. I must think that she has often been forgetful or ignorant of the treasures of her own code when she had recourse to Parliament, thereby parting with some of her dignity, and at the same time depriving herself of the possession of a flexible system of jurisprudence, based on great principles which, under the direction of prudence and firmness, might have been well adapted to her successive exigencies."

Pusey said that "the Majesty of the House of Lords fastened upon the English Church, for the time, a Court of Appeal utterly unconstitutional."[3]

"What sent so many of our friends from us, and turned

---

[1] Sewell, *Vindiciae Ecclesiasticae*, 1839, p. 85.
[2] *The Study of Civil and Canon Law*, 1843, p. 53.
[3] *Unlaw*, p. 10.

servants and sons of the Church into its deadliest antagonists, was, that a State-appointed Court claimed, in the name of the Church, the supervision and determination of its doctrine."[1]

In his book on the Royal Supremacy Pusey[2] insisted that it was limited by the laws of the Church; that "the Acts of the Church cannot be rescinded, nor explained, nor expounded authoritatively, by any authority less than the Church." The fundamental defect of the Court of the Judicial Committee of the Privy Council was that the doctrines of the Church should, for any purpose, be authoritatively determined by any other than the Church itself. The Church of England had never intended by its acknowledgment of the Royal Supremacy to concede anything of the kind which the Privy Council had created. He did not believe that Queen Elizabeth meant to claim it.

Keble, in a series of popular tracts, declared that the Clergy of the Church of England never assented to the powers claimed for the Judicial Committee of the Privy Council of deciding doubtful points of doctrine. "It is no part of the system to which we are pledged by our engagements: we have not, even ignorantly, committed ourselves to it in any manner. I do not mean that we are not bound by it in the sense in which all men are bound by the laws of their country, whether those laws be right or wrong; that is, we ought to obey them, if we can do so with a safe conscience, and if not, we ought to submit to the penalty. We are bound to admit this Court's doctrinal authority in the same sense as a conscientious Dissenter was bound to obey those old Acts of Parliament

[1] Pusey, 1871, *Letter to Liddon*, p 64. [2] 1850.

The Spiritual Independence of the Church

which fined him for not going to Church. We must demur to the law, and quietly take the consequences."[1]

Gladstone, in his Essay on the State in its relations with the Church (1838), put the case as follows:—

As to anomalies and contradictions—"it is enough here to observe that if anything has been done of late years in the way either of anomaly or of usurpation, it has been done by the collective legislature in its capacity of political omnipotence, making use of the occasion while the Church organs (i.e. Convocations) are in abeyance; but it does not bind or commit the Church, which is not a consenting party, and which is only bound to show that in the regal headship, as acknowledged by her, which claims a negative upon all Church acts and upon all sentences in mixed matter, there is nothing unscriptural or unecclesiastical."

The alliance between Church and State is dependent on the continued consent of both the contracting parties.

"And if the conscience of the Church of England should, by its constituted rulers, require any law, or any meeting to make laws, as essential to its well-being, and such law, or the licence of such meeting, should be permanently refused, it would then be her duty to resign her civil privileges, and act in her free spiritual capacity." Gladstone devoutly hoped this contingency might be thought improbable. He was sure it would be deplorable. But he could not deny that it was possible.

One of the very ablest expositions of the Catholic conception of the true relation between Church and State was that published on the occasion of the Gorham Judgment in the *Christian Remembrancer* of 1850. It

[1] Keble, *Pastoral Tracts*, 1850.

The History of the Anglo-Catholic Revival
was reprinted in 1899 as a contribution to the discussion of those questions which had returned in an even more perplexing and formidable shape. The writer (R. W. Church, afterwards Dean of S. Paul's) contended that "there is no reason why Parliament should consider itself capable of discharging all necessary functions of Church administration or legislation, any more than administering or legislating for the internal affairs of the Great Western Railway Company or the Baptist body. There is no reason why the Church should find more difficulty in gaining Parliamentary Sanction to the exercise in a restored form of her own intrinsic and constitutional powers, or even of new and hitherto unknown ones, than other religious or secular bodies. There is no reason why she should not be allowed, under Parliamentary sanction and guarantee, to carry on reforms of her own, to adjust her position to altered circumstances, to administer her own laws, to take counsel for her own interests. There is no reason why in her case all these important matters should be kept out of her own hands, and left in those which are not her own.

"The English Church in the middle of the nineteenth century, suddenly, and certainly to her own surprise, finds herself caught as it were, and brought to a standstill, by an effect—the unintended, apparently, and unexpected effect—of what is called the Royal Supremacy."[1] This totally unexpected result raised the question, What is the nature of that power, which has led, in such a perfectly legal way, to results so anomalous and perplexing; and how ought Churchmen to view it?

Church contended that the primary idea of the power

[1] Church on *Relation Between Church and State*.

The Spiritual Independence of the Church
of the Crown in the Church seems to be what may be called a visitatorial power. "It was a power which presupposed other powers, and laws to which they were bound—powers derived from a divine source, and laws having a divine sanction; and its peculiar function was to keep those powers to their duty according to their own laws. It was a power of supervising and inspecting; not of creating, but of keeping it. It did not profess to supersede other powers by its own, but it watched that those powers were duly and lawfully used. Its interference might be very wide and very strict, but, in form at least, it regulated itself by already existing laws—laws whose independent origin and sanction it respectfully owned, while conferring on them its own sanction outside. But this visitatorial power was itself also claimed by divine right, and as of divine origin; not as a delegated but an independent authority, inherent in the royal function and office."

In previous centuries the Church found itself related not to a mere State or Government, but to a Kingly person: "a person having a conscience, owning personal responsibility, and one with her in faith, in practice, in sentiment, in purpose, acknowledging her laws, sympathising with her objects; and further, as the real depository of power, really able to aid as well as to govern."

Thus when the Church admitted the Crown to a share in its concerns, it was to a real King understood to be both a Christian and a Churchman that the Church consented to yield this power. Moreover, this consent was conditional on the Church's own laws and canons being the rule of its government, which rule the King was to see observed. In the historic relation of Church and

The History of the Anglo-Catholic Revival

State "the existence both of Church powers and Church laws—sanctioned, authorised, enforced, it may be, by the King, and on his own responsibility, but yet separately and distinctly subsisting—is everywhere taken for granted."

History shows, and this fact was profusely illustrated in the Essay before us, that the Royal interference in the affairs of the Church was accepted when the Sovereign was not only on good terms with the Church, but sympathised heartily with its faith, its system, its discipline and its objects. The clergy knew that their spiritual powers were as fully believed in and recognised by the King as by themselves. "The idea of a Christian and responsible King, embarked in the cause of the Church, and identified with her interests, still existed even under Henry VIII—to revive with greater force at subsequent periods. And further it is plain that the idea of the essential distinction of the spirituality, drawing its peculiar power from more than earthly sources, was still a clear and strong one; and as plain that the spirituality was a real and acknowledged complement and coefficient of the Crown in the government of the Church."

The contrast is then drawn between this relationship between the Royal Supremacy and Church in the past, and the condition into which things had changed in later years. The former understanding no longer exists.

As a Person, the Crown now stands at the head of a Nation broken up into recognised and tolerated parties, and therefore bound to neutrality. In temporal matters the Crown is still a power, but restricted, and acting only concurrently with other powers. "But as to ecclesiastical matters, the minds even of keen statesmen are, or seem to be, under a singular confusion. They cling, with incon-

The Spiritual Independence of the Church

sistent tenacity, to a notion of ecclesiastical supremacy entirely different from that which they entertain of temporal supremacy; and are taken aback at the idea of limitations on the one, which they have all their lives assumed as first principles in the case of the other."

"Things are altered from the original understanding if, what the Church asks, the Crown *cannot* grant, except its ministers advise it. But if the Supremacy is no longer to be viewed in this personal light, then there is no reason why it should not be subject to the same constitutional system which it acknowledges in civil government. The Church is, of itself, a substantive and organised body, and has hitherto been always supposed to be so—supposed not only in the theories of divines, but by the law of England. But if, when a question of doctrine deeply interesting to the Church is decided in such a way as to change her position as to that doctrine, she has no opportunity—the opportunity is denied her—of expressing her sense on this change in her position, this is not acknowledging her substantive existence and laws; it is a valid and just proceeding only on the assumption that she has been transformed, or has melted away, from a Church, which she once was, into a phase, a peculiar aspect or side, of the nation of England, for which the Parliament and Courts of England are the only rightful authorities, as they fully and fairly represent its mind, in the making and execution of laws. And those, to whom such an assumption comes as a contradiction of those principles on which they have hitherto held the Christian faith, have but one course left them. They must get it overthrown."

After the Gorham Judgment, Gladstone sent to the

The History of the Anglo-Catholic Revival

Bishop of London an open letter on the Royal Supremacy, representing the impossible situation in which the Privy Council decision had placed many members of the English Church. They could not "accept a system under which, while the legislative organs of the Church are in abeyance, her laws are to be judicially construed and applied, even in the very highest and most solemn subject matter, by a Court essentially temporal and civil, and a Court which, as they conceive, has already, on the very first occasion of its reversing a sentence of the ecclesiastical judge, made practically null one article of the Christian faith, and established principles that must involve the nullification in due time of the rest."

Gladstone maintained that at the Reformation the Papal Prerogatives were not carried over to the Crown. The unvarying doctrine employed by the Church in formulating a Canon was significantly different from that employed by Parliament in formulating a law. "In the Canons we find the words, We decree and ordain; that is, we, the members of the two Houses of Convocation. But in our laws, Be it enacted, by the King's most excellent Majesty, with the advice and consent of the Lords spiritual and temporal, and Commons. Whereas in the Canons the King does everything except enacting; with a remarkable accumulation of operative words he assents, ratifies, confirms and establishes; propounds, publishes; and enjoins and commands to be kept. Everyone of these words recognises that the Canon has a certain force of its own, while it purports to convey, and does convey, another force. In the one case the Crown is the fountain of the whole authority of the law; the Lords and Commons are its advisers. In the other, the Convocation decrees

The Spiritual Independence of the Church

and ordains; the King gives legal sanction and currency to that which, restoring the ancient regal jurisdiction, abolishes one that had been usurped."

Regarding the evidence as it stands, Gladstone said: "I cannot find the slightest trace of anything beyond control given to the Crown, with respect to the enactment of Church canons. The Reformation statutes did not leave the Convocation in the same position relatively to the Crown, as the Parliament. It was under more control; but its inherent and independent power was even thereby more directly recognised. The King was not the head of Convocation; it was not merely his Council. The Archbishop was its head, and summoned and prorogued it. It was not power but leave that this body had to seek from the Crown, in order to make Canons. A Canon without the royal assent was already a Canon, though without the force of law; but a bill which has passed the two houses is without force of any kind, until that assent is given."

Gladstone further pointed out that "In statutes, the King enacts with the advice and assent of Parliament; in Canons, the Convocation enacts, with the licence and assent of the Crown."

The Preamble of the great Statute of 1532 declared that this Realm of England is an Empire governed by one supreme head and king, "unto whom a body politic, compact of all sorts and degrees of people divided in terms and by names of spirituality and temporality, been bounden and owen to bear, next to God, a natural and humble obedience."

Gladstone insisted that "it would be easy to show that until about the accession of the House of Hanover, that

The History of the Anglo-Catholic Revival

is to say, for nearly two centuries, these two great rules of the policy of the English Reformation were observed with substantial fidelity:—(1) that the Convocation should be the instrument of legislation for the doctrine of the Church; (2) that the ecclesiastical law should be administered by ecclesiastical judges. In truth it is not enough to call these rules of policy; for, as to the State, they were constitutional principles, so to the Church they were solemn engagements."

Moreover, looking back to the Reformation struggles Gladstone urged that "we must discriminate and set aside that which belongs to the political character and bent of the particular period of the Tudor sovereigns and especially to that of Henry VIII. It is not to be denied that all liberty was in danger then; and Church liberty among the rest. If we wonder at the clergy who promised to make no law but with the King's prior and posterior consent, what shall we say of the Parliament which gave by statute the force of law to the King's proclamation? The excess in the exercise of royal power over the Church during the sixteenth century is probably due to the absolutism of the period more than to its Erastian tendencies."

If, therefore, the Royal Supremacy in relation to the Church is to be accurately understood the original facts of the Reformation period must be remembered.

"When therefore we review our Church history from the time of the rupture with Rome, let us endeavour to take a candid and dispassionate estimate of that to which the Church of England is committed, of the conditions under which she is committed to it, and of that to which she is not committed at all. She is most formally com-

The Spiritual Independence of the Church

mitted to placing the enactment of Canons under the restraint of prior permission and posterior confirmation by the Crown, but by a Crown of which the wearer is able to act for himself and not through the medium, or under the control, of ministers, virtually chosen by a majority in a Parliament of mixed belief."

And further: the Church "is committed to the exercise of all jurisdiction for her own purposes, subject to the Authorisation of the sovereign; but from a sovereign in her Communion, and having no political relation to maintain of such a kind as to impair the freedom of his personal conscience as a member of that communion, to impose upon him the duty, or supposed duty, of maintaining a spiritual relation with other and like bodies, or to reduce, in fact, to neutrality, or a moral *zero*, that sonship to the Church for which a King has shed his blood upon the scaffold—from a sovereign, the head of a civil government, all whose component members owed to that Church spiritual allegiance...."

Gladstone insisted that as to Courts of Appeal appointed by Parliamentary majorities, and assented to by the Sovereign on the advice of ministers, whom those majorities had constrained him to accept, the Church knows nothing. "Of the permanent suspension of her legislative organ, on pretence of its defectiveness, but without any attempt to amend it, the Church knows nothing—that is, knows nothing by way of acquiescence or approval, though she knows, and to her cost, the stagnation of religious life, and the loss of command over her work, and over the heart of the nation, which it has brought upon her."

In Gladstone's opinion the suppression of Convocation

The History of the Anglo-Catholic Revival
was an act of gross injustice, the most eminent example of tyranny, or the law of the strongest, acting under constitutional forms.

But further, beyond all historical theories and State encroachments, Gladstone maintained that the surrender of the Church's independence is a surrender which the Church cannot make. No assembly of Bishops and clergy inheriting the injunction of Christ to feed His sheep can by any agreement whatever make over to any other body than the Church itself that function. It cannot in the smallest degree derogate from its own awful responsibility for the fulfilment of its trust. If such a compact was ever made it was null and void from the beginning. If a compact was made which was not originally to that effect, but which became so in process of time, then from the moment that it became so it is null and void in spirit, and its nullity would entail the duty of putting an end to it at the earliest practical moment after the fact itself had been clearly established.

Among the changes brought about in the relation of the State to the Church during recent centuries were the suspension of the sittings of Convocation; the change in the personal composition of the Nation and of the State; the fact that the personal will of the Sovereign has lost its ancient place in the constitution of the country; and the progressive alteration in the composition of the Courts by which ecclesiastical causes were to be tried. "From the time when Parliament began to coerce the sovereign, to the time when, perhaps we may say in the year 1829, there was no more struggle, because the sovereign had ceased to resist, the Church was drifting from her position; instead of one master she was coming to have many;

The Spiritual Independence of the Church

it is now the majority of the Commons House of Parliament to which she must look as being in effect the Crown's capital adviser with respect to the exercise of its ecclesiastical supremacy."

A widely prevalent popular view of the English Church was represented in *Fraser's Magazine* in 1864. The Church of England was simply regarded as an institution established by law—and comprehending in fact, for some purpose, the entire Nation. Its Bishops, as Bishops, help to legislate for the whole Nation. It is supported by the Nation. It is governed by Parliament which represents the Nation. It is a National Institution. And "if the National principle were carried out to its fullest extent the Church would be considered as an institution intended for the benefit of the whole Nation, without distinction of religious belief." A National Church might be established which was not more connected with one scheme of theology than another. It might be made up of Protestants, Catholics, Unitarians, Deists and Jews, each with their own religious service and their own place of worship. A National Church, in the widest sense of the word, might contain a Unitarian and a Trinitarian party, just as at present it contains a High Church and a Low Church party. If the national principle was carried to its extreme limit, unity of religious opinion would be treated not necessarily as unimportant, but as irrelevant to Church membership, just as unity of political opinion is at present irrelevant to citizenship.

That is Nationalism in Religion carried out to its logical results. There is, of course, as the writer proceeds to show, another idea about a Church. This he designates the Sectarian view. The sectarian view of the Church is that there is a body of doctrine, communicated by God to man, of which there are in the world authorised expounders. This doctrine is the property of the Church which has the power of deciding when questions about theology arise. According to this sectarian view, uniformity of doctrine is of the very essence of the Church. And a Church which has no determinate doctrines is no Church at all.

The author declares that both these ideas about the Church—the National and the Sectarian as he calls them—are perfectly intelligible and also they are exhaustive, mutually exclusive. Which of them is true he has no intention to discuss. But he is absolutely convinced that the National view is the only one on which in the present state of feeling and knowledge the State can possibly act. If the Sectarian idea of the Church is true, the connection between Church and State ought to come to an end, and the sooner the better.

This is an illustration of widely prevalent opinion in 1864.

As a corrective to the above may be set the following, written about the same time on the Catholic side. After pointing out the two aspects of the Kingdom of Christ, not of this world yet in this world, it was remarked that these are the two aspects of the Kingdom of Christ, the Catholic and the National. "The Church is a spiritual body under a Divine Head, and existing with a spiritual life flowing from that Head, irrespective of human politics—antecedent to them, independent of them, and ordained to outlive them: this is the Catholic aspect."

The Church is an institution coextensive with the

The Spiritual Independence of the Church

political framework of a people, intricately blended with their social life, embedded in their laws, protected by their magistracy ... amenable to the control, and also forming an integral portion of the legislation and judicial departments of the State: this is the National aspect.[1]

Wayland Joyce,[2] a well-known authority on ecclesiastical principles, published in 1869 his treatise on the Civil Power in its relation to the Church. His argument against the Privy Council as a Final Court in Church matters was based on the ground that such a Court contravenes great principles of religion. The principle on which the Church is founded is that the teaching of the Word belongs to those called to the Christian ministry, and not to others. But a Court such as the Privy Council, being a Court of Final Appeal, not only interprets but actually constructs. It was no doubt replied that it is no duty of the Court to construct doctrine, but only to apply a doctrine already settled to the particular case in hand. But in practice this distinction is not really maintainable. "For though the Court is not charged with Authority to construct new doctrine, it is clear that the practical effect of its decisions may be to do so. And while the Judicial Committee itself disclaims either the power or the intention to frame new doctrine, yet every one must know ... how much of the Law of the land has been made by decisions of the judges. Every decision of a point of doctrine by the Judicial Committee would form, as other Courts of Appeal, a precedent. Such precedents settle or modify the law, and at last become law themselves." "And this thought may perhaps throw some light on the wisdom of our forefathers in the Church,

[1] *Christian Remembrancer*, 1868, p. 212.   [2] 1869.

who made Synods and not Courts the tribunals of final appeal in cases of disputed doctrine."

"It is indeed quite clear that the ancient and time-honoured principle of our constitution in Church and State, so early laid down, so often subsequently ratified, that the Church should be 'free in her judgments,' was established under the firm and reasonable conviction that final authoritative judgments on questions of faith or doctrine are the very highest expression of the teaching of the Word."

"The Judicial Committee of the Privy Council is a new statute Law Court, depending for its existence on a late Act of Parliament, and is now unmistakably and unequivocally a creature of modern legislation."

Wayland Joyce appealed to Hooker's words:—"Of this most certain we are, that our laws do neither suffer a spiritual Court to entertain those causes which by the law are civil, nor yet, if the matter be indeed spiritual, a mere civil Court to give judgment upon it."[1]

No plainer illustration could be given of the ideas about the constitution of the Church in relation to the State which prevailed among Englishmen late in the nineteenth century, than the attitude of Archbishop Tait towards Convocation and the House of Lords. Tait's biographer relates that when bent on securing the passage of the Public Worship Regulation Act through Parliament, the Archbishop "carefully avoided any statement which should seem to recognise an inherent right in Convocation to veto or delay Parliamentary action upon a subject of this kind, connected with legal procedure not with doctrine. . . ."[2] A subtle and untenable distinction. As

[1] *Eccles. P.*, iii.   [2] *Life of Archbishop Tait*, ii. 220.

The Spiritual Independence of the Church

if the regulation of the Ritual expression of the Church had nothing to do with doctrine; and as if the proper procedure of the Bishops was to appeal to Parliament in Church affairs without the consent of the synodal constitution of the Church. However, the Archbishop held that Convocation possessed no privilege of concurrent action. "As a matter of courtesy he was anxious to give the assembled clergy the fullest information as to the intention of the Bishops in Parliament." But he sternly resisted the request of Convocation for further time for discussion. Whereupon the biographer is constrained to admit that "the Lower House was not to be appeased, and the measure and its authors were denounced with increasing vehemence as the week's debate went on."[1]

One result of Archbishop Tait's over-riding Convocation was that a Memorial contrary to his policy was presented to the Upper House by Bishop Magee of Peterborough, and to the Lower House by Dean Church of S. Paul's.

On the very day on which the P.W.R.A. came into operation, July 1, 1875, Archdeacon Denison of Taunton denounced it in characteristic style from the pulpit of the Church served by Bennett of Frome. He denounced it as a law touching matters spiritual, a law for putting down Ritualism, framed by the Imperial Parliament, and to be administered by Civil Courts created by Act of Parliament. Parliament making laws about Primitive and Catholic worship was denounced as "a sorry and indecent spectacle." He maintained that "almost as if it were a part of the scheme that no element of Erastianism, of dishonour to the Church, of repulsiveness and alienation

[1] *Life of Archbishop Tait*, ii. 222.

should be lacking, the first Judge appointed under the Act by the two Archbishops is an ex-Judge of the Divorce Court."

Canon Carter of Clewer wrote a public letter[1] to Archbishop Tait in 1877, maintaining that through the policy of 1874 an excess of State interference had been reached, wholly unprecedented, leaving far behind all previous steps taken in this direction. The Court of Lord Penzance created by the P.W.R. Act involved that the matter of judgment was "surrendered to the control of the State." The difference is between the Church's independent right and the State's intrusive control; between the Church's hereditary order of jurisdiction and one of a quite novel character. Thus Mr. Tooth was "imprisoned by an unconstitutional stretch of the civil power and therefore unjustly, for he was judged as to the exercise of his spiritual functions by a judge appointed under merely parliamentary enactment."

Canon Carter declared that "nothing can be fairer or more consistent with a just compact between Church and State than the declarations of the Act (of Henry VIII) which abolished the appellative power of the Pope in this realm. The Preamble to that Act expresses its object "to render and yield justice and final determination to all manner of folk . . . within this his realm, in all causes . . . without restraint or provocation of any foreign princes or potentates of the world: the body spiritual whereof having power, when any cause of the law divine happened to come in question, or of spiritual learning that it was declared, interpreted, and shown by that part of the said body politic, called the Spirituality. . . .

[1] Carter on *Constitutional Order*.

The Spiritual Independence of the Church

Which has also been reputed of that sort, that both for knowledge, integrity, and sufficiency of number, it hath always been thought, and is also at this hour, sufficient and meet of itself, without the intermeddling of any exterior person or persons, to declare and determine all such doubts, and to administer all such offices and duties, as to their vows spiritual do appertain."

Canon Carter proceeded to quote Harold Browne, afterwards Bishop of Winchester, as to the intention of the Articles.

"The supremacy of the Crown must not (according to our constitution in Church and State) be considered as an arbitrary and unlimited supremacy. Everything in England is limited by law, and nothing more than the power of the Sovereign. In matters of State, the power of the Crown is limited by the two Houses of Parliament: in the affairs of the Church, it is limited also by the two Houses of Convocation. Legally and constitutionally the Sovereign, or the Sovereign's Government, can do nothing concerning the state of the Church, her doctrine, and discipline, without first consulting the clergy in Convocation, and the laity in Parliament: so that, when we acknowledge the supremacy of the Crown, we do not put our consciences under the arbitrary guidance of the Sovereign, or the Ministry; for we know that legally nothing can be imposed upon us but what has received the consent of our clergy and laity as represented respectively."

Archbishop Tait evidently regarded Canon Carter as representative and influential, otherwise he would certainly not have replied publicly in a pamphlet of thirty pages.[1] He owned that he differed from Carter in many

[1] *The Church and Law*, 1877.

most important points, but was glad that Carter should freely express to him his thoughts on the present condition of the Church. With regard to the evidence from eminent Divines since the Reformation, the Archbishop thought that Carter had unwarrantably deduced from their statements the dangerous principle that private individuals are entitled to add to the prescribed ceremonial of our Church any ceremonies which they themselves, or the circle of Divines among whom they move, believe to be consonant with Catholic usage. His Grace would like to know whether that principle was applicable to a regiment of soldiers. He was glad to find that Carter did not encourage violent resistance to the existing authorities of the Church. The proposal to obey no court or authority in the Church or realm, so long as such courts and other authorities are bound to conform to the interpretations of law given by the Judicial Committee of the Privy Council, the Archbishop characterised as intemperate and foolish. Carter's authority, continued the Archbishop, "is deservedly so great with a large section of Churchmen," that his Grace fully trusted and believed that he would be able to restrain many who, without his guidance, might be led into dangerous and self-willed courses, injurious to their own souls and to the Church which we all love. His Grace was unable to see why the State, which rearranged ecclesiastical fees and relaxed the terms of subscription to the Articles, should be regarded as violating principles in the decisions of the Courts. The Archbishop reminded Carter that he was in a very small minority among the attached members of the Church of England. "Please to remember," said his Grace, "that the persons whom you have to persuade are

The Spiritual Independence of the Church

a very large body indeed, not merely the comparative few who will accept your views as to the complete independence of the ecclesiastical power from lay control; but that overwhelming Protestant majority which constitutes the very backbone of the English Church." The Archbishop of Canterbury did not hesitate to say quite frankly that in his belief "the one very real objection felt by many to the legislation of 1874 is that it puts an end to that system of trifling with the decisions of Ecclesiastical Courts which had long proved an obstacle in the way of securing obedience." The official Principal of the Archbishop—that is to say, Lord Penzance—"is now able to give peremptory effect to his sentences."

The same reply to Canon Carter included a sermon preached in S. Margaret's, Westminster, in which his Grace observed, "men speak often nowadays as if Christ's Kingdom not being of this world, implied that it was free, in its character as a Church, from all obligation of obedience to the laws of the Christian State. This cannot be."

Carter felt himself completely misunderstood. The Archbishop's conception of the Church was profoundly different from his own; consequently it was inevitable that his Grace's conception of its relation to the State should also be profoundly different. Accordingly, Carter wrote "a further plea for constitutional liberty," published in a second letter[1] to the Archbishop of sixty pages. In this he dissociated himself from individual extravagances, which he would not justify or excuse.

What the adherents of the Oxford Movement contended for was "not any change in the constitution of the Church, but the carrying out into act of the Constitution as it now

[1] 1877.

exists." We hold, said Carter, "that the rights pledged to the Church under the constitution have not been fulfilled, and we believe that the dissatisfaction which so widely prevails, and the disinclination to obey the Courts as at present constituted, which is such an extremely dangerous symptom of the time, is owing to their want of authority, which alone can be secured by a truer concordant action of Church and State, pledged to us, as we believe, by the principles of our constitution."

In explanation of this position, Carter said: "In respect of the Queen's power over Convocation, it is important to note, that while the Act of Submission binds the clergy to seek both the previous permission to deliberate and the subsequent confirmation of the result, from the Crown, yet the Queen is also bound by solemn promise, made at her coronation, to uphold the rights and liberties of the Church. What these rights and liberties are has been explained by no less an authority than the late Baron Alderson, who, commenting on the terms of the Act, says: 'The Queen in the Coronation Oath swears that she will maintain the rights and privileges of the Church, one of which clearly is that no alteration in discipline or doctrine shall be made without the consent of the Church in Convocation, to be afterwards, no doubt, confirmed or rejected by Parliament, but clearly requiring the united act of both and the previous Act of the Church itself. The State has a veto on all changes, but cannot originate any.' (*Life of Baron Alderson*, pp. 118–19.) . . .'If then the power of Convocation is limited by that of the Crown, so likewise is the power of the Crown limited by Convocation.'"

"The Archbishop of York," said Carter, "in his

The Spiritual Independence of the Church

address to the Convocation of his province, has expressed surprise that the clergy should so greatly resent the action of the new Court towards Mr. Tooth, when the district of S. James, Hatcham, and the settlement of the incumbent's stipend, were wholly dependent on Acts of Parliament." To this criticism Carter, addressing the Primate of Canterbury, replied: "To me, my lord, the distinction between such cases and those on behalf of which our contention lies, is of a radical kind. There appears the greatest possible difference between the territorial division of dioceses and parishes, or the financial arrangements of an incumbent's salary, on the one hand, and on the other, questions touching the doctrine, sacraments and discipline of the Church. The one is of things spiritual, the other of their temporal accidents."

Carter was also able to contend that the Public Worship Regulation Bill had met with the distinct disapproval of the Lower House of both provinces of Convocation. Nor was it possible for the Church to forget that this Bill was ushered into the world under the patronage of the Prime Minister—Disraeli—and with the purpose which his memorable expressions (about putting down Ritualism) have stamped upon it for ever.

How deeply the feelings of the Catholic Revival were moved is shown by the manner in which Carter referred to the Seven Bishops who paid the penalty of their obedience to a higher law by incarceration in the Tower; though, added Carter, under circumstances of triumph which can never be forgotten. The co-operation of Disraeli and Tait had roused a spirit on which they had not calculated, and which it was not in their power to allay.

The History of the Anglo-Catholic Revival

"Perhaps," said Carter, "the greatest national blessing of these latter days, the fruit of long struggles, in this country, has been that we have learnt the full lesson of the principle on which those Bishops acted, namely, what law truly means; that it is not the overbearing prerogative of one estate of the realm to the subjection of another, nor the claims of the State against inherent rights of any institution within its borders, but that it means constitutional order, or the mutual respect for all true claims by the concurrent and harmonious action of all rightful authorities."

What less had the Great Charter itself affirmed when it claimed "that the Church of England be free and enjoy her whole rights and liberties inviolable"?

"I am aware also, my Lord," Carter continued, "that the 'overwhelming Protestant majority,' of which your Grace speaks, at the present holds the reins of power in its hands, and is the obstacle to obtaining what many of us heartily desire. But though this majority forms the bulk, does it also constitute the strength and the life of the Church of England? Is it not the case that all movements of life spring from below, and work their way upwards against seemingly overwhelming majorities? It was so with the great evangelical movement. This was confronted by a dense and serried phalanx of popular prejudice, which yet it completely overcame, and happily established itself in the heart of the Church of England. It needed the complement of the Tractarian Movement, which also was the work of the few against great forces, and won its way under great discouragements. Mr. Keble, for instance, never being permitted a licensed curate, and Dr. Pusey inhibited from preaching for two years,

The Spiritual Independence of the Church

and this because of doctrine which has since been pronounced legal by the Courts. But the Movement thus initiated transformed at length the whole character of the Church of England, in our dependencies equally as at home. And now what is called Ritualism, which in its truest sense is but an application of Tractarianism to the practical life and worship of the Church, cannot fail to advance. Its day of triumph may be delayed, and many who now bear the burden and heat of the struggle may not live to see what is reserved for another generation; but already the changed aspect of our sanctuaries and our services, our multiplied communions, our sisterhoods and brotherhoods, our missions and our retreats, our guilds and confraternities, are the characteristic fruits of the Ritualistic Movement, and the unmistakable attestations of its power."

A representative illustration of inability to see the difference between the functions of the State and of the Church occurs in the remarks made by Bishop Fraser of Manchester to his Diocesan Conference in 1875: "I have never been able to ascertain what is the exact kind of Court it is which the Church Union would consider to be spiritual: why a Chancellor appointed by the Bishop should be more a spiritual judge than the same man appointed by the Queen. Why Sir Robert Phillimore should be a secular judge in the Admiralty and a spiritual judge in the Court of Arches." He commented on the new theory put forward in some quarters that the tribunals of the Nation have no authority in matters ecclesiastical: "an *imperium in imperio* never has existed in England. Such talk is the mere rant of fanaticism."[1]

[1] Hughes, *Life of Bishop Fraser*, pp. 222, 238.

The History of the Anglo-Catholic Revival

Few charges have been repeated more persistently against Anglo-Catholic clergy than that they combine exalted views of the Episcopal office with constant refusal to submit themselves to episcopal direction. The criticism sounds telling. And the opposition is admittedly unfortunate. The clergy both by their doctrine of the Episcopate and by their ordination vows are bound to obey their Bishop's monition unless that monition transgresses the function of their office. But as Stuckey Coles said, the Bishops in issuing ritual directions were not using their spiritual powers, but as agents of the State were enforcing the intrusive jurisdiction claimed by the Crown. "It was when the Crown in Council had declared the Vestments illegal that Bishops began to issue monitions."

The accusation of Lawlessness made in the House of Lords in 1874 by the Archbishop of Canterbury against those who declined to obey the decisions of the Privy Council in spiritual matters, was deeply resented. As an instance Wagner, the builder of so many Churches in Brighton, and Chancellor of Chichester Cathedral, published a protest to the Archbishop desiring to repudiate the charge most emphatically. He considered the action of the Privy Council as an attempt on the part of the Civil power to supersede the teaching office of the Church, and to degrade it into a mere function or department of the State. If the oath of the Royal Supremacy required this, it was unquestionably an oath unlawful to take, as being contrary to the express institution of Christ. He insisted that in the Royal Declaration the Crown undertakes to refer to the Church's Convocations all religious disputes and differences which may arise about doctrine and affairs belonging to the Church.

The Spiritual Independence of the Church

Among the reasons for disobeying on principle the ecclesiastical judgments of the Privy Council Wagner gave the following: "Because the Court in question was created without any Synodical assent or consent of the Church, and, therefore, obedience to its decisions is a virtual admission that the Secular Parliament may legislate for the Church in matters affecting Spiritual things, without the Church having any voice in such legislation.

"Because obedience to a Court thus created subordinates the Spiritual and Divinely given powers of the Clergy to the powers of this world, degrades the Church to a mere department of the State, and ignores the Divine basis and supernatural character of Christianity."

It has been constantly urged on the Catholic side that the Scottish Presbyterian Established Church enjoys complete self-government.[1] It is absolutely independent of such Judicial Supremacy of the Crown as is imposed upon the Church of England. Parliament did attempt to interfere in the Established Church on the rights of patronage. The result was the great secession of 1843, and the Free Church independent of State Control.

In the Presbyterian Church in Scotland "no appeal lies to a Civil Court in matters of discipline.... Nor, it is believed, in any case would the Civil Court entertain an appeal from the judgment of an Ecclesiastical Court on a question of doctrine.

"No coercive power is allowed to the Church Court to execute their sentences, but these can be enforced by application to the Civil Court, which would as a matter of course give effect to them."

"The result of this historical independence is that the

[1] Spencer Holland, p. 252 ff.

Civil Courts of Scotland are extremely reluctant even to appear to interfere in any way with the jurisdiction of the Church Courts."

The contrast between the freedom of the Established Church in Scotland from State control and the subserviency of the Established Church in England provokes the question why the independence which is consistent with Establishment in the North of this Kingdom shall not be just as consistent in the South. And it is undeniable that theoretically there can be no reason against it. What is commonly urged against such freedom for the English Church is that it is the heir to a different history and tradition. The relation of the Church of England to the State has been entirely different to that of Presbyterianism ever since the Reformation. The legal and judicial traditions are entirely of another kind.

The differences are undeniable and they are great. But nevertheless, the encroachment of the State on the independence of the Church cannot change the facts of the Church's nature, nor its real and inherent rights.

The duration of an intrusion of secular power into the province of the spiritual over some centuries may make its reform more difficult and intricate, but it can never make that intrusion anything other than it really is, namely, an abuse. How far, both for its own sake and for the sake of the State, the Church should acquiesce in or tolerate this encroachment on its spiritual independence is one of those deep problems which Churches ought seriously to lay to heart. The question is whether this acquiescence in anomalies does not largely account for the religious ineffectiveness of the Church and for the disregard of its authority.

The Spiritual Independence of the Church

Fraser, Bishop of Manchester, represented undoubtedly much popular opinion when he wrote, in 1883, that "People are of course at liberty to say that they do not like the present constitution of the Courts, or that their decisions do not carry conviction to their minds; but this only means that people are at liberty, by lawful means, to reconstitute the Tribunals, and to get the unpalatable decisions reversed. It cannot mean, unless anarchy is to be substituted for order, that the Courts themselves, as existing, are to be ignored, and their most solemn decisions trampled under foot. The President of the English Church Union has indeed proclaimed that the party with which he acts will not be satisfied till they have destroyed the Apellate Jurisdiction of the Privy Council in matters ecclesiastical[1]; but till he has destroyed it by substituting for it a more perfect system, he must bear the present burden with as much patience as he can command. The Church of England cannot afford to be deprived at once of the protection and authority of all law; for if you destroy the authority you destroy at the same time the protection."[2]

This statement of the obligation of obedience to the law of the State would naturally commend itself to every law-abiding citizen. It is, in fact, as a general principle unquestionably right, and would be altogether unanswerable so long as every reference to any other authority than the State is left out. Its implication is that there is only one ultimate and absolute authority, and that authority is the State. But if there is beside the secular Authority another Authority of a spiritual kind, each possessing independent principles of its own, then the invariable

[1] Written in 1885.   [2] *Life of Bishop Fraser*, pp. 279–80.

obligation of obedience to the laws of the State is by no means so easily determined. What if the State exceeds its function, and invades the province of the Church? What if, through confusion induced by historic circumstances, the State has come to pronounce on matters spiritual which are in their very nature beyond its sphere, and belong not to the State but to the Church? This invasion of the Church's province and function by the Courts of the State is precisely what High Churchmen declared had actually happened, and this was the substance of their complaint. It was this invasion which they felt in conscience bound to resist. The consequence was that men of the type of Bishop Fraser of Manchester and men of the Anglo-Catholic type were at cross-purposes. The Bishop's appeal to what seemed the common-sense view of a citizen's duty to the State was to the Anglo-Catholic the Statesmen's view, and failed to realise the limits which the spiritual authority of the Church imposed upon unrestricted obedience to the laws of the State when those laws invaded the province of the spiritual.

Bishop Stubbs of Oxford, in his historical contribution to the Ecclesiastical Courts Commission (1883), held "that the appellate jurisdiction of the Judicial Committee of the Privy Council having been brought about by no conscious act of the legislature, and by no conscious acquiescence of the Church, but rather by a series of overlookings, and takings for granted, by the assumption of successive generations of lawyers, and the laches or want of foresight on the part of the clergy, the maintenance of the existing jurisdiction of the Judicial Committee of Privy Council, as a final tribunal of appeal in matters of doctrine and ritual, is not to be regarded as an essential

The Spiritual Independence of the Church

part, or necessary historical consequence of the Reformation settlement."

When the Report of the Ecclesiastical Courts Commission was issued in 1884, Lord Halifax, representing the convictions of the English Church Union, reiterated the demand that spiritual questions, meaning by that term matters of Doctrine, ceremonial and the Church's internal discipline, should be decided by the Church's accredited representatives. Catholics repudiated the interference in spiritual matters of the Judicial Committee of the Privy Council, and of Courts which derive authority from the Church. They further repudiated that theory of the Royal Supremacy by which the recognition of the Crown as the source of all coercive jurisdiction had been transformed into an acknowledgment of the right of the Sovereign to decide on appeal spiritual questions. And they were prepared to support to the utmost of their power those who might be called upon to suffer in behalf of their principles. They were not content to see the authority given by Christ to the Episcopate left in the hands of a Committee of Lawyers. The Church cannot surrender her rights in such matters.

Lord Halifax pointed to the actual existing situation. "The state of things to which the Church consented, is not the state of things in which she finds herself. In the first place, the position of the Crown is altered, the Church, instead of dealing with the Crown personally, has to look to the majority of the House of Commons, as being, in fact, the Crown's capital adviser in respect to the exercise of the Royal Supremacy; and, in the next, the appellate jurisdiction of the Crown has been

The History of the Anglo-Catholic Revival

progressively altered, till it has been thrown entirely into lay hands."

It is interesting to find Dr. Fairbairn arriving at the same conclusion.[1] "The practice was intelligible and logical enough *on the theory that Church and State were*, though formally different, *materially identical*: each was the same thing viewed under a different aspect, the civil legislature being at the same time in its own right also the ecclesiastical. So long as the theory even tolerably corresponded with fact, the system could be made to work; but once the Church and State ceased to be, and to be considered as being, co-extensive, the system became at once illogical, unreal and impracticable."

With the twentieth century a better condition has been reached in the relation of Church and State. The Royal Commission of 1906 acknowledged that the Jurisdiction of the Privy Council in ecclesiastical affairs cannot be retained. The Royal Commission declared that "a court dealing with matters of conscience and religion must, above all others, rest on moral authority, if its judgments are to be effective. As thousands of clergy, with strong lay support, refuse to recognise the jurisdiction of the Judicial Committee, its judgments cannot practically be enforced."

What is most important is the new conception which has arisen concerning the relative independence of bodies within the State. No English writer has illustrated that more clearly than Fr. Figgis in his book, *Churches in the Modern State*. In the opinion of a large majority of English people the Established Church has no inherent rights. The prevalent theory is the omnipotence of the

[1] 1899.

The Spiritual Independence of the Church

State. The State is the one and only association which exists of right. Confronted with that supreme authority are simply individuals. The Omnipotent State ascribes to groups of men by a legal fiction a sort of personality. But there is no real corporate Institution except the State. There is nothing in human existence but the State on the one side, and the individual on the other. The rights or actions of the one are private, those of the other are public. There are "no real social entities, no true powers, except the Sovereign State on the one hand with irresistible authority, and the mass of individuals on the other. Societies, so far as they exist, are mere collections of individuals who remain unchanged by their membership, and whose unity of action is narrowly circumscribed by the State, and when allowed is allowed on grounds quite arbitrary. Under such a view there can be no possible place for the religious body, in the sense of a Church living a supernatural life, and the claim is quite just that no Church should have any standard of morals different from those of the State."

Against this false conception of the State Figgis insisted that it is not the individual but the family which is the real social unit, and that personality as a fact never grows up except within one or more social unions.

Figgis, basing himself on historical Jurists such as Gierke and Maitland, maintained that "the State in the sense of an absolute superhuman unity has never really existed, and that it cannot exist. In theory it represents a despot ruling over slaves: in practice even a despot is limited by the fact that the slaves are after all, human; deny their personality as you like, there comes a point

The History of the Anglo-Catholic Revival

at which it asserts itself, and they will kill either the despot or themselves. At bottom the doctrine represents a State, which is a superman ruling individuals who are below men."

What we actually find in human life is not a sand-heap of individuals, unrelated except to the State, but an ascending hierarchy of groups, family, school, Church, etc. These groups have each of them a real life.

It is the principal function of the State to see that justice is done. Property must come under the control of the civil power. Now the claim of the Church is for freedom within the limits of civil society. Figgis held that as soon as men began to think of the State and the Church as each of them a perfect Society, they were on the way to a more reasonable theory of the relation between the two than was possible to a mind dominated by the idea of an absolute State.

Applying this to present conditions, Figgis urged: "We are both citizens and Churchmen. We have to try to look at all these matters alike from the ecclesiastical and from the civic standpoints. We have, as members of the Church, the right and duty to claim freedom within this society for its own laws, ideals, and development: as members of the State we have to think and to vote for what is the wisest course in a nation of which many of the Christians refuse to submit to our discipline, and many are not Christians at all."

Figgis illustrated this in the case of changes in the marriage law of the land coming with all the authority of a Royal Commission. "We need to have it perfectly clear . . . that any change in the law of the land shall leave entirely unchanged the freedom of the Church to

The Spiritual Independence of the Church

insist on the observance of the Christian law of marriage by all her communicating members, and to exclude all who do not."

Bishop Gore, in evidence before the Royal Commission,[1] said that at the time of the Reformation the State and the Church were so identified in England that some confusion between the authority of either was natural, if not inevitable. The State is committed to the Church, and the Church to the State. But in the subsequent period the Church of England has become only one of many religious bodies in the State, enjoying practically equal toleration and completeness of civil privileges. The consequence of this is that the legislative and judicial authorities of the State have ceased to be in any real sense representative of the Church, or capable of claiming the allegiance of Churchmen in spiritual matters. Thus it has come about that a great number of the decisions and orders, including orders given by Bishops on ceremonial matters, which have been given for many years past, have failed to appeal to the conscience of High Churchmen, or to command their obedience, because directly or indirectly they have represented an authority which they would feel it treasonable to the Head of the Church to accept in spiritual matters, though they would not of course hesitate to recognise in the civil legislature and the Civil Courts their proper functions towards all communities in the State, and their special relation towards an Established Church.

Bishop Gore contended that the whole idea of Establishment had been completely and quite fundamentally changed by the introduction of the wide-spreading idea of toleration. At the Reformation the idea was that the

[1] *Royal Commission Eccles. Discipline*, 1906, ii. 499.

The History of the Anglo-Catholic Revival

State identified itself with one particular religious opinion, with the Church which it accepted as National, so that to be a citizen and enjoy the privileges of a citizen it was necessary to belong to the Church and be in obedience to the Church. Thus at the Reformation over both Church and State there was the King, but the same body was both Church and State, and the State was committed to the Church and the Church to the State.

This idea of Establishment has been gradually but completely changed. Civil privileges have been extended to all kinds of religious opinions. But the completely altered status of the Church has not been fully and fairly faced and realised. Whereas this altered situation of Church and State involves a deep alteration in the relation between the legislature and judicial functions of the State towards the Church. And while the State must always have the power of saying that if the Church persists in certain courses it can no longer be recognised as established, yet the fundamental change which has taken place in the relation of the State to the Church, involved in the principle of toleration, has never been adequately faced, and must be faced. And this is the legitimacy of the High Churchman's plea.

"I was what people call a ritualist from the time I was a boy, and I have been more interested in this subject through all the time of my growing up into manhood than in almost any other. I was full, in all the time when one forms one's young enthusiasms, of this particular plea, and of all that was involved in it; and what I have felt all my life—passionately—has been that here was this plea being made by those whom I most venerated, and being made in a form which appeared to me to be

The Spiritual Independence of the Church

profoundly scriptural, to correspond profoundly with the claim of the Church of England to antiquity, and at the same time I felt, as I read Bishops' charges after Bishops' charges or utterance after utterance in Parliament, that this plea was never being adequately faced in its implications. And the result of course has been that, though I have lived all my life among people who certainly were as indisposed as any Englishmen can be to be lawless, I have known so as nobody could know better, why it is that legislation and episcopal charges and demands have failed to carry effect; why we have got on the High Church side, so far as it has come about, into a condition of lawlessness. It has been I am quite sure not nearly so much on account of particular things which have been asked, as on account of this great principle which has underlaid the difficulties.

"I believe that until it is fundamentally faced, as it seems to me never yet to have been, by the Episcopate collectively or by Parliament, we shall not be on the way to any satisfactory solution of ceremonial difficulties."

In the Report presented to the Church Assembly in 1926 the real reason for the refusal of Anglo-Catholics to recognise any spiritual authority in Privy Council decisions in Church affairs was plainly given. "The principle upon which the objections to the present Court of Final Appeal is based is that the right of declaring, interpreting, and showing the teaching and use of the Church belongs to the authorities of the Church, and not to a tribunal which receives its jurisdiction exclusively from the State."

At the basis of all modern conflict between the Church and the State lies the modern theory of the State as the one and only possessor of jurisdiction.

The History of the Anglo-Catholic Revival

This theory of the nature of the State, propounded simply by Jurists, such as Von Gierke among German authorities on law, and brought into English circles of thought by Maitland, and applied in the case of the English Church by Fr. Figgis, was set before the Episcopate in Convocation by the Bishop of Truro in 1929. Von Gierke's masterly work[1] "claimed for a corporation that it had a right as against the State; and that it had not only the right to exist, but it had natural rights of its own which it possessed, and which its members possessed; and that it did not depend for its rights upon the State."

This principle, as the Bishop of Truro said, affects all corporations of every kind. It applied to every social institution within the State. It applied to the family. It applied to the Church. Every man as a matter of fact was under a great number of jurisdictions. The Church was asserting its own jurisdiction, claiming and securing the allegiance of its members to a degree which in England had been for long unusual. But the members of the Church were also under the jurisdiction of the State. And as a man was living under various jurisdictions, if he did not get justice in one jurisdiction he might have to seek it in another. That might happen in a family, or in the Church. But the essential thing in case of such appeal was to remember that he had gone from an Ecclesiastical Court to a Court of the Crown, that is to say, from the spiritual jurisdiction to the political. It would, of course, be much better that he should not have to make any such appeal; but if it was made, the distinction between the different kinds of jurisdiction must be clearly appreciated.

[1] *Chronicle of Convocation*, 1926, pp. 140–53.

The Spiritual Independence of the Church

It must also be borne in mind that a Corporation within the State might refuse to be bound by the State's decisions. The result would then be a condition of persecution. Modern instances could be found in the conscientious objector, in the Passive Resisters, in the Quakers. Numerous instances were found in the history of the primitive Church in the Roman Empire. The ideal certainly was the reduction of such irreconcilable collisions to a minimum.

In the week before the Convocation heard this speech important new proposals with regard to Ecclesiastical Courts were recommended to the Church Assembly by the Archbishop of York. It was fully agreed that the Judicial Committee of the Privy Council could no longer be the final Court of Appeal in Ecclesiastical affairs, nor could the Courts of the Church be bound by its decisions. The appeal so far as the Church was concerned should be from the Court of the Diocese to the Court of the Province. The Court of the Province should be the Supreme Spiritual Court. It was greatly to be hoped "that the members of the Church, even when they have to have recourse to litigation, will regard the Court of the Province as the supreme spiritual court, accepting its decisions as having spiritual authority and not go beyond it. But if in any particular case there is a complaint of lack of justice in the spiritual Courts, it is the right of any claimant to carry his appeal to the Crown." It is, said the Archbishop, "essential to clearness of thought that the Appeal to this Court must be recognised as an appeal from the Ecclesiastical Courts to the Crown. It is an appeal to the Crown for remedy in particular cases, based upon the contention that justice in the

The History of the Anglo-Catholic Revival

Ecclesiastical Courts has not been done, or that those Courts have improperly exercised their authority. It follows that it is from the Crown that the jurisdiction of the Court is and must be derived." Dr. Temple owned "that there is no reason in theory why the Crown should not delegate to a purely spiritual Court the exercise of its supremacy over all causes Ecclesiastical and civil." "But there is not the slightest chance of any such Court being established in England at the present time."

It was distinctly maintained that it does not follow that in case of heresy or of ritual the Crown Court should determine what is or is not the doctrine or use of the Church. In proof of this the Archbishop of York referred to the well-known words of the Preamble to the Henrician Statute of Appeals—which declares "that the final determination of matters and jurisdiction to render justice belongs to the King, who, nevertheless, if any cause of the law divine or of spiritual learning happen to come in question, is to have it declared, interpreted, and showed by the spirituality of the English Church." In accordance with that principle the function of the Court of the Crown would be as follows: "What may be the actual teaching or use of the Church is a fact which the Court is not to determine but to ascertain, and it is to ascertain it from those who have the authority to state it. It is for the Court to apply the fact so ascertained to the case in hand."

As the Report of the Commission presented to the Church Assembly said, "in the past it has often been through the interpretation of words, sometimes highly technical and containing within them a long theological and liturgical history, by a State tribunal not specially

The Spiritual Independence of the Church

qualified by religious learning, that difficulties have arisen." We desire, added the Archbishop, that those difficulties should not arise again.

Finally it was insisted that "any system of reconstructed courts must receive the formal assent of the Church." That was interpreted to include the Church Assembly, but also "in a matter so deep-reaching, affecting as it does so closely the whole constitution and life of the Church, we think that a special place must be given to the ancient Convocations or Synods of the Church. Therefore we lay it down that the assent of the Convocations should be obtained in the most formal manner by licence duly received, confirmed and promulgated and ratified by the Crown."

Whatever may be thought of these proposals, whether the Church should be satisfied with this degree of independence suggested on the ground that a purely spiritual final Court of Appeal was what the Church of England at the present time had not the slightest claim to get—in any case the scheme which the Archbishop of York set before the Assembly, and the Bishop of Truro set before the Provincial Synod of Canterbury, presents a striking advance, and is a frank recognition of the justice of the claim which the Oxford Movement made in the Church's behalf.

CHAPTER XI

THE REVIVAL OF RELIGIOUS ORDERS IN THE ENGLISH CHURCH

ONE of the greatest achievements of the Catholic Revival is the restoration of Religious Orders to the English Church. Wherever Catholicism prevails Monasticism appears. This has been the case both in the East and in the West. Community life is a persistent characteristic of Christendom. This is natural, since Christianity is founded in Sacrifice, the greatest, most awful, sacrifice ever conceived, and Monasticism is a noble expression of the sacrificial spirit. A community wholly dedicated to the service of Religion has in its very nature capacities for completer renunciation and self-surrender to the one undivided aim than can be found elsewhere. The individual acquires immense access of strength from the corporate spirit of his Order. The cause of Religion is promoted not only in the ordinary domestic way. It is not only the Creeds of Christendom and the Liturgies, it is also the Monastic orders which link the Church of to-day with the Church of the centuries.

Newman, as early as 1838, reminded Oxford, in his public letter to the Margaret Professor of Divinity, that Archbishop Bramhall in the seventeenth century had spoken favourably of Monasticism as consistent with reformed devotion. The Irish Archbishop thought that:

"So as monasteries were restrained in their number and in their revenue, so as the monks were restrained from meddling between the Pastor and his flock . . . so as the

Revival of Religious Orders in the English Church

abler sort, when not taken up with higher studies and weightier employments, were inured to bestow their spare hours from their devotions in some profitable labour for the public good, that idleness might be stripped of the cloak of contemplative devotion, so as the vow of celibacy were reduced to the form of our English Universities, so long a fellow, so long unmarried . . . so as their blind obedience were more enlightened and secured by some certain rules and bounds . . . and lastly so as all opinion of satisfaction and supererogation were removed, I do not see why Monasteries might not agree well enough with reformed devotion."[1]

The need of religious Communities in the English Church was set by Pusey before the Archbishop of Canterbury in 1842. He called "Monastic institutions a refuge from the weariness and vanities of the world, and a means of higher perfection to individuals, which many sigh after, and which might be revived in a primitive form, but which as yet we have not."[2]

It is a memorable indication of vitality in the English Church that the very year 1845, in which Newman's secession filled many with a discouragement something approaching despair, saw also the opening of the first religious community in that Church since the Reformation. It was in the parish of Christ Church, Albany Street, a church which Pusey had largely helped to build, and where Dodsworth was Vicar. Lord John Manners, afterwards Duke of Rutland, was the moving spirit. A little group of devoted women lived together under a simple religious rule. The movement thus begun extended.

[1] Letter to Godfrey Faussett, p. 23.
[2] Letter to the Archbishop of Canterbury, 1842, p. 10.

The History of the Anglo-Catholic Revival

From this little community in the parish of Christ Church, Albany Street, Miss Sellon was inspired to found the community which she established at Devonport, under the sanction of the Bishop of Exeter, and of which she became the Superior. The dress of the sisters, their special form of devotion, their Oratory, was in the popular opinion of the district nothing else than a sinister and provocative indication of Popery. Miss Sellon was hooted and pelted on several occasions. But she gathered out of the streets the poorest and most neglected children, took them into her house, fed and clothed and trained them.

One of the odious features of the opposition was that published attacks upon the Devonport Community were chiefly conducted by clergymen. In a dignified public defence of his daughter's work Commander Sellon wrote:

"I admit it is a great trial to part with such a child, but neither I nor her mother have any desire to prevent it. She is of age, and gifted with a sense to enable her to act and judge for herself. She fully knows what the life is; I feel she is fitted for the work; and I give her and her future portion to God's service, in the full assurance that she has a far greater prospect of happiness, both as regards this life and that endless one to which it leads, in the path she has chosen than she could have in any other."[1] Owing to reiterated attacks the Bishop of Exeter felt obliged to institute a public inquiry into Miss Sellon's work, at the conclusion of which he addressed her in terms of deep respect.

"Most heartily, Madam, do I your Bishop thank you for having come here on this mission of Christian love;

[1] *A Contradiction*, by Commander Sellon, R.N., p. 36.

Revival of Religious Orders in the English Church

for having laboured so devoutly, and by God's blessing so usefully; for having endured more than yet I ever knew a woman to be called upon to endure."

The Bishop of Exeter's public commendation of Miss Sellon's work was given in face of a fanatical Protestant resentment. It was at that period an act of conspicuous courage. The Bishop's action, and the unreasoning prejudice of her opponents, roused widespread sympathy with the Sisterhood. A priest in Liverpool, the Rev. J. Martin, set the facts before the Churchmen of that city in fervent terms. The preacher declared himself "not surprised at finding people insensible to the grandeur of a sacrifice, and the purity of motives, which they have neither the capacity nor the virtue to adorn." It was natural for men to criticise coldly an enthusiasm which they cannot love. But he urged that "it is not natural even for the bitterest partisan to oppress, insult, and traduce defenceless women; to impugn their motives, to watch their way of life, and intrude into the sanctity of their home, that they may insinuate odious suggestions misrepresenting their character, and paralysing their usefulness." He declared that "the world, whether Christian or not, will always visit with unrelenting criticism what is too high for its comprehension." He insisted that "while we do not love the errors of medieval Christianity, as little do we love the corruptions of the last three centuries. But we do love the Catholic doctrines and pious practices of more primitive ages. Had the Church of England fostered high enthusiasm, had it been a rallying point for ardent minds, how strong it would have been in the affections of its people, how nobly it would have fulfilled its mission." In Wesley's case the

The History of the Anglo-Catholic Revival

English Church "knew not how to employ this powerful instrument, and his enthusiasm sought other channels and exceeded its due commission."

The character of this remarkable woman is illustrated in the published defence which she felt obliged to write.

"I am ignorant of controversy, and know little of our present divisions. I believe the Creeds, and pray to love our Lord Jesus Christ in sincerity, and to obey Him by His grace as well as I can. The Church of England is my Mother Church, and I love her with a true and hearty love. What she has taught me that I have received; what she has allowed, that I have not refused; what she has forbidden, that I have not looked into, and I pray God to keep me dutiful, submissive and true. . . .

"I cannot close my defence without an inexpressible yearning of the heart towards those who are so offended with me, and who have so rashly written words which are not true against me. Perhaps we may never meet on earth, but would to God they would listen to the words of one who has known more than once what it is to lie, as it were, on the verge of eternity. Then when the fever of life is subsided, there is nothing worth a thought but the love of Jesus and of each other. There is no room then, no wish for thoughts of dissension and disunion, for Protestant or Papist outcry. . . ."[1]

Lord Coleridge's comment on the treatment of the Devonport Sisterhood illustrates the impression made on a judicial mind.

"I have been very nearly worked into an Article about this Plymouth and Devonport business, which seems to me nearly the worst case I ever heard of low-

[1] Pamphlets. Church Subjects.

Revival of Religious Orders in the English Church

Church blackguardism and jesuitry. How beautifully Miss Sellon contrasted with . . . her enemies. . . . The chief imputation . . . being that they (the Sisterhood) had a cross on their private rooms. I do really think the awful profanity of low Churchmen, in this and such like things, is more like Anti-Christ than anything one reads or hears of nowadays. What would the wildest heretic of early times have said if he had heard of the Sign of the Cross being an object of aversion and attack?"[1]

The beginnings of the Wantage Community date from 1848. Under Butler's[2] strong and inspiring leadership, aided by Manning, it began well, but passed through a disastrous period, owing to Manning's secession, followed by that of Miss Lockhart, the Mother Superior. Still further troubles ensued, and the little community seemed destined to disappear. Yet it had within it the element of permanence. In course of time the Sisterhood became devoted to Penitentiary work, and to the work of teaching. Butler's own preference was with the active rather than the contemplative career. In his instructions to the Community he drew an admirably balanced comparison of the functions of Martha and Mary.

"To serve is Martha's special work, to contemplate is Mary's. Martha provided that Mary may have leisure to gaze. Mary could not contemplate did not Martha serve." Butler suggested that "the two characters form a perfect whole. Each may, neither need, fail." He also reminded the Sisterhood that "Martha may be cumbered about much serving, Mary may sit at Christ's feet and despise her sister. Yet while Martha serves for the love of Christ,

---

[1] *Life of Lord Coleridge*, i, p. 189.
[2] *Life of Dean Butler*, 127-173. Cameron, p. 42.

gladly aiding Mary, while Mary sits for the love of Christ, gladly praying for Martha, His blessing is on each, each has a portion of the blessing of the other." Mary has chosen that good part which shall not be taken away from her. But also Martha has served Christ and shall follow Him where He is. To which the instructor added, "in this present time surely Martha's work must be the fittest preparation for Mary's."[1]

The Sisterhood of S. Margaret, East Grinstead, was founded in 1854. It was, to quote the words of Canon Stucky Coles,[2] "the work of an isolated, unbeneficed, almost unbefriended priest, hindered by weak health, persecuted and opposed, with the habits of a scholar and the temperament of a poet, called away at the early age of 48, but one who has his own unapproachable place in the history of the Revival: Dr. J. M. Neale."[3]

When the Sisterhood of S. Margaret, East Grinstead, was first formed, the Bishop of Chichester authorised the use of his name in connection with it. He viewed it as an association of ladies for the training of nurses, which none could question was a praiseworthy and a Christian object. But when he came to realise that the Community was under Dr. Neale's direction, which, considering that he was its founder, was not unnatural, the Bishop wrote to the Superior informing her that Dr. Neale was a clergyman in whose views and practices he had no confidence, particularly in the matter of habitual Confession, a practice which the Bishop not only denied that the Church of England authorises, but asserted that those

---

[1] *Life and Letters of W. J. Butler*, 1897, pp. 152–153.
[2] Neale's *Letters*, p. 233.
[3] *Memoir of V. S. S. Coles*, p. 175.

Revival of Religious Orders in the English Church

who practised it manifest thereby the inadequacy of their direct faith in Christ's promises. The Bishop accordingly withdrew his name from any connection with the Sisterhood. This was in 1857.[1]

The Sisterhood of S. John the Baptist was founded through Canon Carter at Clewer in 1851. Harriet Monsell was instituted as Superior by Bishop Wilberforce. Carter's ideal for the Community at Clewer was to cultivate the counsels of perfection and to practise active service both in spiritual and corporeal works of mercy.[2]

Dr. Littledale, a name famous in Catholic controversy, placed his learning at the disposal of the revival of Religious Orders. In 1864 he wrote a remarkable Essay on Religious Communities of Women in the Early and Medieval Church. This placed at the disposal of the British public much historical knowledge with which that public was totally unfamiliar, related, moreover, without the anti-monastic bias with which the same public was only too well acquainted.

The question of vows, apart from its intrinsic gravity, was beset with peculiar difficulties at the period when Community life was revived. It raised serious misgivings on the part of Church people otherwise well disposed towards the movement. It was deprecated by those in authority. No vows were taken in the early years of the revival. Hutchings, in his *Life of Canon Carter*, shows that the desire to take vows originated in the Communities themselves. Carter said that the Sisters had always assumed that their mission implied lifelong dedication. The notion of being a Sister for a time, and then going

---

[1] *Kirwan Browne*, p. 442.
[2] Hutching's *Life of Carter*, 1904, p. 101.

away to live a different kind of life as if she had never been a Sister, was foreign to the whole animus of the body. Carter himself did not wish that vows should be taken. And the rule of the Community which was read to the Community from time to time definitely stated that a Sister was free to depart if at any time her mind was changed. Nevertheless, the conviction grew and increased that the religious life was not a temporary experience, but an abiding self-surrender. Members of the Community felt that their life would be strengthened by deliberate profession of permanent absolute dedication. Three successive occupants of the See of Oxford were consulted: Bishop Wilberforce, Bishop Mackarness, and Bishop Stubbs. The first objected to vows, and would not have the rule altered, yet allowed Carter to do what he thought best. The second let the rule be changed. The third allowed it to be inserted in the rules that vows were actually taken.

Writing in 1866, Carter of Clewer discussed in Orby Shipley's Volume of Essays on the Church and the World[1] the subject of the relation of vows to religious communities. The question raised was how far is it expedient to introduce vows as a formal and integral element into the religious communities now increasingly being formed in the English Church. Carter held that this was not a question of necessity, but of expediency. The early history of the Religious Orders proved that vows were not necessary to the integrity or security of such communities. Yet, on the other hand, to deny the lawfulness or moral expediency of making vows on the ground that such actions presumed unduly on the stability of the

[1] *Church and the World.*

Revival of Religious Orders in the English Church

soul's purpose, or bound what ought not to be bound, is to ignore the very principle of special Divine vocations. It is to cast distrust on the power of God to sustain the Life in which He has predestined His own elected ones to serve Him. Of course it is vital to use all diligence to guard against mistakes. But it strikes at the very root of the principle of Divine vocations to question their enduring power. At the same time Carter, cautiously balancing one reflection with another, admitted that there was great reason for supposing that in refounding Religious Houses, which he regarded as "perhaps the most momentous work of our own eventful days," great caution was needed, at least in the early stage of their existence, as to the general introduction of vows as a formal part of the bonds of Community life. It ought, he held, to be remembered that "vows were a later development, not an initiatory step, in the organisation of Communities of Religion, and that a graduated system of dispensations became a necessity after their introduction." Not that these facts form any argument against vows. They only mark the progressive order which such forms of life tend to assume. They show the natural working of the inner desires of the soul.

"A Sisterhood, as distinguished from other kinds of associated communities of women, implies a vocation to live and work wholly and undividedly for God, as a permanent state; an aptitude for devotion and useful service; a religious rule; fellowship in prayer and work, binding all together; a gradation of offices with recognised authority; rights and customs carefully guarded; and a systematic way of adapting the capacities and dispositions of the different members of the community to the necessities of the work undertaken. The organisation becomes complete when through the Bishop's sanction the seal of the blessing of the Church is upon it."[1]

Carter[2] thought it advisable to take precautions on the legal aspect of religious vows. He therefore consulted Judge Coleridge whether such vows subjected to prosecution those who take them or those who impose them, and whether from a legal point of view such vows are binding. Sir J. Coleridge replied that so far as he was aware, the law had taken no notice of the matter in a Protestant Sisterhood, and that the vow is nothing except as it binds the conscience, and with this the law will not interfere.

Bishop Jackson of London, in 1879, in his Charge to the Clergy of his Diocese, spoke of Sisterhoods in the following terms: "The devotion, perseverance, and tenderness with which these ladies discharge the offices of charity to which they have given their lives, is beyond all praise, and enhance the regret which is occasioned by the adoption in *some* of the Sisterhoods of rules and ritual alien to the mind and practice of the Church of England, and of vows which it is difficult to reconcile either with the rights of conscience or the teaching of the Word of God."

It is of course quite impossible to present in a limited space any adequate idea of the splendid services which Conventual Institutions have conferred on the English Church during the century. A mere enumeration of the names of the various Orders and their daughter Houses would convey very little. Much information will

---

[1] Carter, Church Congress, Stoke-on-Trent, 1875.
[2] Hutching's *Life of Carter*.

Revival of Religious Orders in the English Church

be found in the pages of Cameron's *Religious Communities of the Church of England*. All that is possible here is to give selected illustrations.

There was a similar revival among men. The Society of S. John the Evangelist, Cowley, was the first great example. In 1866 the beginnings of this memorable Community were made. In that year Father Grafton, afterwards Bishop of Fond du Lac, and Father O'Neill took vows with Father Benson as their Superior. The Society has attracted to itself a succession of very remarkable men. No finer products of the Monastic life are anywhere to be found in Christendom. Many a Community which has since arisen owes its inspiration or its encouragement or its guidance to Cowley.

The Order of the Sacred Mission, now at Kelham, owed its inception to Fr. Kelly. It was founded in 1891. Its great work in the training of young men for the priesthood has conferred invaluable service on the English Church. It has made ordination possible for many young men who otherwise would have been lost to the priesthood.

The Community of the Resurrection was founded in 1892. Some years before a sermon had been preached by Dr. Westcott, afterwards Bishop of Durham, in the Chapel of Harrow School, on the work of S. Benedict, S. Dominic, and S. Francis. The preacher ended with a prayer that one among his hearers might be called of God to do for the Church in our day something of what these great leaders of Religion had done for Europe long ago. Among his hearers was Charles Gore. Years afterwards, when Gore became head of the Pusey House, the preacher's prayer was answered. The Community of the

The History of the Anglo-Catholic Revival

Resurrection was formed. Its first members were James Nash, George Longridge, Cyril Bickersteth, Walter Frere, Paul Bull, Gerard Sampson, and Richard Rackham. This was the beginning of that great Institution at Mirfield which within thirty-five years included a college with more than a hundred students training for priesthood, and the little company of the original brethren in the Community increased to 50.

In 1889, the Canterbury Convocation,[1] agreed that the time had come for the Church to avail itself of the voluntary self-devotion of Brotherhoods, both clerical and lay. This was advocated with all the eloquence of Archdeacon Farrar, who paid a tribute of admiration to "that excellent Father Benson and the work that he had done at Cowley." After Farrar's speech the Brighton Working Men's Branch of the Church Association passed a resolution expressing their indignation at the reactionary proposal made by the Archdeacon of Westminster in Convocation to establish a Monastic Order in the Church of England. They considered it as practically repealing the Act which makes the Jesuit and other religious Orders in England illegal, as inculcating false views of the Christian life, and as calculated still further to alienate the working classes from the Church. This was recited by Farrar in Convocation.[2] Farrar declared that the Wesleyans had assured him that for five years their ministers are also bound by conditions, whether they be called vows or not, of poverty, celibacy, and obedience quite as stringent as here proposed. On the alternative of marriage and celibacy he repeated Bishop Lightfoot's inquiry, "is it not unreasonable, when God has not only permitted, but sanctioned, both states

[1] *Chronicle*, 1889, p. 235.   [2] Ibid., 1890, p. 21.

Revival of Religious Orders in the English Church

of life alike, to hold that all the advantages lie on the one side to the exclusion of the other?" Farrar himself only advocated a temporary postponement of marriage. "We do but follow the example of many great saints before us when we say there may be times and conditions in which celibacy does distinctly aid in the exceptional efforts of the Church. We are not asking members of the Brotherhoods to live celibate lives; but only asking that young men should postpone their marriage for a time to add to the efficacy of an imperative work." It is evident that while Monasticism was mentioned in words, the ideal which was being contemplated was far more like the grouping of curates in a clergy house than the creation of a permanent Community with lifelong self-dedication.

The history of the revival of Religious Orders in the English Church has been attended by many difficulties. They had no recent Anglican tradition, no modern precedents, no experience, to guide them. They made—it was almost inevitable—many mistakes. There were pathetic instances of instability, of unsuitable persons. There were defections and secessions. Youthful communities whose future was uncertain looked insignificant beside the agelong institutions of Rome. There was an inflexibility, a want of variety of types.

The number of enterprises towards community life which had not in them the element of permanence witnesses to the extensive prevalence of the monastic ideal. It certainly inspired many persons to ascertain by experiment whether they had or had not a vocation. It brought into transient existence many a little group. There were failures both among leaders and followers. There is nothing to surprise in this. But it has its lessons.

The History of the Anglo-Catholic Revival

Fr. Paul Bull, of the Community of the Resurrection, writing on the *Revival of the Religious Life*,[1] lays considerable stress on the principle that differentiation of function is essential in every highly developed body. He suggests that a century ago the medical profession was practically undifferentiated, and the ordinary practitioner was expected to be adequate for every emergency. But modern needs compel the medical profession to develop a high differentiation of function. This principle applies to the Church. He thinks that history can show no period when parochial work was at a higher level of earnest endeavour, and no body of men more anxious to do their duty than our parish priests. But at the same time the ordinary practitioners require supplementing by the Religious Orders, "and by specialists who can be highly trained in our monasteries to meet unbelief on every battlefield of modern thought." There is need of missionaries who are specialists in the work of conversion, of students also. Fr. Bull urges that "many of our best thinkers are quite unfitted for the routine work of parish priests, but can consecrate their great gifts to the service of God in the cloister."

That was written in 1917. But it can hardly be denied that this principle of differentiation of function still needs to be pressed upon the general mind of the Church. The fact is that the Church of England has suffered from a narrow uniformity in the prevalent idea of a clergyman. But of course the religious life requires its own gifts and its distinct vocation.

The highest importance of the restoration of Religious Orders within the Church of England is that it presents

[1] Fr. Bull, *Revival of the Religious Life*, 1917.

Revival of Religious Orders in the English Church
an ideal of unreserved self-surrender which English Churchmen from the sixteenth to the nineteenth century only knew of as a fact in the distant past, or occasionally encountered as an alien phenomenon existing in other lands, but never contemplated as a living reality enshrined within their own precincts. The example set by the Anglican Religious Orders has contributed immensely to raise the standard of devotion throughout the English Church.

It is of interest to read the reflections of an eminent German Lutheran on this Anglican revival.

Heiler says that the best powers of the Roman cloister life are developed in the Anglican Religious Orders, and these will become the most effective propaganda for Catholicism in the English Church.[1]

[1] Cf. Heiler, *Im Ringen*, p. 426.

CHAPTER XII

THE MOVEMENT IN THE TWENTIETH CENTURY

WITH the twentieth century the atmosphere has greatly changed. The Revival seems passing beyond the period of Ritual prosecutions. Decisions of the Privy Council on the Sacramental Doctrine of the Church sound strangely remote. No desire appears to exist for the repetition of such procedure. The contested doctrine and ritual have immensely extended.

Biblical criticism in Germany, conducted quite independently of Catholic pre-suppositions, is found in certain matters to be on the side of Catholicism rather than against it. The old familiar division, between the Protestantism of Scripture and the Catholicism of the Church, is by no means so readily accepted by Continental criticism as it used to be. Distinguished Biblical critics have detected the Sacramentalism of the Church in the Epistles of S. Paul. He is recognised to be in principle a powerful cause of the Catholicism which followed. Indeed a German critic has gone so far as to describe S. Paul reproachfully as the first great perverter of Christianity. Where, however, the Bible is regarded as the source of Christian Truth, account has to be taken of the Catholicism of S. Paul. His institutionalism, his sacramentalism, are in that case original elements in the Gospel. And the opposition to the Catholic Revival is discounted.

Probably the most characteristic examples of the influence of the Movement in the twentieth century are

The Movement in the Twentieth Century

seen in three departments: Revision, Reservation, and Reunion.

I

The Catholic Revival has been greatly concerned with the *Revision* of the Book of Common Prayer. It seems at first sight singular that for years the English Church Union should have been a resolute opponent to all Revision. But the singularity disappears when we remember the determined and reiterated efforts made during the nineteenth century to secure a Revision in order to remove Catholic elements of doctrine from the Prayer Book, and to obstruct the progress of Ritualism by cancelling the Ornaments Rubric, or by altering its character. Attempts were made by Bishops antagonistic to the Catholic Revival to secure approval of the Revision in Diocesan Conferences, the motive manifestly being in the Protestant interest. There were occasions when a favourable vote for Revision was only secured by the personal influence of the Diocesan. Facts like these intensified dislike and resistance on the part of the English Church Union.

When, however, it was clear that Revision would take place, it became the function of the Catholic-minded to secure the retention of all Catholic elements, and to secure also such liturgical changes as would bring the Anglican Rite into closer harmony with the ancient liturgies of Christendom. During some twenty years the long-protracted debates in Convocation proved at least how utterly ill adapted for such work as detailed liturgical Revision any large Assembly is. They proved this most conclusively.

The History of the Anglo-Catholic Revival

The process of Revision displayed in a most remarkable way the influence of Anglo-Catholicism in the Councils of the English Church. For it resulted in the production of an alternative Rite in which the Prayer of Consecration was considerably reconstructed on the lines of the ancient liturgies, and on the lines of the first English Reformation Book of 1549. The production of an alternative use was unprecedented in the Church of England. It was certainly not suggested in the interests of Evangelicals, nor of the Broad Church School. It was due to Catholic influence. Liturgical learning was very largely the property of Anglo-Catholics, whether within Convocation or beyond it. It is, of course, quite true that various elements which the Catholic School did not desire were introduced into the new alternative Rite. It is true that a very singular departure was made from the principles of Eucharistic Consecration which had prevailed in the Church of England, not only ever since the Reformation, but also before it. The Authorised Anglican Rite had beyond all possibility of dispute regarded consecration as effected by our Lord's own words—"This is My Body." "This is My Blood." That this is the doctrine of the Authorised Anglican Rite is certain, because when a second consecration is required, the Words of our Lord are ordered to be repeated, and nothing else. This ascription of consecration to the Words of Christ is the Western use. But in the alternative Rite a remarkable alteration has been introduced. An appeal to the Holy Spirit to consecrate the Elements is introduced immediately after the recital of Christ's own Words: the intention, of course, being to assimilate the Anglican Rite to the belief of the Eastern Church, that consecration is the divine response to the

The Movement in the Twentieth Century

Church's invocation of the Holy Spirit. Now if the Invocation came first, and the Words of our Lord had followed, both Eastern and Western principles of consecration would have been reasonably combined. For in that case we should first appeal to the Spirit, and then recite what Christ has spoken. But as the order is reversed, the Alternative Rite recites the words "This is My Body," which the Church of England hitherto has regarded as effecting the consecration, and then goes on to appeal to the Holy Spirit to consecrate in spite of the previous recital of Christ's Words. This alteration appears to deny the consecrating power of Christ's Words, which, nevertheless, the Church of England has always hitherto implied.

Yet still, although in this respect other influences have prevailed, with the result that many of the Catholic-minded could not use the alternative permissive Rite, it is none the less true that Catholic influence over the revision has been very remarkable. It is certain that the Catholic Revival could not have effected anything approaching to this in the nineteenth century.

The alternative form of the Prayer of Consecration, on which both Convocation and the Church Assembly agreed, was criticised with great severity by the Evangelical section in the country at large. It was complained that the idea of Eucharistic Sacrifice therein involved was another religion. It rested on a different idea of the relation between God and man. It re-erected the barrier of a Priesthood interposed between God and man; a barrier which it was the work of the Incarnation and Atonement to throw down. And it put the Church in the place of Christ. This was the substance of the accusations. These criticisms were presented to the Archbishop of Canterbury to be set before the House of Bishops, in a petition signed by more than three hundred thousand adult Communicants of the Church of England.[1] It was, however, admitted by the composer of the petition that many persons had written asking him to cut out his reasons, which advice he declined to adopt.

The relation of Anglo-Catholicism to the Church of England as Reformed appeared to the Evangelical group in 1925 as a hopeless contradiction. We differ, said the Evangelicals, fundamentally. "Two radically opposed systems of thought are contending for the soul of the Church of England." Anglo-Catholics were challenged to define their attitude to the Reformation, to make clear their loyalty to the Church of England, and their loyalty to the larger thing called Catholicism. And yet Evangelicals themselves acknowledged that the independence of the Church of England was subject to acceptance of those fundamental beliefs which are common to the Catholic or Universal Church. According to an Evangelical group, there is no room for sacrificial priesthood in the Church of England. And the words, "This is My Body," when spoken by our Lord, meant simply, "This is a symbol of My Body." The possibility that these words were prophetic, that our Lord spoke in anticipation of the value which the Eucharist would possess in the future, although suggested by the phrase, "which is being shed for you," was not even considered. It was asserted that to regard the Consecrated Elements as being in reality Christ's Body is to give our Lord's words a totally different meaning from that which they had when He uttered

[1] Bishop Knox, Letter, 1924.

The Movement in the Twentieth Century

them. The fact that the historic Church has thought otherwise was not alluded to, although an interpretation of Christ's Words which contradicts the belief of the Historic Church about their meaning ought surely to be regarded as liable to be mistaken. It is also noteworthy that no notice was taken by Evangelicals of the fact that the Anglican Archbishops, in their reply to Leo XIII, maintained that the consecration of the Eucharistic Gifts is in order that they may become to us the Body and Blood of Jesus Christ. Between Evangelicalism and Anglo-Catholicism the differences were declared to be fundamental. There are two radically opposed systems of Sacramental doctrine. That this is so is shown in the two rival interpretations of Christ's Eucharistic utterance —"This is My Body."[1]

The sequel to the Revision is not less significant in the History of Anglo-Catholic influence. The rejection of the Revised Book by the House of Commons was in itself indirectly a tribute to Catholic influence, for it was expressly based on the ground that the book was an advance in a Catholic direction. And certainly from the Protestant point of view they were perfectly right. A liturgy which emphasised the Eucharistic Sacrifice, which admitted Prayers for the Departed, and which sanctioned, with whatever restrictions, the practice of Reservation of the Sacrament, was in reality decidedly adverse to Protestant tradition, and was progressing towards its contrary. It was quite impossible to reduce the Revision to a level which would have contented the House of Commons. The Lutheran, Heiler, thinks that if the Anglican Episcopate had issued a total prohibition

[1] Storr, *Crisis in the Church*, 1925.

The History of the Anglo-Catholic Revival

of Reservation they might have precipitated a disastrous schism.

The rejection of the Book by Parliament placed the Authorities of the Church in a critical position. What should their action be? Were they to refuse submission? But that would be a challenge and a defiance. Were they to acquiesce and consign the Revised Book to oblivion? But that would be a virtual abdication of the Church's right to decide for itself the language of its prayers. That would practically deny the spiritual independence of the Church. Did not the Primate officially declare before Convocation, in sentences careful and guarded and warmly approved, that ultimately the Church must claim the right to decide for itself the expression of its devotions? Accordingly the Book, although rejected by the Nation, was regarded by the Church as a basis for Synodical discussion. Individual Bishops acted independently, each in his own Diocesan sphere. One Bishop affirmed a Diocesan's liturgical right within his Diocese. He will see that the services respond to the spiritual requirements of his people. Another Bishop allowed 160 of his priests to continue reserving the Sacramental Elements as before, subject only to the rules in the Book of 1928.[1]

Now in all this, and it might be extended to other instances, the result was Diocesan variations, encouraged by the varieties of Episcopal outlook and opinion. There is little in it that can be called collective action of the whole Episcopate. But the significant thing is that the rejection of the Revision by Parliament has led Diocesan Bishops to claim their spiritual independence in a manner

[1] Cf. Stewart, *Anglo-Catholicism*, p. 381.

The Movement in the Twentieth Century

which would not have happened last century. And this spiritual independence is one of those great principles on which the Catholic Revival has resolutely insisted through the whole of its laborious and sacrificial career. Thus the whole process of Revision, including its sequel, is a witness to the wonderful influence which the Movement has exerted.

II

A second characteristic of the Movement in the twentieth century has been its concern about *Reservation* of the Blessed Sacrament.

Pusey, in a letter written in 1882, said on Reservation: "there is absolutely no authority in the early Church for Reservation, except for the sick, nor for placing the Blessed Sacrament in a monstrance, or censing, still less of blessing, the people with it. This last seems to me a most unjustifiable use of the Presence which He vouchsafes us. He gave it for one end. He has never authorised us to use His gracious Presence for another. No one has told us that He does bless us so. It is this imitation of modern practices in the Roman Communion which repels people from us. It was a panic from things much less than this, which brought upon us the P.W.R. Act. That panic still exists. I agree with Vernon Staley entirely that our Blessed Lord instituted the Sacrament to give us His Body and Blood, and that we might plead the memorial of His sacrifice, that adoration is a natural result of that Presence, but not the object of the institution, and that reservation for the purpose of adoration is not

The History of the Anglo-Catholic Revival

according to the primitive usage which we profess to follow."[1]

Canon Bright, writing from Oxford in 1882, held that the Reservation of the Blessed Sacrament for the Sick is not permitted by our Rubrics, although there may be cases in which the breach of the rubric in the Communion Office might be well condoned. Still less is Reservation for the purposes of adoration simply, and with the additional rite of Benediction. This is purely Roman.

In the same year (1882) Canon Liddon wrote "as to the Benediction Service which you describe, it is certainly without any sanction from our own Church language or authorities. And no wonder, since it did not exist before the Reformation period, but is of later growth. I agree to your formula that adoration is a necessary incident or accompaniment of the Eucharistic Presence, rather than the object with which that Presence has been bequeathed to the Church."

Perpetual Reservation of the Blessed Sacrament hardly came within the Tractarian horizon. If Reservation was mentioned, it was regarded from a purely theoretical standpoint unknown by experience. It was sometimes distinctly disapproved. Its introduction into extensive notice in the English Church belongs almost entirely to the twentieth century. It must, however, be remembered that Reservation was made the subject of a long essay in Orby Shipley's *Studies in Modern Problems*, 1874.

The Sacramental teaching of the Catholic Revival on the consecration of the Elements, on the Reality of the Presence, produced its natural result, in an enormous increase of the demand to receive the sacred Gift. The

[1] *Hierurgia Anglicana*, 1904, iii. 341.

The Movement in the Twentieth Century

conditions of modern life in many classes of work rendered access to the ordinary hours of administration impossible. Hence Reservation became a necessity. In large parishes, the communion of the sick, and of those unable to attend the service in Church, would have been impossible unless the Sacrament were reserved. Accordingly, Reservation became the practice in many places, and gradually became continuous. Reservation was simply for the purpose of reception. This always was the intention from the earliest beginnings of the practice. But where the Consecrated Elements are, whether in the Eucharistic Rite, or in its extension for the purpose of communicating the absent, there is Christ. The effect of Consecration is not intermittent, but perpetual. The consecrated elements are an indication of His Presence. The natural result is worship. Individuals resorted to the place where they knew the Sacrament was reserved. It became a centre of private devotion. Experience proved it to be impressive. So far the devotion before the Sacrament was spontaneous and individual. A further stage was reached when the priest himself encouraged, organised, and officially led, the devotions, which now became corporate, congregational. Extra-Liturgical Devotions came into use. Evensong was arranged to lead up to this. Ceremonial accompanied it. There were many—by no means all—to whom it made considerable appeal, which probably only those who have shared in it can rightly appreciate. So far for the actual process of its development.

Authorities in the Church viewed this latest phase of the Catholic Revival with grave anxiety. They greatly wondered whereunto this would grow. Some from a doctrinal standpoint questioned the theological basis on which the practice rested. Was the continuance of the Presence certified in an extended use of the Sacrament beyond what the Lord had authorised? Did not this habit of resting in the external presence militate against the deeper fact of the presence within the soul? Others, from a very different point of view, disputed the whole doctrine of any real presence in the Consecrated Wafer, and suggested that the Consecrated Elements should be subjected to scientific analysis.

The case in behalf of the practice of Reservation was argued by Canon Lacey in an open letter to the Archbishop of Canterbury, published in 1899. It was written in view of the Archbishop's intention to hear arguments at Lambeth officially on the subject. Lacey made no attempt to prove that Reservation was legal, but maintained that a practice which is not forbidden may be allowed. He appealed to the canonical principle that it is not in the power of an individual local Church to reject rites observed by the Universal Church, or to observe rites rejected by the same. He argued, first, that the statement in Article 28 (that "the Sacrament of the Lord's Supper was not by Christ's ordinance reserved") merely says that our Lord Himself did not actually command it. Lacey's second contention was that the provision of a service for the Communion of the Sick did not imply the prohibition of any other use. Bishop Beveridge, for instance, only condemns as contrary to Christ's ordinance such reservation as withdraws the Sacrament from its proper use in Communion. The practice of Reservation was allowed to pass away. And this for two reasons. The chief reason was the fear of abuse. But the other was that the ancient law required the renewal of the Reserved Sacrament at least

The Movement in the Twentieth Century

once a week. The observance of that rule became impossible when weekly celebrations of the Eucharist passed, not merely out of use, but beyond the region of imagined possibilities. Thorndike, for instance, thought that if only a more frequent celebration of the Mystery could be revived, perpetual Reservation would follow as a matter of course.

The third argument was on the Rubric of 1662, which says that "if any of the Bread and Wine remain unconsecrated, the Curate shall have it to his own use; but if any remain of that which is consecrated, it shall not be carried out of the Church, but the Priest and such other of the Communicants as he shall then call unto him, shall, immediately after the Blessing, reverently eat and drink the same."

Bishop Cosin explained that the purpose of this Rubric was to correct a profane misuse. The earlier rubric had said merely that if any of the bread or wine remain the Curate shall have it to his own use. The result was that the Elements, whether consecrated or not, were then appropriated to the Curate's use. That abuse, the addition to the Rubric—that if any of the consecrated elements remained it shall not be carried out of the Church—was intended to prevent. An attempt was made to set this explanation aside on the ground that a legal ruling must be interpreted from its actual wording. "The language of the legislator must be taken to express his mind; it is only when the language is obscure that we investigate his aims and purpose, in order to arrive at his meaning." Lacey, however, contended that a Rubric is not a Law. It is nothing else than a direction. And this particular Rubric only directed what reverence required. "Being read as a reference to the law of the Church it cannot be taken to prohibit Reservation. The law of the Church knows no such prohibition." Lacey concluded that "the practice of Reservation is not forbidden, expressly or implicitly, either by the terms of the 28th Article, or by the appointment of the Prayer Book for the Communion of the Sick, or by the Rubric ordering the consumption of the Eucharist. It does not, therefore, come within the category of things illegal."

The practice therefore is discretionary. And the question is, Where does that discretion reside? Reservation had gone out of use. May it be revived by the authority of the local priest? Or does its revival rest on the discretion of the Bishop? Lacey argued that the administration of the local Church is committed to the priest. And when jurisdiction is given, all things necessary to the exercise of that jurisdiction are included. The priest is, of course, guided by regulations. A wide field, however, is left to his discretion. "He is a dispenser of the Sacraments, and apart from what is expressly enjoined or allowed, he may do all things necessary for their efficient dispensation." Accordingly, Lacey held that the priest is bound by general principles, by the law of reverence, by the obligations of the faith, and may not do anything that conflicts with the truth of the sacrament or that would mar its efficiency. At the same time, "when exercising his judgment seriously, and knowing the needs of his people, he resolves to set apart at the open Communion a portion of the Lord's Supper for the sick and dying, always supposing the practice to be not forbidden ... he is lawfully using the power given him for the government of the Church." Lacey held that the inception or revival of such a practice is not reserved to the Bishop as one of his Episcopal rights. Such practices as Exposition of the Blessed Sacrament, however justifiable, are altogether apart from the original institution of the Eucharist, and therefore their adoption is not within the priest's general commission, which is to administer the Sacraments according to their normal uses. "But in reserving the Eucharist for the Communion of the Sick and Dying, the priest is putting the Sacrament to its original and appropriate use, for which he needs no authorisation beyond his general commission."

The Bishop "may require such a mode of Reservation as will ensure a proper respect for the Sacrament according to the ordinance of Christ and the dictates of natural reverence." Moreover, the Bishop "has the power to regulate the practice and even to forbid it in certain places." But "he ought not to forbid it until grave cause carefully weighed and declared in every case." "The priest who has the cure of souls knows better than anyone else the difficulties he has to meet, and the responsibility is laid on him of taking steps to remove them."

Archbishop Temple's decision on Reservation, delivered early in 1900, was as follows: "After weighing carefully all that has been put before us, I am obliged to decide that the Church of England does not at present allow Reservation in any form, and that those who think it ought to be allowed, though perfectly justified in endeavouring to get the proper authorities to alter the law, are not justified in practising Reservation until the law has been altered."[1]

The influence of Bishop Gore did much to encourage

[1] *Memoirs of Archbishop Temple*, ii. 308.

The History of the Anglo-Catholic Revival

and promote the movement to restore the ancient practice of reserving the Sacrament. When invited by Bishop Watts Ditchfield to address the clergy of the Chelmsford Diocese on the subject, he said: "I, at any rate, do not see that there is anything to be said against it. I deeply deplore that it ever was abandoned, and I have always, ever since I thought about the subject, greatly desired its restoration. If anybody had told me, however, when I was made a Bishop that within fifteen years I should see it restored by universal agreement among the Bishops of our own province, I should have thought that that was too good to be true: but it is the fact now. It is agreed to admit Reservation for the communion of the sick, but not under such conditions as admit free access to it by the faithful for the purpose of devotion. That is implied in the words of our proposed rubric on which we are agreed to act—'For no other purpose whatsoever,' except the communion of the sick.[1] About that proposal I should like to say that I think there is no question of real difficulty, if only there is the will to accept the limitation."

But while Bishop Gore cordially welcomed this unexpected agreement of the Bishops of the Southern Province to approve Reservation, he set himself resolutely to justify this limitation "for no other purpose whatsoever." He laid very great stress on the exclusive use of the Reserved Sacrament for Communion. He thought that to put the Eucharist to a new use totally different from any use recognised in the Church for a thousand years, different from any use recognised in the Eastern Church up to the present day, different from any use which is directly or indirectly suggested in the New Testament, is some-

[1] Bishop of Chelmsford, *Reservation*, 1917.

The Movement in the Twentieth Century

thing which has about it a great venturesomeness, a great presumption.

"It is no doubt," concluded the Bishop, "very distressing to be obliged to resist the establishment or maintenance amongst us of this specially Roman cultus of the Blessed Sacrament, when there is such a weight of emotion and desire pressing for its adoption and sanction. But there is a similar emotional pressure behind other claims, doctrinal and practical, which are made from other quarters. And in each case the Church must learn to discriminate: the authorities must learn carefully and wisely to bind as to loose: and the body of the Church must learn to submit sectional desires to the common good."

It was hardly to be expected that Reservation could be excluded from the debates when the Prayer Book was being revised.[1] Much anxious thought was given to the question of directions about it. These proposals gave rise to the Conference on Reservation, held at Farnham Castle in 1926, called together by the Bishop (Woods) of Winchester. Among the members were Dr. Warman, Bishop of Chelmsford, Dr. Headlam of Gloucester, Dr. Temple of Manchester, Dr. Strong of Oxford, Dr. Frere of Truro, the Regius Professor of Divinity in Oxford, the Principal of Pusey House, and others.

Bishop Gore, in opening the discussion, urged that toleration, though it be strained to the uttermost, was safer in the interests of the Church than any project of discipline which lays itself open to the charge of onesidedness. "I hope," he said, "with all my heart that reservation for the communion of the sick will be secured. And

[1] 1926.

The History of the Anglo-Catholic Revival

though I greatly shrink from the admission of communicating *the whole* from the Reserved Sacrament, I do not see how it can be excluded in all cases.

"But the practice which I think could legitimately be prohibited, even though it will cause resentment in certain quarters, is that of *Devotions attached to Evensong* or any other Prayer Book Service. I found myself exiled from attending or preaching at Evensong in what are called advanced Churches, because I am likely to find myself assisting at the following function: Evensong; Sermon; then a procession bearing the Reserved Sacrament to the high altar, where it is exposed so far as that the door of the Tabernacle is open and the veil withdrawn; then follows the service of Benediction. . . . The introduction of this rite I believe to have been a grave disaster on the whole; though no doubt a joining to the Lord in the Sacrament is not transitory, but permanent, the adoration is not to be restricted to the time of the Liturgy, but is right also when the Sacrament is reserved."

Dr. Temple, Bishop of Manchester, held that individuals privately might be permitted to say their prayers before the Reserved Sacrament if they liked, but that no such devotions should be organised or conducted by a priest.

The case for extra-liturgical devotions was presented by Dr. Darwell Stone. This was summed up in four propositions. First, that the presence of our Lord in the Holy Sacrament is to be associated with the appointed rite, not with the faith of the communicant. Secondly, that there is no reason to suppose that this presence of our Lord is so limited that it cannot remain after the offering of the sacrifice, and the giving of Communion

The Movement in the Twentieth Century

in the rite itself are over. Therefore, this presence is the presence of our Lord Himself. And therefore in the Sacrament He is to be adored. Fourthly, that if it is true that the presence of our Lord in the Sacrament is not transitory but permanent, the adoration is not to be restricted to the time of the liturgy, but is right also when the Sacrament is reserved.

From a different aspect the reasonableness of extra-liturgical devotion was supported on the ground that this cultus began in what was the golden age of the Church; that its development was mainly due to a desire for new methods of stirring the sluggish spirit of devotion; and that its growth since the Reformation was simultaneous with a growth in the frequency of Communion.

According to statistics given in Hughson's *Reservation and Adoration*, it appeared that in more than half of the jurisdiction of the American Episcopal Church there has been perpetual Reservation. Bishop Hall, however, of Vermont, opposed any use of the Reserved Sacrament beyond the communion of the sick and of those unable to be present at the regular service.

In favour of Reservation it was urged at the Farnham Conference that it is just as right to base a practice on the doctrine of the Real Presence as on that of the Eucharistic Sacrifice. Into the question of the legality of Reservation the Conference refrained from entering. It was significant that all such question-begging epithets as fetish, idolatry, superstition, were never urged against the practice at Farnham.

At the same period as the Farnham Conference the subject of Reservation was frankly introduced by Bishops into their Diocesan Synods. This was courageously done by Bishop Watts Ditchfield in the Chelmsford Diocese, and by Bishop Garbett in the Diocese of Southwark. The voting in the latter Diocese illustrates the enormous increase of the desire for Reservation. 419 of the clergy voted approval of Reservation, while 111 opposed it; 485 agreed that the place and mode of Reservation, and all matters relating thereto, should rest with the Diocesan Bishop, while only 31 disagreed, mostly because they disapproved of Reservation altogether. To the question, Should the Reserved Sacrament be used for any purpose of corporate devotion or adoration? 78 answered Yes, and 441 answered No.

The conviction that Reservation of the Blessed Sacrament was imperatively required by modern conditions of life increased in volume greatly, and found powerful expression in Convocation when Prayer Book Revision was discussed. Opposition to the revival of the practice would undoubtedly have been far less if Reservation of the Sacrament had not led to acts of devotion before it, and the tendency to organised Congregational extra-liturgical devotions had not developed. It was explained on the Catholic side that the purpose of Reservation was, and always had been, Communion, and that the Worship associated with it was not the purpose, but only an incidental result. But the distinction did not carry conviction to opponents, especially when the development of extra-liturgical devotions as an organised system of habitual Sunday Services was beginning to appear. Dislike of developments of this nature accounts for the resistance displayed to Reservation when the subject came before Convocation in debate. The consequence was that while it was felt to be quite

The Movement in the Twentieth Century

impossible that Reservation should be altogether prevented, misgivings and hesitation pervaded the minds of many. They were determined that precautions should be taken to prevent the slightest move in the direction of devotion before the Sacrament when reserved. This spirit is displayed in every line of the Rubrics then composed.

The New Rubrics directed that "when the Holy Communion cannot reverently or without grave difficulty be celebrated in private [words which give decided preference to private celebrations], it shall be lawful for the Priest, with the sick person's consent [the priest's discretion is thus dependent on the decision of the sick person], on any day when there is a celebration of the Holy Communion in the Church, to set apart at the open Communion so much of the consecrated Bread and Wine as shall serve the sick person or persons, and so many as shall communicate with him, if there be any. And the open communion ended, he shall, on the same day and with as little delay as may be, go and minister the same."

A second Rubric contemplated a further case. "If further provision be needed in order to secure that any sick person may not lack the benefit of the most comfortable Sacrament of the Body and Blood of Christ, the Priest, if licensed by the Bishop so to do, may to that end, when the Holy Communion is celebrated in the Church, reserve so much of the Consecrated Bread and Wine as is needed for the purpose. And the Bishop shall grant such licence if satisfied of the need, unless in any particular case he can see good reason to the contrary."

A third Rubric declared that "the consecrated Bread and Wine set apart under either of the two preceding

The History of the Anglo-Catholic Revival

rubrics shall be reserved only for the Communion of the Sick, shall be administered in both kinds, and shall be used for no other purpose whatever. There shall be no service or ceremony in connection with the Sacrament so reserved, nor shall it be exposed or removed except in order to be received in Communion, or otherwise reverently consumed."

Archbishop Randall Davidson, placing the final form of the Revised Book before the Lower House of Convocation in 1927 (February 7th), said with reference to these directions about Reservation, "there is no question that with the stress laid, rightly or wrongly, by many on the obligation of the priest to celebrate fasting, and yet more with the increased frequency of the reception of the Holy Communion by the faithful, a demand has grown up which calls for consideration. Accordingly, the Rubrics prefixed to the alternative Order for the Communion of the Sick make provision for the reservation of the Elements to be used for the Communion of the Sick, and for no other purpose. Whatever rules it may be necessary for the Archbishop and Bishops acting together, or for the Convocation of the Province, to issue, the conditions under which alone we authorise Reservation are set forth with unmistakable clearness in the proposed Rubric."

III

The Reunion Movement in Anglo-Catholicism suffered a decided setback from the action of Pius IX and the Vatican Decree on Infallibility. Pusey's Eirenicon thenceforward took the title, "Is healthful Reunion impossible?" It was reserved for the twentieth century to take what further

The Movement in the Twentieth Century

steps seemed reasonable in the direction of Reunion with Catholic Communions alike of the East and of the West.

Anglo-Catholics had always based their allegiance to the Anglican Episcopate on the ground of the Catholic character of the Anglican ministry, and its inheritance of the Apostolic Succession. The Tractarians had set this principle in the forefront of the Revival, not indeed as something new, but as their fathers of the seventeenth century had done before them.

The leaders of the Oxford Movement revived this doctrine in an age in which it was largely undervalued or ignored. It was obvious that one of the main obstacles to any right relation with Rome was its inability to credit the existence of the Apostolic Succession in the English Church. The whole history of Anglican Orders had been seriously obscured in Roman writers since the seventeenth century by the fiction about the Nag's Head Tavern. And although this had been long ago abandoned by some of their ablest historians, such as Lingard, it still lingered in various places. There were also other misapprehensions which hindered Roman theologians from an impartial or accurate estimate. Indeed the members of the *Curia* were not usually well informed in the history of the Anglican Church. Consequently there had grown up an adverse tradition in the Roman Church about Anglican Orders, and a habitual denial of their reality in the case of the converts. However, in 1894, various theologians in the Roman Church, trained in a more objective, less controversial, school of historical study, were more or less prepared to regard the matter with an open mind. Some indeed were disposed to think that there was much more to be said for the Anglican Succession than previous

The History of the Anglo-Catholic Revival

opinion had allowed. No one on the Roman side was more hopeful about this change of attitude than the Abbé Portal. He successfully imparted his optimism to the President of the English Church Union. There were unquestionable evidences confirmatory of this more historical outlook on the Roman side. The Roman theologian Gasparri owned that he had blundered on the subject of Anglican Orders through unhistoric ideas imparted to him by eminent teachers of his own Communion. Lord Halifax was convinced that misconceptions might be removed. The historian, Duchesne, advised that a treatise on Anglican Orders should be written in Latin, in order to be read in Rome. The Roman *Curia*, said Duchesne, do not know English. In Latin you will be read: in English you will be translated. The superior advantage of being read rather than translated, in a case where accuracy depends on exact equivalents, was of course self-evident. For this task, few in the English Church were better qualified than Canon Lacey. He was a master in Ecclesiastical Latin, and well read in the writings of modern Roman theologians. In collaboration with Edward Denny he composed the *Dissertatio Apologetica de Hierarchia Anglicana* for the use of Italian readers.

A little group of Anglicans went to Rome and were resident there during some months. Lord Halifax, the Abbé Portal, Fr. Puller, S.S.J.E., and Canon Lacey worked together. The two Anglican priests placed their learning at the disposal of Italian clergy, who were none too familiar with the intricacies of the Anglican Reformation.

With regard to the attitude of Cardinal Vaughan on

The Movement in the Twentieth Century

the discussion of Anglican Orders at Rome, it is well to remember the impression made on the historian Thureau-Dangin,[1] himself a member of the Roman Church. Thureau-Dangin contrasts the wide difference between the sympathetic attitude of the first Roman Archbishop of Westminster, Cardinal Wiseman, and the conduct of his second successor. Wiseman recalled the attitude of Bossuet and Leibniz. Vaughan did his utmost to discredit the movements of Anglo-Catholics. Thureau-Dangin says that Cardinal Vaughan regarded Anglicans as obstinate heretics, and viewed them with profound dislike and distrust. His attitude, however sincere, was unjustifiable. And he acted against the counsels of moderation imparted to him by English members of his own Communion. He sent the Pope's letter *Ad Anglos* to *The Times*, but accompanied by comments of his own, emphasising precisely those passages which were most adverse to Anglican convictions. Whereupon the *Guardian* observed that Leo XIII had been very badly assisted by his representative in England.

The Cardinal greatly resented the intervention of certain French priests in the question of Anglican Orders. He viewed it as an unwarrantable intrusion into a matter which was no concern of theirs. The *Tablet*, which was under his control, spoke contemptuously of Duchesne and those ecclesiastics whom Lord Halifax was said to have enrolled in his party. Not content with this, the Cardinal felt that he must intervene in person at Rome. There he gradually exerted influence over Leo XIII, and secured finally the pronouncement against the validity of Anglican Orders. As a natural result the Journal which

[1] *Le Cardinal Vaughan*, par P. Thureau-Dangin, 1911.

The History of the Anglo-Catholic Revival

promoted the Anglican cause, the *Revue Anglo-Romaine*, expired, and the French clergy who favoured the cause were silenced. Cardinal Vaughan, however, by a singular act of indiscretion, declared publicly that Leo XIII had been requested to set apart a considerable sum of money to meet the needs of the Anglican ministers who, by their conversion to the Roman Church, would be reduced to poverty. But the expected Anglican ministers did not arrive. Thureau-Dangin's comment is that Mgr. Vaughan showed once more how little he understood the mentality of the Anglican world. But the Archbishop of Westminster's controversial style is displayed in his conviction that when Anglicans appropriate the doctrines and practices of Catholicism they are the marionettes of Satan and agents of his malice against God.

After the failure in 1895 to secure a better mutual understanding between Rome and the English Church, another considerable interval elapsed before any further intercommunications were resumed. The deep yearning after larger unity, and the exceptionally sympathetic character of the saintly Primate of Belgium, seemed to open out a prospect of a better attitude on the Roman side towards the English Church. Cardinal Mercier made possible the Malines Conversations, and welcomed certain Anglo-Catholics in his own Archiepiscopal palace. The ideal of Reunion was dominant in the English Church in an entirely novel degree. And however greatly individuals and schools might differ as to the direction in which Reunion should be promoted, it could not be denied that no Reunion of Christendom could be anything but partial if the Roman Church were left out. The reasonableness of Anglo-Catholic movements in that

The Movement in the Twentieth Century

direction might and did rouse considerable misgiving and apprehension on the Protestant side, but could not possibly be ruled out if Reunion was ever to be complete. Such movements were involved in the principles of the Lambeth Conference of 1920, and the Malines Conversations were at least in principle approved by the Primate of the English Church.

This movement towards a better understanding between Rome and England in 1921 was due to the splendid enthusiasm of Lord Halifax, combined with the sympathetic attitude of Cardinal Mercier, the Abbé Portal greatly assisting, as he had done five-and-twenty years before in the days of Leo XIII. A new Papacy had just begun in the election of Pius XI. The Archbishop of Malines issued a Pastoral letter to his Diocese, which he asked Lord Halifax to translate and reprint in England. It contained, of course, the usual emphasis on the value of a centre of unity. Lord Halifax distinctly said, "the question of reunion, if it is to be approached with any hope of success, must depend upon how far a way can be found to reconcile that claim with those of the Orthodox and Anglican Churches."[1]

Lord Halifax was most careful to assure his fellow Churchmen that this overture involved no assent to Roman principles. "They may see in it a surrender to Roman claims, and imagine a change in myself which implies disloyalty to that *Ecclesia Anglicana* in whose service my life has been spent. Let me assure them—for their friendship and confidence are very dear to me—that such is not the case. From the time of my Confirmation, some seventy years ago, I have tried, however

[1] *Call to Reunion*, p. 15, 1922.

imperfectly, to conform my life to the requirements of the Book of Common Prayer. My Communions and Confessions have been governed by it. Every one of those seventy years has only strengthened and confirmed my conviction of the truth and reality of the Sacraments I have received. Throughout those years the Blessed Sacrament has been the guard, the security, and the happiness of my life. I hope and believe that I would gladly die rather than any action of mine should cast a doubt upon the reality of those Sacraments, or the purposes of God in regard to the Church of England. It is because of the absolute security of faith as a member of that Church, that I do not hesitate to advocate the duty of our endeavouring to recognise the need of a visible centre for the Catholic Church throughout the world."

The Anglican position was still more plainly reasserted by Lord Halifax in his address to the English Church Union in 1925, when he said that "if we in England have to consider, with a view to its acceptance, the claim of the Holy See to a primacy *jure divino*, the Holy See has, on its side, to take into consideration, with a view to reunion, the question of Anglican Orders."[1] He urged that there was nothing to prevent the decision of Leo XIII from being reconsidered. He reminded his hearers that "the Anglican bishops in the interests of reunion at the last Lambeth Conference stated their willingness, if agreement could be arrived at on other points, to accept such a rectification of their orders as might facilitate their recognition by the Roman Church." But he insisted in the most definite terms that "it is impossible on the Anglican side for Anglicans to consent to anything which

Reunion and the Roman Primacy, 1925, p. 27.

The Movement in the Twentieth Century

in their eyes would seem to invalidate the orders conferred by the English Episcopate."

At Rome the Conversations at Malines were for a while favourably regarded. The Monastic Community of Amai was entrusted with a special mission to study and promote Reunion work. The Journal *Irénikon* was created as a literary organ for that purpose. And for a while Anglican as well as Roman writers were allowed to contribute to its pages.

A very appropriate theologian was chosen on the Roman side, the French theologian Batiffol—learned, courteous, careful, sympathetic, a voluminous writer, well read in S. Augustine's principles, and well aware, from painful personal experience, how liable a Roman theologian is to find one of his own works on the Index of books condemned. At Malines Batiffol appeared as a moderating influence, disposed to place a minimising interpretation on that greatest of all obstacles to Reunion with Rome—the Infallibility Decree.

The main difficulty lay in the Infallibility dogma rather than in the Primacy. Heiler[1] thinks Bishop Gore's outlook was more unroman than that of Bishop Frere or Lord Halifax. But they were agreed that Episcopal authority was immediately derived through Christ, and not derived from the Primacy; and that the Papal decisions could only become infallible when the Pope, in and with the entire episcopate, and ultimately with the entire Church, propounded a doctrine.

By far the most astonishing document produced at Malines was the anonymous Memoir entitled *L'Eglise Anglicane Unie non Absorbée*, read to the Conference

[1] Cf. Heiler, *Im Ringen*, p. 431.

The History of the Anglo-Catholic Revival

by Cardinal Mercier himself. It took the view that the Anglican Church, historically regarded, appeared with a certain insularity, self-governed and in splendid isolation —while nevertheless firmly attached from its origin to the Roman See. A Patriarchal character was conferred on Augustine of Canterbury by Gregory the Great. Urban II, at the Council of Bari in 1098, placed Anselm of Canterbury beside himself *quasi alterius orbis papa*. The inference from these facts was drawn that the notion of the Anglican Church absorbed by Rome, and the notion of it as separated from Rome, are equally inadmissible conceptions.

It was further observed that Patriarchal authority still exists in the Uniat Churches which retain their own rights and customs, and are ruled by their own Synods. Leo XIII, in his Constitution on the Oriental dignity in 1894, undertook that neither he nor his successors would suppress their patriarchal privileges.

The document proceeded to contemplate the possibility of the application of this Patriarchal principle to the English Church; the re-establishment of the Archbishop of Canterbury in the traditional rights of Patriarch of the English Church; the Canon Law of the Latin Church not being imposed on the English Church: on the analogy of the case of the Oriental Churches whose Code is different from that of the Latin Church. Thus the celibacy of the clergy need not be imposed on a Uniat Anglican Church any more than it is in the Eastern Churches similarly placed. Further, in the case of such Reunion, the Anglican Church would retain its own liturgy. Then came the most original clause of the whole document. It contemplated that all the historic ancient

The Movement in the Twentieth Century

Sees of the English Church would be maintained, and all the new Roman Catholic Sees created since 1851, such as Westminster, would be suppressed. *"Evidement, c'est une mesure grave"* adds the author. But he remembers that Pius VII, in the Concordat with Napoleon, suppressed existing Dioceses in the Church of France, and required the resignation of their Diocesans to the number of more than a hundred.

The document proceeded to reflect what Rome would think of this proposal. Admittedly it involved a scheme of decentralisation which was not in accord with present-day tendencies of the Roman *Curia*. The author did not think it possible to foretell what would be the answer of the Vatican.

The Malines Conversations, like the discussion of Anglican Orders at Rome, were very repugnant to Westminster Cathedral and to the journals under its direction. There were Roman priests in England who represented the Belgian Primate as meddling in a matter which was no business of his. And as time advanced there was a very apparent decrease of sympathy or approval at the Vatican. With Cardinal Mercier's death, the journal *Irénikon* confined itself to other than Anglican affairs, no Anglican writer contributed any further to its pages, and no probability appears that Malines Conversations are likely to be resumed.

Yet although it was not to be expected that they could be of any immediate effect, still they mark a stage in the History of Reunion Movements. They stand in various ways as a unique endeavour. It was much, even for a brief space, that Roman and Anglican theologians should meet and confer under the presidency of a Cardinal

The History of the Anglo-Catholic Revival

of the Roman Church. The significance of it may be suggested when we look back and ask whether such a move would have taken place over half a century ago.

Bishop Gore's reflection on the Conversations at Malines was that "it is a great matter for thankfulness that once again, after long centuries, frank and serious conversations have taken place in perfect friendliness between representatives of Rome and of the Anglican Church. Anyone acquainted with the history of the Church since the period of the Reformation must recognise how deeply different Rome to-day is from the Rome of the sixteenth century, both in respect of discipline and doctrine, though the difference does not on the whole tend to make reunion easier: and I cannot pretend to see any way at present opening through the dogmatic obstacles between us. But the power and moral and spiritual influence of the Roman Church grow from decade to decade in the world at large, and the vastness of its position in the whole of Christendom makes any *ignoring* of it, such as is common among Protestants, foolish and blind indeed. There is at least an urgent duty laid upon us to seek sympathetically to understand this tremendous organ of spiritual power, and to watch the movements of mind and energy within it."[1]

Reunion with *the Eastern Church* was an early vision in the Catholic Revival. It had strongly appealed to the Nonjurors before them, and indeed it arose from time to time when Catholic principles prevailed. It has naturally seemed a simpler enterprise than Reunion with the West, since the problem of the Papal Infallibility, indeed the whole problem of Papal primacy, does not enter.

[1] Bishop Gore, *The Anglo-Catholic Movement To-day*, 1925.

The Movement in the Twentieth Century

It is unquestionably the Anglo-Catholic element in the English Church which attracts the *Eastern Churches*, and with which it would be congenial for them to unite. In the early period of the Catholic Revival nothing very promising could be effected. Now that the Revival has its assured position and its extensive influence, the English Church naturally grows more attractive to the East. The determination of the Catholic-minded to frustrate attempts of Low Churchmen in Jerusalem to detach Eastern Catholics from their allegiance, increased the sense of brotherhood between the Anglo-Catholic and the Orthodox. The main obstacle to Reunion between the Eastern Church and the Church of England is the Protestant element in the latter.

In the Declaration of Faith, signed by 3,715 Anglicans, presented by the English Church Union to the Ecumenical Patriarch of Constantinople in 1922,[1] it was affirmed that the one saving faith is the Faith of the Undivided Church and that, notwithstanding individual departures therefrom, this Faith has not been forsaken by the English Church. Also "the essential necessity of the Sacrament of Order, according to the institution of Christ, the practice of the Apostles, and the constant tradition of the Church. This is secured in the Churches of the Anglican Communion by the transmission of the several orders of the hierarchy by the imposition of the hands of the Bishops, to whom it has been transmitted in like manner by an uninterrupted succession from the days of the Apostles." It is further declared that "our Lord through the ministry of the successors of the Apostles has conferred on us and on all the members of the clergy

[1] Bell, *Documents*, 1924, p. 90.

The History of the Anglo-Catholic Revival

of the Anglican Communion the Sacrament of Order, with the purpose that we, who are priests, should preach and teach the Word of God; offer the Sacrifice of the Eucharist for both the living and the departed; sacramentally absolve sinners who repent and confess their sins; and otherwise minister to the flock of Christ according to the ancient faith and practice of the Universal Church." It was also affirmed that "by consecration in the Eucharist, the bread and the wine, being blessed by the life-giving power of the Holy Spirit, are changed and become the true body and the true blood of Christ, and as such are given to and received by the faithful. We hold, therefore, that Christ thus present is to be adored. As to the actual manner of the change, and the mode of the presence, no doctrine on this point is laid down by any Ecumenical Council, and therefore, while believing the fact, we do not venture to define the mode. We agree with the Holy Orthodox Eastern Church that honour should be given to the holy and ever-virgin Mother of God and the saints departed; that there is a legitimate use of sacred images; and that, alike in our public and in our private prayers, we should ask for the benefit of the intercession of the saints." Finally, "We account the 39 Articles of Religion as a document of secondary importance concerned with local controversies of the sixteenth century, and to be interpreted in accordance with the faith of that Universal Church of which the English Church is but a part."[1]

Overtures towards reunion with the Roman Church, or even with the Orthodox Churches of the East, were naturally repugnant to those who rejected the Catholic conception of the Sacraments and of the Ministry. The

[1] Bell, *Documents on Christian Unity*, 1924, pp. 90–92.

The Movement in the Twentieth Century

affinities of the Evangelicals were rather towards the Nonconformists. This contrast of purpose produced the Kikuyu difficulties in 1915. Whereas in England both Catholic-minded and Evangelical are intermingled in every diocese, in Africa separate dioceses were created by missionaries from different schools of thought, with the result that the Diocese of Mombasa was exclusively Protestant, whereas that of Zanzibar was as exclusively Catholic. The practice of Intercommunion with non-Episcopal bodies seemed perfectly reasonable to Mombasa and perfectly reprehensible to Zanzibar. On the proposal of open Communion the Archbishop of Canterbury (Dr. Randall Davidson) advised that interchange of pulpits was in certain cases legitimate. And members of other denominations, deprived for a time of the ministrations of their own communion, although they have not been confirmed, and have no intention of being confirmed, might be admitted to communion at the Altars of the English Church. But Anglicans were not authorised in receiving Communion from ministers not episcopally ordained.

The Archbishop of Canterbury's opinion on this subject—it was deliberately given only as an opinion, and not as an authoritative rule—compelled the Catholic-minded to resist. Bishop Gore, then Bishop of Oxford, openly declared himself unable to accept it.[1] He insisted that "in the long run there is no justification for refusing full recognition of Nonconformist ministers, in view of the spiritual fruits of their labours, except the belief (1) that the episcopate is of the essence of a valid ministry, and (2) that an episcopally ordained priest is necessary

[1] *Crisis in Church and Nation*, 1915.

for a valid eucharist." He maintained, therefore, that "to accept a non-episcopal ministry is an act of explicit rebellion against the authority of the ancient and undivided Church, than which there can be no rebellion more complete."

CHAPTER XIII

THE PAST AND THE FUTURE

Now that the century of the Catholic Revival in the English Church has approached its completion, it is appropriate to look back upon its course in order to estimate the principal lessons to be learnt from its history, and the prospects of its future.

I

The first and most obvious reflection on the Catholic Revival is its wonderful Achievements. It is literally true that the Revival has simply transfigured the whole appearance of the English Church. It has driven out the spirit of neglect and numberless abuses which had become conventional. It has restored the outward signs of reverence and dignity and beauty. It has profoundly affected the whole conduct of devotion. Its influence has extended beyond its own adherents. It has altered the externals of devotion among Evangelicals and Broad Churchmen also. Its ideals have been largely followed in most forms of English Nonconformity, except the Society of Friends.

But the influence of the Revival with regard to outward expressions of devotion is after all only the minor part of its astonishing work. It has restored to the English Church a Sacramental belief which has made the Eucharist once again realised as the indispensable medium for the communication of spiritual vitality, and therefore in a totally new degree valued. Even in 1865, Harold Brown,

The History of the Anglo-Catholic Revival

Bishop of Ely, was compelled publicly to complain to his clergy that there were still some parishes in which this Blessed Sacrament was offered to the worshippers not oftener than four times in the year. Dean Church said something not dissimilar.

"Fifty years ago there were Churches which hardly saw the Eucharist from year's end to year's end. Fifty years ago, except in the Prayer Book, except in the ideas and perhaps the shy practice of a few obscure students or devout observers of ancient usage, that which is the foremost and indispensable part of Christian worship was looked upon as something meant exclusively for the stricter and more devout few, or as the rare and occasional incentive to a flagging faith. . . ."[1]

The influence of the Catholic Revival extends much further still. It is very widely claimed at the present day that the appointment of Bishops in the English Church must not be made by men who are not necessarily its members, or even necessarily adherents of the Christian Religion; that it is not the rightful function of politicians and statesmen to determine who shall rule the Church. It is also insisted to-day in popular assemblies, and advocated by clergy and by Bishops who are by no means in agreement with Anglo-Catholicism, that we are bound to secure the spiritual independence of the Church. These claims have grown to be among the commonplaces of ecclesiastical Reform—recognised as long overdue by the generality of the Church's members.

But it must be remembered that, self-evident and generally accepted as these principles are to the present generation, they were by no means self-evident to the

[1] Dean Church, *Pascal and other Sermons*, p. 344.

The Past and the Future

generality of Churchmen a century ago. They were either ignored or rejected by the majority of clergy and laity alike when the Oxford Movement began, and for a very long time afterwards. It is the Catholic Revival which has wrought this change, because it has insisted as fundamental that the Church is a Divinely created Institution whose nature is essentially spiritual, and therefore contrasted with all State and National Institutions whatsoever. The right of a Divinely created Institution to choose its own leaders, and to possess its own independence within its proper sphere, follows as the inevitable consequence of the principles which the Catholic Revival has brought home convincingly to the Church's members.

The astonishing character of the achievements of the Catholic Revival impress every one who studies the course of its development. One or two weighty judgments may be here given. Here is the estimate of an English Historian. Bishop Stubbs, contemplating the Movement, wrote as follows:

"The results of that short work were wonderful; to be seen in every village Church, to be heard in every sermon, to be felt in the administration of every parish. Never since the Reformation had there been such a change, and the influences that wrought it were more intellectual and more spiritual than those which effected the Reformation."[1]

The German Lutheran, Heiler, surveying the century of the Anglo-Catholic Revival, confesses himself amazed. The Movement has inspired new life into a dying Church. It has restored the Catholic tradition into a communion in which it was almost lost. Most wonderful of all, it

[1] Bishop Stubbs, *Charge*, 1899, p. 349.

The History of the Anglo-Catholic Revival has leavened the whole Anglican Church with the Catholic spirit. Even the keenest opponents of Anglo-Catholicism are under its influence.[1]

II

The opposition to the Catholic Movement has been very formidable. The Movement had against it the Crown, the Authorities of the State, decisions of the Law, the large majority of the Authorities in the Church. The powers of coercion, imprisonment, deprivation, united in a determination to expel the distinctive doctrines and practices of the Catholic Revival from the Church of England. Statesmen and ecclesiastics of the highest ranks combined in a resolute opposition through the greater part of a century. And yet the united efforts of the Throne and the powers of the State and the Church, with all the forces at their disposal, proved powerless to prevent the growth and expansion of Catholic ideals and Sacramental principles. The efforts at suppression failed as completely against Anglo-Catholicism as they did against Methodism, with the significant difference that the one was driven out of the English Church, whereas the other remained within. The Oxford Movement is a remarkable illustration of the futility of coercion in Religion. As Dr. Sanday said, their most effective asset was their willingness to go to prison for their cause. The pathetic feature of the contest is that, given their contrasted beliefs about the Church and the State, the prosecutors could not well do otherwise than prosecute, nor the prosecuted do otherwise than resist. Once more in the history of

[1] Heiler, *Im Ringen*, p. 433.

The Past and the Future

Christendom, they were condemned, they were imprisoned, they were deprived, and yet they multiplied.

With the twentieth century there has come a change. Kensitites could scarcely in the present time cause riots in Church. Even the "no popery" cry, although not altogether ineffective, is unable to raise the passionate fury of a former age.

Opposition to Catholic principles is of course persistent and strong. But it resorts to other methods of procedure. Legal prosecution has ceased. Episcopal denunciation is rarely heard. Priests are no longer imprisoned or deprived for Ritualism. The opposition goes outside the Church of England to secure recruits. The rejection of the Revised Prayer Book by Parliament, in spite of diplomatic, even desperate ecclesiastical assurances of its innocuous nature, illustrates how strong the opposition is. But the opposition assumes more subtle and insidious forms. Whether the method resorted to in the creation of Protestant trusts will ultimately commend itself to the Christian conscience any better than the policy of coercion remains to be seen. At present it has aroused the deep resentment of many Churchmen who are not Catholic-minded, and it has also immensely increased the desire for disestablishment. It is in any case inconceivable that a Movement which has made such sacrifices and endured such privations will be reduced to nothing by such attempts at its exclusion from the Parishes of the English Church.

Official opposition to Catholicism on the part of those who are in authority seldom attempts the method of prosecution. Nor as a rule does it openly denounce and refuse to license curates. Nor does it withdraw grants, as it did last century. Nor does it, as a rule, confine its patronage to Modernists and Evangelicals, and frankly leave it to a successor to redress the balance. The methods usually employed against the Movement are more subtle. They consist in replacing an incumbent by a successor of a more moderate type, or in exerting private influence to prevent the continuance of Eucharistic Vestments, or the making the Choral Eucharist the central devotion for the general congregation. Where the clergy and laity are people of strong convictions these efforts to weaken the Movement are never likely to succeed.

In the light of the advancement which the Catholic Revival presents it is instructive to look back to reflections written in 1843 by Frederick Denison Maurice, on right and wrong methods of supporting Protestantism. It was written at the time when Lord Ashley was attempting to suppress the revival of Catholic principles in the University where they arose. Maurice insisted that the Catholic Movement was not towards formalism, but away from it; and that it was recovering the great principle of a social faith, the principle that we exist in a permanent communion which was not created by human hands, and cannot be destroyed by them. The effect of this Catholic teaching, said Maurice, was assuredly very remarkable. The Movement began to Catholicise the Church, and was a blessing to at least one portion of it. They threatened to unprotestantise it. But what was the Protestantism which they seem to mean? It was that spirit of fierce denunciation and contradiction of something else. Popular Protestantism was according to Maurice being degraded. It was a question of life or death. If Catholic and Protestant principles can be brought to work together it is life. If they cannot, the alternative of death is inevitable. He

The Past and the Future

deplored what he called the meagre, negative, spurious Protestantism of his age. The Evangelical clergy must learn that they have a sacred position of their own to maintain, and yet that this position is not exclusive. Exclusive Protestantism cannot be urged by a strong Protestantism in the present century. The very strongest Protestantism is that which is brought out to sustain and balance Catholic principles. Maurice warned the Evangelicals that attempts at suppression of their opponent were certain to fail. "That like most measures proposed with such an object it will utterly fail in its purpose and produce an exactly opposite effect to that which was intended I believe we have abundant warrant for affirming. It has been ascertained by the experience of every University in Europe that in whatever place it is safe to attempt the suppression of opinion, in schools of learning it is not safe. In Oxford the experiment has been tried again and again by all parties: against Wickcliffe—against the Reformers of the sixteenth century—against Laud during the Primacy of Abbott—against the Puritans during the Primacy of Laud—against Episcopalians during the supremacy of the Puritans—against the Methodists in the eighteenth century. In every case the only persons who have profited by the persecution have been those against whom it was directed. They have been seen to gain disciples: a sense of English justice has been raised in their favour; young men have felt that there must be something good in that which was unfairly attacked." Above all things, urged Maurice, do not let us suppose that we can promote truth by destroying freedom.

The History of the Anglo-Catholic Revival

III

There are, of course, many characteristics which have attended the Movement's development. The Catholic Revival, like all Movements of Religion, has suffered from defects.

It is a serious fact that the recovery of neglected Sacramental principles, and the expression in ceremonial of Sacramental beliefs, have been secured by the resistance of the inferior clergy to the directions of their superiors. That the priests were in many cases right in their contentions, and the Bishops were wrong, has been in process of the century admitted by episcopal successors who have themselves sanctioned what their predecessors forbade. The advance has been won by disobedience; or, rather, by obedience to a higher Authority against the demands of a lower. The process was an unhappy one, however inevitable. The inability of the Episcopate, during a considerable part of the century, to realise the nature of the Movement, its legitimate claims, and historical antecedents, is perfectly intelligible, but equally deplorable. It is useless to picture what might have been. But it is wise to remember what was.

1. Looking back across the History of the Movement, it is obvious that one of the hindrances to its larger effectiveness was the periodical secessions to Rome. In the days when it was widely supposed that the English Church was through the silence of its Bishops committed to the Privy Council's decision that the denial of Baptismal Regeneration was consistent with Anglican formularies, it is perfectly intelligible that grave misgivings about the Church's loyalty to the Faith should arise, and consequent

The Past and the Future

unsettlement should prevail. And when subsequently the Authorities of the English Church appeared to be indifferent to an alternative Anglican and Lutheran succession in the Bishopric of Jerusalem, unsettlement among the believers in the Apostolic Succession naturally increased. Given the Tractarian conviction about the Church's principles the tendency to secession is understood. Nothing can be more pathetic than Newman's sorrowful reproach of the English Church. We may feel perfectly convinced that neither Newman nor Manning, nor many of those who in the early period withdrew, would have withdrawn had their lot been cast in the English Church as it is to-day.

Their secession was immensely valuable to the Roman Church. They introduced among Roman Catholics in England a wealth of ideas which did much to change the attitude of the older Roman families.

But their loss was for the English Church an indescribable calamity. It threw back the progress of the Catholic revival in the Nation. The natural result of secessions was the charge that Tractarianism was a deliberate movement to Rome. That accusation was naturally plausible and effective. The public mind was in a state of incapacity to distinguish between what was Catholic and what was Roman. And when an Anglican clergyman here or there, after ardently promoting the Ritual revival, abandoned his charge, denied his own orders, and offered himself to Roman Authorities to be baptised, there is no wonder that a violent reaction from the Oxford Movement resulted. Thus, for example, it was proclaimed in print that the Church, College, and Schools of S. Barnabas, Pimlico, were entirely in the hands of Jesuit priests, and used solely for perverting our people to the Church of Rome.

The tendency to secession has beset the Movement from time to time. What is popularly known in clerical circles as Roman fever has broken out in various places. But quite without the provocation which existed in the case of Newman and of Manning.

It is natural to recall Von Hügel's memorable thoughts about exchanges of Communion. Von Hügel records the matured experience of a Roman Catholic Bishop that he had "seen for many a long year how easy it is to disturb souls from out of what contains much truth and which they can and do assimilate to their spiritual profit, and to push and strain them up to something to which they are not really called, and of which they do not know what to make."[1]

Von Hügel's own inclination was to be very zealous to help souls to make the most of what they already have; and if they come to think of moving, to test them to the uttermost. Fresh converts, he thought, were naturally proselytisers at first. They have not been long enough in the Roman Church to have experienced its human poornesses, nor to have themselves within that Church passed through desolation and reaction. Von Hügel added that one Roman Catholic who falls away gave him more pain than a hundred accessions to the Church gave him joy. The reason being that it is the sticking to it which really matters, and in which the difficulty really consists. It is natural to apply these reflections to the case of Tyrrell with which Von Hügel was so intimately concerned. No one who reads Tyrrell's mature judgment

[1] *Letters*, p. 346.

The Past and the Future

about the reasons for his secession from the English Church is likely to forget it. "Not one of the reasons on which I acted do I now acknowledge as of the slightest validity." If it had not been for Von Hügel's ascendency Tyrrell would in all human probability have returned to the Church which in youth he had forsaken.

The Catholic Revival within the English Church has always drawn the sharpest dividing line between individual secession and Corporate Reunion. Nothing has given greater stability to the Movement than the firmness with which its leading laymen and priests have adhered resolutely to that distinction. There is something inspiring in the assurance that a man will not stultify in age the allegiance and the loyalties of his life. Controversialists will sometimes insinuate suspicions of vacillation between two Communions. They are well aware that misgivings about a priest's unswerving loyalty are demoralising to the congregation which he serves.

The Revival has suffered repeatedly from such secessions. Religious Communities have at times been almost wrecked, and congregations half-paralysed. Founders of religious institutions have been almost heart-broken by the resultant desolation. And yet these failures are comparatively few. The Movement has gone on and prospered in spite of desertions. None the less, individual secessions are a saddening sign of weakness.

This subject of Secession has been a good deal studied of late, as may be seen in the Essays of Professor A. E. Taylor and Dr. Goudge, giving reasons why they are not Roman Catholics.

Dr. Goudge says, "I have prayed repeatedly to God to show me if He wishes my allegiance to be changed,

The History of the Anglo-Catholic Revival

and He has not done so. I have considered and reconsidered the Roman claims, and can find no basis for them anywhere. I have found in the Sacraments as ministered where I am all and more than all that I could have expected to find in them; and, though I have a profound regard for many Roman Catholics, I see nothing in their conduct and character to lead me to suppose that they possess advantages denied to others. Moreover, all that is best in the teaching and practice of Roman Catholics, as in that of other Christians, I can study and assimilate where I am. Thus I have no motive for becoming a Roman Catholic."[1] Dr. Goudge says that in his experience he has never known a deep student of Scripture to become a Roman Catholic.

Professor A. E. Taylor insists that confessional allegiances cannot be changed without deep-seated reconstruction of the whole personality, and that readiness to change them except under the stress of the most imperative necessity is only possible where there is no real depth of personal character. "Facile conversion," he says, "means either or both of two things. Either the convert's old belief meant very little to him, and was not really inwoven into his personality, or his new convictions are very much on the surface, and he is not the sort of convert it is worth taking much trouble to make."

It is worth while that convictions such as these should be quoted, were it only as an assurance that the Catholic Revival is, on principle, utterly hostile to individual secessions.

2. Another reflection is forced upon us by the extensive prevalence of Ritual expressions. Dignified ceremonial is

[1] *Why I am not a Roman Catholic*, pp. 183–4.

The Past and the Future

in use far beyond the adherents of the Catholic Revival. It is to be found in Cathedrals where gorgeous copes are worn such as would have roused the "no popery" cry less than a century ago. But there is attached to these externals no doctrinal significance whatsoever. This broadening range of external observance is at least a reminder that Ritual does not of necessity convey its meaning if divorced from doctrine. It must be remembered that one main characteristic of the Catholic Revival was that instruction in the Faith came first, and the Ritual expression afterwards. Moreover, the great leaders during the nineteenth century never regarded the ceremonial of the Eucharist as an adequate equivalent for Sacramental teaching. It is often asked whether the conspicuous preference in modern life for ceremonial is not rather due to æsthetic causes than to religion. Large numbers of the rising generation have dissociated themselves from the Puritan traditions of their forefathers, and have felt the attractiveness of ornate devotional forms. But it is never safe to assume that the Eucharistic Ritual conveys its meaning unless the worshipper is instructed in the dogmas of the Faith. It is said that the successors of the Tractarians to-day are sometimes relying on ceremonial in the absence of doctrinal instruction. This is what the leaders of the Movement in the past most certainly never did.

The original strength of the Tractarian revival consisted in its strong, definite, dogmatic teaching, not at all in its ceremonial expression. Experience proves that Symbolical action does not by any means necessarily convey its meaning.

3. Yet another characteristic of the Tractarians and of

The History of the Anglo-Catholic Revival

the leaders in the Ritual revival is their singularly sacrificial spirit. Scott Holland spoke of "the old Tractarian instinct of self-repression." That is part of the idea. There was among them a remarkable number of men of independent means, some of considerable wealth, who deliberately devoted their lives to the Church's service without ambition, in altogether uncongenial surroundings, identified with a social class far inferior to that to which they belonged. It is almost invidious to mention names. They will recur to anyone who thinks. They chose to deprive themselves of many of this world's advantages. This was the case both with men and with women. They entered the religious life. Communities arose, multiplied, flourished.

The serious question which the heirs of the Catholic Revival have to face is whether while we inherit their labours we possess their spirit. The criticism is heard that the tendency of Catholics in the present century is appreciation of the self-gratifying elements of Catholicism without compliance with the self-sacrificing elements of the same. A study of the Movement in its noblest phases must provoke reflection whether the sacrificial spirit which is the essential quality of Catholicism, is the quality of its present-day adherents, whether laity or priests. If it is a fact that there is a disposition to offer the Sacrifice without in reality practically uniting ourselves with the Sacrifice; if we delight in the glory of Ritual devotion and recoil from the thought of vocation; if the religious Communities are not adequately recruited; there is evidently something seriously deficient in the Movement to-day. Critics have been engaged in calculating the ordinary duration of a Revival in Religion,

The Past and the Future

and are disposed to suggest that Catholic Revival has outlived its time, has weakened, shows signs of age; and some are quite ready to apply to it the thought that which waxeth aged is nigh unto vanishing away.

4. Like all great Movements the Catholic Revival in its later phases betrays a tendency to form into various groups whose notions of the rate of progress are different, or whose ideals are not exactly the same. It may be that in certain earlier periods of its existence it was held together partly by the force of pressure from outside. Considering that, when all is said, Anglo-Catholicism is only a minority in the Church, however effective a minority, it is self-evident that its strength depends upon its unity.

Efforts have been made to secure a closer unity between the various groups within the Anglo-Catholic Movement. Bishop Chandler's Eirenikon was a commendable effort in that direction. For sympathy, conciliatory spirit, and sweet reasonableness it left nothing to be desired. But it did not win success, or indeed much more than the respectful hearing due to a prelate of high character and Catholic convictions. It is, of course, quite true that no union would serve its aim if it left out a considerable minority of the more advanced. But it is also self-evident that no common basis is possible where diversity exists without some concession in one direction or another. It is also obvious that inability to combine means weakness, since it deprives the Movement of united strength and harmonious co-operation. It lends support to the criticism that the Movement is losing its power.

Bishop Creighton raised the question, in one of his letters, "How much of the results of the Oxford Move-

The History of the Anglo-Catholic Revival

ment are to be permanently incorporated into the Anglican system?" To which the answer surely ought to be, as much as is compatible with the principles of the Universal Church. It seems inconceivable that the Sacramental doctrines and practices which have been so marvellously recovered should ever again be lost. Yet the history of the English Church has been a series of reactions. And the doctrines recovered can only be retained by strenuous effort and self-effacing devotion against the many influences which tend to deprive the English Church of its wonderful gains. Our duty is to keep that which, by the sacrifices of our predecessors, has been committed to our trust.

INDEX

Adoration of consecrated elements, 62
Aggrieved Parishioners, 79
Alban's, S., Holborn (sequestered, 134), 126
Anderson, Rev. V. S. (Leicester), secession, 52
Andrewes, Bishop, Elements in Eucharist, 61
Androutsos, doctrine of Apostles, 41
Anglican Orders, Archbishop Meletios, 43
Apostolic Succession in Catholic Movement, 12
Arnold (Rugby), Losses at Reformation, 15
Augsburg Confession, 33

Barnabas, S., Pimlico, "Jesuits in Charge," 289
Bath & Wells, Bishop of (Bennett case), 65
Batiffol, Episcopate and Apostolic Succession, 31, 273
Bennett, Vicar of Frome, ref. Eucharist, 59
Benson, Archbishop, Court at Lambeth, 153
Benson, Father—
  Loyalty to Truth, 13, 23
  (Cowley) Ritual and Religion, 80
  on Pusey as preacher, 152
Bickersteth (Bishop of Ripon), ref. *Greville Memoirs*, 19
Bishops against Catholic Revival, 23
Bonner, Bishop, 137
Bricknell, Episcopal Charges, 1833, 15

Briggs, Professor, Bishops and Continental Church, 35
Bright, Dr.—
  Professor Ecclesiastical History, Oxford, 21, 141
  Reservation not allowed by rubrics, 254
British Quarterly Review, ref. Privy Council, 138
Brooke, S. John the Divine, Kennington, 158
Bulgakoff, Archpriest, Professor, orthodox ordination, 42
Bull, Father (Mirfield), Revival of religious life, 244
Burne-Jones, Sir E., ref. a funeral in Westminster Abbey, 81
Butler, Dean (Wantage), 235

Cairns, Lord, Public Worship Regulation Bill, 143
Calvin, Theory of Ministry, 35
Cameron, Religious Communities, Church of England, 241
Campbell, Lord Chancellor, Gorham Case, 51
Cardwell, Synods of Church, 18
Carter (Clewer)—
  Doctrine and Ritual, 75
  Freedom of Confession, 121
  Sisterhoods, 237
  State Interference, 206
Catholic Revival, begun by Priests, 14
Chandler, Bishop, Eirenikon, 295
Chasuble, forbidden by law, 101
Christ Church, Albany Street, Community Life, 231
Christian Remembrancer—
  Catholic Movement, 18, 131
  Communicants, 78, 182

297

Christian Remembrancer—contd.
  Convocation, 195
  Church and State, 191
  Church and State, Dr. Liddon on, 147
Church Association—
  Bennett Case, 60
  Appeal to Privy Council, 63
  "Persecution Company," 128–9
  Patronage to High Church, 140
  Prosecutes Rev. S. F. Green, 146
Church, Dean R. W.—
  Oxford Movement, 14, 139
  Bishop of Lincoln Trial, 155
  State and Church, 192
Clay, Rev. E., Ordination of Priests, 115
Clement, S., Apostolic Succession, 28
Coke, Lord Chief Justice, Convocation, 179
Coleridge, Lord—
  ref. Exeter, Bangor, 54
  ref. Miss Sellon, 234
Coles, Stuckey, East Grinstead, 236
Confession, Sacramental, petition for, 140
Confessors, duly qualified and licensed, 119
Convocation—
  Report on Ritual, 86
  Ordered revise Rubrics of Book of Common Prayer, 95
  Henry VIII, Hallam, 176, 183
Cope sanctioned at Holy Communion (not Chasuble), 99
Cornish, Warre, on Tait, 151
Cosin, Bishop, ref. Bread and Wine and Rubric, 61, 257
Cowley, S. John Evangelist, Grafton, Benson, O'Neill, 241
Creighton, Bishop—
  Incense, Candles, 156

Creighton, Bishop—*continued*
  Oxford Movement, how much incorporated in Anglican System, 296

Dale, Rev. Pelham, 146
Davidson, Archbishop, Revised Prayer Book, Reservation, 266
Dean and Chapter of S. Paul's rebuked by Tait, 141
Denison, Archdeacon (Taunton)—
  Real Presence, 55
  Denounces Public Worship Regulation Act, 205
Denison, Bp. E. (Salisbury), Debt to Tractarians, 16
Devotions at Evensong, etc., Bishop Gore, 262
Disraeli—
  and Queen Victoria, Low Church Appointments, 21
  and Public Worship Regulation Act, 145, 211
Ditchfield, Watts, Bishop, Chelmsford, Reservation, 260, 264
Dodd, Rev. E., Convocation, 180
Dodsworth, Rev. W. (Albany Street), Gorham Case, 52
Dolling, Father, Need of impressive Church, 69
Döllinger, Dr., and Archbishop of Munich, 137
Duchesne—
  Episcopate, Apostolic Succession, 31
  Treatise on Anglican Orders should be in Latin, 268

East Grinstead, Sisterhood, 236
Eastward Position—
  (Purchas Case), 135
  Liddon and Gregory, 138
  Bishop Jackson, 147
  Bishop of Lincoln, 155

Index

E.C.U.—
  1860, 128
  Counsel's Opinion, Vestments, etc., 130
Edinburgh Review, ref. Absolution, 111
Eglise Anglicaine unie non Absorbée, 173
Ely, Bishop of, Holy Communion four times in Year, 282
Enraght Case (wafer produced), 145
Essays Catholic and Critical, authority, 170
Eucharistic Sacrifice (Bennett case)(Dr. Phillimore defends list of Anglican Teachers), 62

Fairbairn, Dr.—
  Church and State, 220
  Tracts and *Lux Mundi*, 163
Farrar, Archdeacon, ref. Cowley and Father Benson, 242
Figgis, Father, *Churches in Modern State*, 220
Fisher, J. C., Liturgical Purity, 113
Fraser, Bishop—
  (Manchester), Vestments, 95
  Spiritual Court, 213, 217
  Ornaments Rubric, 101
Fraser's Magazine, English Church, 201

Garratt, Rev. S. (Ipswich), Evangelist, 149
George's-in-the-East, S., Vestments at, 127
Gibson, Bishop, Royal Supremacy, 188
Gladstone—
  Church before Revival, 67, 71
  Reply to Queen Victoria ref. Ritual, 142
  State and Church, 191
  Royal Supremacy, 196

Gloucester, Bp. Ellicott, reply to Randall, Vicar of All Saints', Clifton, 136
Gore, Bishop C.—
  Apostolic Succession, 31
  Church and State, 223
  Devotions, 262
  Malines Conference, 276
  Nonconformist Ministers, 279
  Non-Episcopal Orders, Church Congress, Cambridge, 39
  Reservation, 260-1
  Ritual and Aesthetic Movement, 81
  Vestments in Forty Churches, 102
Gorham Judgment ref. Baptism, 49, 179
Gray, C. N., Vicar of Helmsley, 158
Green, Rev. S. F. (Miles Platting), prisoner, 146, 148
Gregory, Canon—
  Liddon and Bishop of London, 137
  Rubrics and Ceremonial, 102
Greville Memoirs, Low Church Appointments, 19
Guest, Bishop, Vestments and Holy Communion, 97
Gutch, Rev. C. (at S. Mary's, Leicester), 53

Haddan, Arthur, Apostolic Succession in Church of England, 28
Halifax, Lord—
  and E.C.U., 128
  Timidity of Bishops, 156
  English Church Union, Spiritual Matters, 219
  with Abbé Portal, Father Puller, and Canon Lacey at Rome, 268
  Attitude to Rome, 271

299

Hall, Bishop Vermont, Apostolic Ministry, 38
Hallam, *Constitntional History*, 176
Hamilton, Bishop of Salisbury—
  Ritualism, 76
  Church and State, 13
Hampden, Dr. (Regius Professor of Divinity), Opinions of, 46
Harcourt, Sir W.—
  Bishop's authority human only, 145
  Letter to *Times* on Canonical Obedience, Reservation, etc., sent to Bishops from 220 Clergy, 157
Heiler—
  Early Church and Catholic Germs, 28
  Apostolic Succession, 44
  on Dean Inge of S. Paul's, 174
  Anglican Religious Orders, 245
  Reservation, 251
  Anglo-Catholic Revival, 283
Hereford, Dean of, appeal to Queen Victoria ref. Dr. Hampden, and Protest, 48
Hoare, Henry, ref. Church House, Westminster, 180
Holland, Scott, Self-Repression of Tractarians, 294
Hooker—
  ref. Holy Trinity, 129
  Spiritual Court, 204
Howley, Archbishop, Protest against Hampden, 47
Hughson, Reservation and Adoration (America), 263
Hutchins, *Life of Canon Carter*, 237

Ignatius, S., valid Eucharist, 29
Incense (Bishop Creighton on), 156
  in use A.D. 385, 159

Inge, Dean of S. Paul's, Heiler ref., 174
Intercommunion in Africa and Here, 279
Irénikon (Malines), 273-5

Jackson, Bishop—
  Warns against auricular confession, 121
  on Sisterhoods, 240
Jackson, Dr., succeeds Tait as Bishop of London, 22
Jebb, Dr., Legality of Vestments, 86
Joyce, Wayland, Church and Civil Power, 203

Keble, Rev. J.—
  National Apostasy, 11
  Eucharistic Adoration, 56
  Alfred Poole, curate to, 107
  Privy Council, 190
Kelham, Sacred Mission, Father Kelly, 241
King, Bishop Edward—
  ref. Confession, 122
  Petition to Tait, 141
Kingsley, Charles, Queen Victoria ref. to, 21

Lacey, Canon—
  Episcopate indispensable, 40
  Letter on Reservation, 256
  and Edward Denny wrote Latin Treatise on Anglican Orders, 268
Lausanne, Orthodox Church Ministry, 42
Liddell—
  Vestments, S. Paul's, Knightsbridge, 87
  Case of Rev. Alfred Poole and Confession, 105
Liddon—
  Tait and Jackson, 22
  and Gregory, letter to Bishop of London, 137

Index

Liddon—*continued*
  Rebuked by Tait, 139
  Evangelical Religion and Popery, 149
  Rubrics enforced on one side only, 150
  Benediction Service, 254
Littledale, Dr.—
  Communities of Women, 237
  in *Church Times* ref. Vestments, 93
Lock, Dr. W., ref. Keble, *Christian Year*, Eucharist, 51
Lockhart, Miss, Superior of Wantage (secession), 235
Longley, Archbp., successor to Dr. Tait, 22, 129
Lowder, Charles, 145
Lux Mundi—
  Names of Writers, 163–4
  Protest against (8 names), 168

Mackonochie, Rev. A. H., "elevation," 132–3
McNeile, Dr., ref. Absolution, 117
Magee, Bp., Tait and Convocation, 205
Manners, Lord John, Christ Ch., Albany Street, 231
Martin, Rev. J., on Miss Sellon, 233
Martineau, Dr., on Holy Communion Office, 57
Maurice, F. D., Protestantism, 286–7
Meletios (Constantinople), Anglican Orders, 43
Mellor, Dr., against McNeile, 118
Mercier, Cardinal, Malines Conversations, 270
Mill, Prof. W. H.—
  on Gorham Judgment, 53
  Influence of Italian Art on Religion, 77
Milligan, Priesthood, 165

Mirfield Community of Resurrection, 241
Moberly, Bishop—
  "Spiritual Presence," 61
  Bampton Lectures, 107
Mohler, "Symbolism," Episcopate, 41

Neale, Dr. (East Grinstead), ref. Bishop of Chichester, 236
Newman—
  Sermons dedicated to H. J. Rose, 11
  Secession, 1845, 11
  Letter to De Lisle, 17
  Monasticism, 230
  Non-communicating attendance, 141

Origen, God Alone? 164
Origin of Species and Genesis, 166
Ornaments Rubric, 84
  Tait to Alter, 91
  Bishop Jackson, 92
  Revision, 103

Palmer, Bishop (Bombay), Apostolic Succession and Mission Field, 32, 36
Palmerston, Lord, 20 Evangelical Bishops appointed, 19
Penzance, Lord—
  and Mackonochie, 134
  Ridsdale, 145
  against appeal to Law, 150
Phillimore, Dr.—
  Criticism of Bennett of Frome, 60
  Criticism, Martin *v*. Mackonochie, 147
  Position of the Church, 189
Phillpotts, Bishop of Exeter, ref. Gorham Case, 50
Poole, Rev. A. (S. Barnabas, Pimlico), Confession, 105, 107

Pope Leo XIII, reply to English Orders, 30
Portal, Abbé, 271
Presbyterian—
 Ministry, origin, 34
 Scotch Church and Self-Government, 215
Priest in Absolution, 120
Privy Council (Bennett Case), 64
Pseudo-Romanism, *Ingoldsby Letters*, 73
Public Worship—
 Regulation Act (1874), 142, 146
 Archdeacon Denison, 205
Purchas Judgment against ritual in Holy Communion, 76, 135
Pusey—
 (1833) Rule of Vincentius, 11
 Gorham Judgment, 54
 Bennett of Frome, 60
 Letter to Gladstone ref. Bennett Case, 63
 Ornaments, Rubric, 94
 Book on Confessions, 105, 107
 House of Lords and Church, 189
 Royal Supremacy, 190
 Religious Communities, 231
 Christ Church, Albany Street, 231

Quarterly Review, Church and State, 177

Randall (All Saints', Clifton) and Bp. Ellicott, 136
"Real Presence"—
 Denison Case, 56
 Rejected by Archbishop Sumner, 56
 Dr. Phillimore judgment, ref., 63
Record, The, Eccles. litigation undesirable, 149
Reformation, not reject Apostolic Succession, 33

Reservation—
 Montague Villiers, 157, 253
 Archbishop Temple's decision, 259
 Conference on (members), 261
 in Revised Prayer Book, 266
Resurrection, Community of (members), 241
Reunion, Bishop Palmer at Lausanne, 32
Reunion Movement, 266
Revision of Prayer Book, 247
Reynolds, Nonconformist, Absolution in Visitation of Sick, A.D. 490, 119
Ridsdale Judgment against Vestments, 96, 145
Ritual—
 Revival, begun by Congregations, 76
 Movement, Criticism of some, 78
 and Religion, Father Benson, 80
 Convocation, Report on, 86
 Commission, Report on Vestments, 92, 130
Rose, H. J., Newman refers to, 11
Russell, Lord J.—
 Letter of Bishop of Durham, Papal Aggression, Anglo-Catholic Revival, 124
 ref. Bishop Hampden, 47

Salisbury, Lord—
 Ritualism not to be Stopped, 101
 Strong language against Confession, 120
Sanday, Dr.—
 Catholic *not* Roman, 158
 at Sion College, gains by Disobedience, 160
Sanderson (Lancing), *Dublin Review* on Holy Communion, 66

Index

Sandys (later Archbishop of York), Vestments, 93
Secessions, 6 names, 53
Selborne, Lord—
  on P.W.R. Bill, 143
  Estimate of Tait, 151
  Estimate of Pusey, 152
  on Bishop of Lincoln's Case, 154
Sellon, Commander, on his daughter, 232
Sellon, Miss—
  Work at Devonport, 232, 234
  Commendation by Bishop of Exeter, 232
Sewell, Privy Council, 188
Shaftesbury, Lord—
  Church Appointments, 19
  at S. Alban's, Holborn, 126
  ref. Arthur Stanley as Examining Chaplain, 139
Shipley, Orby—
  Church and World vows, 238
  Studies in Modern Problems, 254
Sion College, 160
Smith, Prof. Goldwin, Protestant Appointments, 26
Stanley, Dean, 17, 138, 143
Stanton, Father—
  and Tait, 133
  and Bishop Jackson, 134
Stone, Darwell, Extra-liturgical Devotions, 262
Stubbs, Bishop—
  Archbishop Benson's study not court, 154
  Catholic Revival, 283
  Ecclesiastical Court Commission, 218
  Higher Criticism, 168-9
  Historic Episcopate, 37
  Ritual, rubric, 150
Suckling, Rev. R. J., S. Alban's, Holborn, 158

Sumner, Archbishop—
  Rejects Real Presence Doctrine, 56
  Poole Case, 105
Symbolism—
  Catholic, Sir J. Stevens, 68
  and Artistic Beauty, Bishop of Exeter, 70

Tablet, The, Duchesne and Lord Halifax, 269
Tait—
  for London, Broad Church suggested by Shaftesbury, 20
  to succeed Longley as Archbishop, 22
Tait, Archbishop—
  Ornaments rubric, 91, 99
  Withdraws Licence from Rev. A. Poole, 105
  "Bishops repudiate habitual Confession," 120
  and Mackonochie, 135
Taylor, Prof. A. E., "Facile Conversion," 292
Temple, Dr., Spiritual Court, 228
Tertullian, Churches' identity of Creed, 29
Thirlwall, Bishop Connop—
  Defects of English Church, 15
  on "Real Presence," 59
Thureau-Dangin, Contrast between Wiseman and Vaughan, 269
Times, The—
  Article on Confession, 1855, 109
  Pusey's letter ref. Public Worship Regulation Act, 144
  Sir W. Harcourt ref. M. Villiers, 157
Tooth, Rev. Arthur, in prison, 145,
Tractarianism, appeal to history, 12
Tractarians, Doctrine not Ritualism, 67

Tracts for the Times, 161, 174
Trevelyan, W. B. (S. Matthew, Westminster), 158
Turner, Cuthbert—
  Oxford Movement, 12
  Apostolic Succession, 27, 31
Tyrrell, Reasons for Secession, 290.

Urban II and Anselm, 274

Vaughan, Cardinal, Attitude to Anglican Orders, 269
Vedast, S., Foster Lane, 134
Vestments—
  Canterbury Convocation on Ritual, 83
  Nine lawyers say "legal," but not incense, 130
Victoria, Queen—
  ref. Oxford Movement, 21
  Presbyterian, 23
  Letter to Mackonochie, 132
  Letter to Archbishop Tait, Ritual, 142

Victoria, Queen—*continued*
  Letter to Gladstone, Romanising, 142
  Letter to German Emperor, English Nation Protestant, 143
Villiers, Rev. Montague, 3 Resolutions, 157
Von Hügel, Intercommunion, 290

Wagner (Brighton), "lawlessness," 214
Wainwright, Father, succeeds Mackonochie, 135
Wantage, Community, 235
Wesley, Change of Principles, 36
Wesleyan Movement, 10
Wilberforce, Bishop—
  Palmerston's appointments, 20
  Ornaments rubric, 91
Wiseman, Dr., Archbishop of Westminster, 124

Zankow, Prof. Stephen, Ministry in Greek Church, 41

For Product Safety Concerns and Information please contact our EU representative GPSR@taylorandfrancis.com
Taylor & Francis Verlag GmbH, Kaufingerstraße 24, 80331 München, Germany

www.ingramcontent.com/pod-product-compliance
Lightning Source LLC
Chambersburg PA
CBHW052152300426
44115CB00011B/1634